Inner Sound

INNER SOUND

Altered States of Consciousness in Electronic Music and Audio-Visual Media

Jonathan Weinel

OXFORD
UNIVERSITY PRESS

Oxford University Press is a department of the University of Oxford. It furthers the University's objective of excellence in research, scholarship, and education by publishing worldwide. Oxford is a registered trade mark of Oxford University Press in the UK and certain other countries.

Published in the United States of America by Oxford University Press
198 Madison Avenue, New York, NY 10016, United States of America.

Library of Congress Cataloging-in-Publication Data
Names: Weinel, Jonathan, author.
Title: Inner sound : altered states of consciousness in electronic music
and audio-visual media / Jonathan Weinel.
Description: New York, NY : Oxford University Press, [2018] |
Includes bibliographical references and index.
Identifiers: LCCN 2017057904 | ISBN 9780190671198 (pbk. : alk. paper) |
ISBN 9780190671181 (cloth : alk. paper) | ISBN 9780190671228 (oxford scholarship online)
Subjects: LCSH: Music—Psychological aspects. | Altered states of consciousness. |
Electronic music—Psychological aspects. | Electronic dance music—Psychological aspects. |
Motion pictures—Psychological aspects.
Classification: LCC ML3838 .W33 2018 | DDC 781.1/1—dc23
LC record available at https://lccn.loc.gov/2017057904

9 8 7 6 5 4 3 2 1

Paperback printed by Webcom Inc., Canada
Hardback printed by Bridgeport National Bindery, Inc., United States of America

ACKNOWLEDGEMENTS

In my earliest memories, I discovered ammonites and danced ecstatically to rock 'n' roll cassettes in Sherborne, Dorset, a small town on the Jurassic coast of the United Kingdom. Although the actual writing of *Inner Sound* was undertaken over a two-year period, its formation began long before, and as such I would like to thank everyone who helped me to cultivate my interests in music over the years. This includes my friends and family; the Abbey and Gryphon schools; my guitar teacher Roger Cleverley; my lecturers at Keele University, especially Rajmil Fischman, who supervised my PhD in electroacoustic composition; and my tutors at the Open University. The research and writing of the book proper was undertaken at the following institutions: Glyndŵr University (UK), the British Library (UK), and Aalborg University (Denmark). During this process, I received valuable assistance from my editor at Oxford University Press, Norman Hirschy, and a panel of anonymous peer-reviewers. Additional feedback was also provided from my friends Lyall Williams, Sol Nte, and my partner Jennifer Pickles. All of these inputs were vital in steering *Inner Sound* towards its final form, and as such are highly valued. Thanks is also due to everyone who provided images for the book, who are credited throughout. Jan Robbe deserves a special mention for creating original digital artworks for the front cover. Lastly, I would like to thank all the other artists and musicians whose work I discuss in the book, especially those who took the time to correspond with me about their work.

CONTENTS

Inner Sound

Introduction

Immediately before my eyes are a vast number of rings, apparently made of extremely fine steel wire, all constantly rotating in the direction of the hands of a clock; these circles are concentrically arranged, the innermost being infinitely small, almost point-like, the outermost being about a meter and a half in diameter. The spaces between the wires seem brighter than the wires themselves. Now the wires shine like dim silver in parts. Now a beautiful light violet tint has developed in them. As I watch the center seems to recede into the depth of the room, leaving the periphery stationary, till the whole assumes the form of a deep funnel of wire rings.

—Anonymous participant, *Knauer and Maloney, 1913*

These words relate the experience of a participant in a scientific study, who sees visual hallucinations while tumbling down the rabbit hole under the influence of the drug mescaline. Mescaline is an alkaloid chemical compound that is found naturally in peyote (*Lophophora williamsii*), a small spineless cactus that is common to the southwestern United States and Mexico. Among Native American tribes such as the Tarahumaras, Kiowas, Comanches, and indigenous peoples of Mexico such as the Cora people and Huichol, peyote is valued for its visionary properties and is considered to be a religious sacrament. In these traditions, the top of the cactus is cut off and dried to form 'mescal buttons', which are later eaten in a ritual context. The use of peyote is believed to date back at least 6000 years (Terry et al., 2006), and is known to have been used in Pre-Columbia Mexico by the Aztecs.[1] Indeed, the word 'peyote' originates from the Nahuatl word 'peyotl'. In 1918 mescaline was identified as the active hallucinogenic ingredient of peyote, enabling its chemical synthesis and scientific study. When taken orally mescaline is absorbed and high concentrations reach the brain within 1 to 2 hours (Julien, 2001, p.337). Within 3.5 to 4 hours the individual will experience psychoactive effects, such as distortions to visual and auditory perception, dissolution of ego boundaries and 'dimensions of "oceanic boundlessness"', which may last up to 10 hours.

In 1928 Henrich Klüver carried out his first psychological trials with mescaline, in order to identify the underlying structure and form of the hallucinations that his participants experienced. With regards to the visual aspects of these experiences, Klüver (1971, p.66) revealed what he described as 'form constants': honeycomb, cobweb, funnel, and spiral forms. According to Klüver's research, these form constants are the basis for visual pattern effects such as the 'deep funnel of wire rings' described above. Participants would either experience these forms directly, or versions abstracted from them. For example, while an individual might perceive geometric funnel patterns in the early stages of a mescaline experience, later on such funnel patterns might assume realistic forms such as actual tunnel environments.

Klüver's (1971) work on form constants has since been followed by others, such as Bressloff et al.'s (2001) study, which suggested that the forms perceived were the result of patterns of connection between the retina and the visual cortex. The research also informed a landmark article in the field of anthropology by Lewis-Williams and Dowson (1988), which investigated the basis for certain symbolic markings that were found in Upper Palaeolithic parietal art (art on cave walls or stone). While the presence of various animal forms in rock art from this era was clear, Lewis-Williams and Dowson proposed that other seemingly abstract signs could in fact be representations of 'entoptic phenomena': phosphenes[2] and form constants seen during altered states of consciousness (ASCs). Thus, they argued that the presence of images resembling the form constants in rock art suggested that those who created them were likely to have been part of shamanistic societies. These hunter-gatherer shamanic societies would have used ASCs in order to contact spirits and supernatural entities, heal the sick, and affect animals and the weather (Lewis-Williams, 2004, p.133). The artists who created these markings were representing aspects of the visions that they considered to be sacred.

Lewis-Williams and Dowson's (1988) argument is compelling since it suggests that some of the earliest known art may have been based on the visual forms experienced during hallucinations. If correct, the representation of ASCs could be among the oldest of human enterprises.[3] If this is the case, then surely the topic is one that calls for our attention, and it is to this call that this book responds. However, the book will not re-tread the anthropological grounds covered by authors such as Lewis-Williams (2004). Instead I will focus on the ways in which recent technologies in electronic music and art provide new capabilities for representing or inducing these states. This will not mean an extended technical discussion regarding the use of neural imaging techniques to directly extract inner experience.[4] Rather, the book will provide an in-depth exploration of the ways in which time-based electronic audio and audio-visual media of psychedelic rock, electronic dance music, experimental film, and modern video game culture have allowed ancient practices involving the production and representation of ASCs to be developed since the 1950s. In addition, just as the shamanic art and music related to ASCs forms an essential part of the shamanic world-view, we shall also see how electronic music and audio-visual media related to ASCs reflects the ethos of various sub-cultures.

Over the past few millennia humankind has woven an intricate history with intoxicating plants, resulting in various associated artefacts. Exploring this area, Devereux (2008) finds evidence to suggest that the use of intoxicating plants extends back to prehistoric times. For example, Ralph Solecki's (1975) discovery of the Neanderthal 'flower burial' at the Shanidar Cave in Northern Iraq indicated the possible use of herbal stimulants from the *Ephedra* genus 60,000 years ago. Perhaps as old, the ancestors of today's Australian Aborigines may have used the stimulant pituri 40,000–60,000 years ago.[5] Scattered evidence gathered from various archaeological finds also point towards the use of opium and cannabis in Neolithic and Bronze Age Europe,[6] while the Ebers Papyrus in Egypt describes the medicinal use of opium (Merlin, 1984, pp.274–275). In the Indus Valley region (now northern India, Afghanistan, and Pakistan), the sacred Aryan text of the Rig Veda describes 'soma', a sacred drink of unknown contents that transports the individual to ecstatic realms.[7] Similarly enigmatic are the Eleusinian Mysteries, an initiation cult in Ancient Greece that continued for nearly two thousand years, in which various ecstatic rites were enacted, and a sacred drink known as 'kykeon' was consumed (Eliade, 1978). Though the contents of kykeon remain unknown, it is believed that the drink may have contained a hallucinogen similar to LSD (lysergic acid diethylamide) that was derived from the ergot (a parasitic fungus) of barley (Wasson, Hoffman, and Ruck, 1978).

While the full details of many of these early examples may have been lost in the sands of time, more recent recorded history provides a clearer impression of the ritual use of hallucinogens. Modern use of the term 'shaman' derives directly from Siberian shamanism and the Tungus word meaning 'to know' (Laufer, 1913). In Siberian shamanism *Amanita muscaria* mushrooms are ritually used for their psychoactive properties, by either eating directly or drinking urine (since the active ingredients are passed this way). Anthropologist Weston La Barre (1972, pp.181–182) has argued that the origins of shamanism in the Americas may lie in Siberian shamanism, having been transported there via the Bering land-bridge which connected Eurasia with the Americas around 25,000 years ago. When Spanish conquistadors landed in the Americas, Bernardino de Sahagún (1499–1590b, p.130) found the Aztecs using *teonanácatl* (meaning 'flesh of the gods'), *Psilocybe cubensis* mushrooms. Fascinating mushroom-shaped stones found throughout Guatemala, Mexico, and Honduras suggest that the use of these mushrooms may date back to at least the first millennium BCE.[8] Today the shamanic use of mushrooms continues in the Huichol and Mazatec peoples of Mexico, who are descendant from the Aztecs. Elsewhere in North America, Native Americans use peyote, while in South America shamans of the Peruvian Amazon use ayahuasca (or 'yagé'); a hallucinogenic brew that contains a natural source of DMT (*N,N*-dimethyltryptamine, a powerful hallucinogen).

Returning to Europe, prior to the sixteenth century 'wise women' (folk healers) were commonplace (Thomas, 1971). Typically located in wilderness areas outside of towns, wise women performed magic rituals, sometimes involving the use of 'hexing herbs' with intoxicating properties.[9] For example, Harner (1973, pp.125–150) discusses the use of belladonna, mandrake, datura, and henbane in the preparation of witches' 'flying ointments'. Harner argues that the hallucinogenic properties of these flying ointments may account for the tales of witches flying through the air and cavorting with spirits and demons at Sabbat. With the advent of the Reformation and modern medicine, witchcraft saw a decline in the sixteenth century, though various natural hallucinogens such as *Psilocybe semilanceata* mushrooms are still found throughout much of Europe today.

In 1938 Albert Hofmann synthesized LSD, a compound with remarkable hallucinogenic properties. Such drugs came to be known as 'psychedelic', meaning 'mind manifesting', as coined by British psychiatrist Humphry Osmond in reference to their powerful consciousness altering capabilities. The use of LSD was initially explored for therapeutic and military purposes during the 1950s, later rose to prominence in the public sphere through its popularity in the 1960s counter-culture, and was subsequently banned in the United States and most other Western countries (Roberts, 2012). The euphoric stimulant MDMA (3,4-methylenedioxymethamphetamine, commonly known as 'ecstasy'), originally synthesized in 1912 by Anton Köllisch, followed a similar pattern. Alexander Shulgin promoted the drug for use in psychiatry in the late 1970s and early 1980s, before it became popular in the emerging electronic dance music culture and was subsequently outlawed. Modern use of psychedelic drugs is predominantly characterized as hedonistic, though in hippy cultures and some neo-shamanism groups they are used as 'entheogens'[10] for spiritual purposes.

Throughout history the use of ASCs has ranged from religious ritual to hedonistic indulgence, and has often been a source of conflict. In shamanic societies where ASCs play an integral role in shaping beliefs, the plants that produce these states are seen as sacred medicines. Yet such beliefs are not always shared between societies. When Spanish conquistadors found the Aztec shamans using hallucinogenic mushrooms, they violently suppressed these practices, forcing them underground. The fate of witches using hexing herbs in Europe followed a similar pattern, as the Christian Church sought to eradicate pagan practices and beliefs. In more recent times, Native Americans were unable to carry out their religious use of peyote without breaking the law, until a legal exemption was passed in 1991. Conversely, in Peru, shamanic tribes have profited from the booming 'ayahuasca tourism' sought by Westerners seeking exotic forms of spiritual awakening. Yet parts of the Amazon are also battlegrounds for groups that have vested interests in the international drugs trade. Fuelled by demand in the West for cocaine and heroin, drug trafficking has claimed thousands of lives in Mexico and other countries through which packages are moved. There are also consequences for individual users at the end of this chain, as these drugs carry risks due to toxicity and the potential for addiction. For example, heroin addiction can have devastating personal and social consequences. These consequences may lend some credence to the argument in support of regulation, but this is a double-edged sword as it perpetuates illicit trading and invariably does little to reduce harm (Godlee, 2016). Of course, the substances themselves are not inherently evil and neither are the ASCs they produce; opiates are also extremely valuable in healthcare for their medicinal properties in pain-relief.[11] It seems then, that much depends on the context in which intoxicating substances are used. Furthermore, some ASCs such as meditation or dreaming can also be accessed without the need for plants or drugs. While the latter types tend to be less controversial, certainly there has historically been much disagreement over who can access ASCs and how they may do so.[12]

PSYCHEDELIC ARTEFACTS

It may not come as a surprise that the presence of ASCs in culture over thousands of years has resulted in a great deal of art, literature, and music related to these experiences. As discussed, early examples include spiral patterns in rock art, or mushroom-like stone figures, which some anthropologists consider to be related to ASC experiences.[13] In surviving shamanic traditions, the ASC experience frequently permeates the art and music of those cultures. For example, peyote is reflected both symbolically and through the brightly contrasting colours and hallucinatory geometric designs of Huichol art (Eger and Collings, 1978), while Shipibo art also incorporates geometric patterns and designs inspired by the ayahuasca experience (Schultes, Hofmann, and Rätsch 1996, pp.131–133).

In modern Western culture, we find further examples of painting and visual art related to ASCs. Beginning in the 1920s, the surrealist art movement explored ideas of dreams and the unconscious as discussed by Freud. Later on, the 1960s saw a major boom in psychedelic artwork, which emerged as part of the counter-culture of the era, and permeated everything from concert posters and fashion to the pop art and op art movements (Grunenberg, 2005). Rubin (2010) discusses the extensive influence of psychedelic culture on the visual arts of the late twentieth century, referring to the paintings of Fred Tomaselli, Kenny Scharf, Alex Grey, and others. Johnson (2011, pp.35–40) also explores these themes, drawing attention to the presence of designs that are similar to Klüver's form constants in the work of various visual artists.

In Western literature of the eighteenth and nineteenth centuries, ASC-inspired literary accounts are found in works such as Samuel Taylor Coleridge's 'Kubla Khan' (1797) or Thomas De Quincy's *Confessions of an English Opium Eater* (1821). In the twentieth century, Paul Bowles's *A Hundred Camels in the Courtyard* (1962) used a literary mosaic technique to reflect the effects of smoking hashish; Carlos Castaneda's *The Teachings of Don Juan: A Yaqui Way of Knowledge* (1968) described visionary journeys and shamanic metamorphosis precipitated by various hallucinogens; Tom Wolfe's *The Electric Kool-Aid Acid Test* (1968) recounts his experiences touring America with the Merry Pranksters; and William Burroughs provides us with his extensive enquiries into heroin, yagé, and other techniques of altering consciousness through his various works (e.g. *Junky*, 1953; *The Naked Lunch*, 1959; *The Yage Letters* [with Allen Ginsberg], 1963, 1975).

Music appears to have a special connection with ASCs. In their respective work, Rouget (1985) and Becker (2004) have discussed the use of music in trance cultures such as those of Southeast Asia. In these trance cultures, and in many shamanic traditions, music is often used to conduct the ritual and plays an important role in inducing ASC states. Field recordings such as those available on the Folkways record label provide a recorded document of these (e.g. María Sabina's *Mushroom Ceremony of the Mazatec Indians of Mexico*, 1957; Harry Smith's *The Kiowa Peyote Meeting*, 1973). In modern Western music, surf rock preceded the arrival of psychedelic music in the 1960s, as popularized by acts such as The Beatles, The Jimi Hendrix Experience, Jefferson Airplane, and the Grateful Dead. As Hayward (2004, pp.15–18) has discussed, this era also saw science fiction themes and psychedelic music becoming entwined, in the Afrofuturist space jazz of Sun Ra and John Coltrane; or in the space rock of Pink Floyd, Gong, and Hawkwind. Veal (2007, pp.209–210) also highlights that these themes saw parallels in dub-reggae music, which he suggests could be viewed as 'psychedelic Caribbean' music. The sound system culture of dub also prefigured the electronic dance music culture that would emerge in the late 1980s. From its origins in Chicago, acid house music subsequently spread to the United Kingdom, developing alongside the MDMA-fuelled 'rave' culture (discussed in Collin, 1998; Reynolds, 2008; St. John, 2009). Electronic dance music culture subsequently became a global phenomenon that included both mainstream commercial forms and underground counter-culture strains; the latter often remaining explicitly orientated towards psychedelic drug culture.

In the emerging audio-visual culture of the twentieth century, ASC themes also appeared in experimental films such as Storm De Hirsch's *Peyote Queen* (1965) or in Jordan Belson's visual music films (e.g. *LSD*, 1962), which Wees (1992) compared to Klüver's (1971) form constants. In Hollywood, hallucinatory sequences were also featured in many films: *Easy Rider* (Hopper, 1969), *Altered States* (Russell, 1980), and *Fear and Loathing in Las Vegas* (Gilliam, 1998) are just three examples. Meanwhile, as Turner (2008) has discussed, many individuals involved in the early computer culture were formerly involved in the 1960s counter-culture movements, and were instrumental in fostering utopian attitudes within some sections of the cyberculture.[14] As one of the manifestations of this intersection of cultures, the 1980s and 1990s saw psychedelic computer graphics visualizations, from the programs of Jeff Minter's *Colourspace* (1986) to the *X-Mix* (Studio !K7, 1993–1998) VJ mix series. As PlayStation culture and rave music flourished in tandem, at the turn of the millennium psychedelic themes were seen in such interactive video games as *LSD: Dream Emulator* (Asmik Ace Entertainment, 1998) and *Rez* (United Game Artists, 2001). In recent years titles such as *Far Cry 3* (Ubisoft Montreal, 2012) and *Grand Theft Auto V* (Rockstar North, 2013) have also incorporated drug experiences into interactive gameplay, with increasing levels of detail and sophistication.

Just as the use of ASCs throughout history has occurred in relation to various cultures and systems of belief, so too do these various artefacts reflect differing attitudes towards ASCs. For example, shamanic art and music can be seen as a means to invoke and communicate with the spirit world that ASCs allow one to experience. Romantic literary works such as 'Kubla Khan' (Coleridge, 1797), and later the surrealist movement, can also be seen as responses to a perceived loss of connection with inner experience. Subsequently, the psychedelic art, literature, and music of the 1960s can be seen as part of the counter-culture movement towards expanded forms of consciousness and social revolution. In this context, drugs such as LSD were seen by some as a means through which to achieve revolutionary forms of consciousness, and the associated cultural artefacts embrace this ethos by representing such experiences, or by actually seeking to induce them. Some of these ideas also extended into the electronic dance music culture of the 1980s and 1990s, though here the ethos was frequently a more hedonistic celebration of euphoric drug-induced states. Of course, not all cultural artefacts within these domains celebrate ASCs, and in some cases music and art may avoid these aesthetic approaches, and be seen as sufficiently powerful in its own right. Other examples may also express cautionary tales or present anti-drug positions. This is especially the case in recent mainstream media, where drugs are often viewed in negative terms and used for their shock value; hence some of the most recent films and video games that represent ASCs do so within the context of the horror genre.

INNER SOUNDS

Perhaps the most famous literary work related to ASCs is Aldous Huxley's *The Doors of Perception* (1954–1956) in which the author discusses his experiences after taking 400 mg of mescaline. Huxley uses the technology of the written word (if we may consider it as such) to provide descriptive accounts of hallucinations. However, the examples we have discussed also indicate the use of both audio and visual media for representing ASCs. Considering visual technologies first, these have advanced since the days of early cave paintings so that impressions of ASCs can now be rendered with the full benefit of modern oil paints and canvas. Yet the capabilities provided by technology for rendering these subjective visual experiences go much further with digital technologies, which also allow the rendering of complex mathematical patterns, fractals, and 3D graphics. These allow vast potentials for creating almost any environment or visual experience imaginable. Such capabilities support the design of visual images such as Klüver's (1971) form constants, which can be described using mathematical functions (as discussed by Bressloff et al., 2001). When combined with immersive technologies that surround the viewer's visual field and trick the eye with false perspectives, digital artists have been able to create psychedelic hallucinatory experiences. Similarly, 'projection mapping' techniques work by projecting light on to objects such as sculptures, creating illusions of movement and transfiguration through the manipulation of video. In the context of psychedelic trance parties and elaborate electronic dance music stage shows, such technologies bring fixed objects alive, making visual experiences of funnels, rotating wire rings, or other wild synaesthetic fantasias concrete. From simple early markings on cave walls to animated luminescent digital projections, technology has radically advanced our capability for creating illusory visuals based on the subjective experience of ASCs.

ASCs may act not only on the visual system, but also upon the auditory senses, enhancing or distorting sensory perception, or causing auditory hallucinations. Audio technologies may represent these experiences by imitating changes to auditory perception. This function, if not new, is at least significantly enhanced by developments in technology over the last century that have provided new possibilities for creating and manipulating sound. The beginnings of this emerge with analogue technology for the recording and manipulation of sound in recording studios. More recently in the field of electroacoustic music, high-quality loudspeakers and spatial audio algorithms enable the construction of convincing sonic spaces and events. This technology can be used not only to recreate the sound of real spaces or locations but also to design illusory or imaginary sound worlds such as those that might be experienced during states of hallucination. Furthermore, while sound may represent ASCs, it can also be used to induce them by promoting heightened states of emotion. The ritual use of music for this purpose is an ancient practice, yet in modern times, similar principles are enhanced through the use of sound systems—the throbbing hypnotic pulses of electronic music replacing the acoustic drums of the past.

When both the audio and visual elements described are combined in interactive systems, 'ASC Simulations' are possible. This concept has been demonstrated to an extent through the video games mentioned, yet remains an area that is relatively new. ASC Simulations may be designed in various ways, and when combined with immersive visual displays and spatial audio, the possibility for them to closely resemble actual experiences of hallucination emerges. Within the next hundred years, they could even become indistinguishable from traditional forms of ASCs. These simulations could have useful applications not only in the world of video games, but also as therapeutic tools. More generally, in a world where human interaction is increasingly mediated through digital information networks, the potential to simulate the subjective experience of human consciousness could have important implications not only for art, music, and entertainment, but also for day-to-day communication.

Yet the construction of any such ASC Simulations first requires a theoretical basis in order to properly consider how the material design of audio-visual media can achieve this effect. This is the call to which this book responds. Through an analysis of ASCs in electronic music and audio-visual media, *Inner Sound* develops a theoretical model that allows us to consider the design of these simulations. In order to achieve this goal, the book takes a tour through various material artefacts such as sound recordings, films, and video games, so that we may see how they represent or induce ASCs. Along the way we shall travel from Amazonian chicha festivals to a Mazatec mushroom ritual in Oaxaca, Mexico; from the wonderlands of psychedelic rock to the synaesthetic assaults of neon raves; and from an immersive outdoor electroacoustic performance on an Athenian hilltop to a mushroom trip on a tropical island in virtual reality. Through consideration of these various art forms, we shall see how electronic processes have enabled new capabilities, and how the material design of works reflects the ethos of a variety of subcultural groups. These discoveries ultimately feed into a conceptual view of ASC Simulations that allows us to not only look back but also to look forward to see what is possible at the frontiers of digital cultures for representing and transforming consciousness.

THE CHAPTERS

The chapters following this introduction are organized in such a way as to establish a common basis in ASCs and their relationships with art and music in shamanic traditions. Following this, a discussion of various electronic music and audio-visual media is provided, allowing the ways in which these may represent or induce ASCs to be considered. This discussion will feed into the development of a conceptual model that will allow us to consider how sound can be designed in order to provide ASC Simulations. Throughout the book, the relationships between musical aesthetics and ethos are explored, ultimately allowing the reader to consider not only how these simulations may be designed, but also how and why they might be used in digital society.

Chapter 1 commences with an introduction to consciousness. This enables us to explore the variety of ASCs that may occur, and the changes they cause to subjective experience, which can be considered in terms of dimensional models. The possible ethical implications of ASCs are also reviewed, with regards to their physical and psychological effects, and how these may be considered in different cultural circumstances. We also begin to see how sound may be used to either represent or induce ASCs.

Chapter 2 discusses how shamanic traditions may invoke visionary experiences of the spirit world through art and music. This is explored through an analysis of material artefacts such as ethnographic field recordings, which are among the earliest examples of electronic media that incorporate the concept of ASCs. Through the course of the discussion, the chapter establishes the relationships that have traditionally existed between music and ASCs in shamanic and trance cultures, which will allow comparisons with electronic music and audio-visual media to be made later in the book.

Chapter 3 explores how audio technologies and electronic studio processes relate to ASCs in popular music. The capabilities of sound recordings and studio electronics are considered through the analysis of examples in rock 'n' roll, surf rock, psychedelic rock, and space rock/space jazz. Through the course of the chapter I argue that electronic technologies allow the energetic properties of rock 'n' roll music to be adapted in order to elicit various concepts, including that of ASCs.

Chapter 4 extends this discussion into the area of sound system culture and electronic dance music. I argue that the sound system places the communicative properties of electronic studio productions within a social context, eliciting powerful affective experiences that are framed by conceptual meaning. The extent to which music may complement or reflect the use of intoxicating substances is considered, while also acknowledging that some artists have actively spoken out against the use of drugs in electronic dance music culture.

Chapter 5 explores the possibilities of electroacoustic music for representing the sensory experience of ASCs with varying degrees of accuracy. The chapter commences with a general explanation of electroacoustic music, and how it may allow illusory representations of real and unreal sounds and spaces. Various works of electroacoustic music that engage with themes such as dreams, shamanism, and hallucination are then considered, leading to a conceptual model that defines possible approaches for sound design.

Chapter 6 expands my discussion of time-based media into the area of audio-visual media. I discuss the presence of ASCs in avant-garde films, feature films, visual music, psychedelic light shows, and VJ culture. Continuing to use the conceptual model of the previous chapter, this chapter expands our discussion by exploring the role of sound to represent or induce ASCs in an audio-visual context.

Chapter 7 advances this discussion further by considering ASCs in interactive video games and virtual reality applications. Through examples ranging from action adventures to meditation games, we shall see how ASCs can be simulated in virtual environments using sound, graphics, and interactivity. This ultimately allows the concept of ASC Simulations to be defined: interactive audio-visual systems that represent ASCs with regards to the sensory components of the experience.

Chapter 8 consolidates my analysis of ASCs in electronic music and audio-visual media. By drawing connections between shamanic art and music, and modern ASC Simulations, we find that there are some similar underlying principles. However, we also see how electronic technologies enable new capabilities for simulating ASCs in ways that are more accurate than ever before. Looking forwards, the ethics and implications of these ASC Simulations are considered, allowing us to reflect on how they might be used for various social or therapeutic purposes. Through the concept of ASC Simulations and its exploration then, we will have seen the limits of technology for representing and manipulating consciousness at the frontiers of electronic music and art.

Throughout the book examples are drawn from the material artefacts of sound recordings, films, and video games. The original analysis of these works forms the substance of the book, from which underlying relationships with ASCs are revealed. In each case the examples chosen have been selected in order to evidence a particular important function or paradigm in the use of sound. Some of these works are well known, while others are relatively more obscure; yet most are readily accessible with the benefit of online digital media services, and I would encourage the reader to make use of these, in order to complement reading with listening, viewing, and playing.[15] Frequently the innovations described with regards to one work are idiomatic, evidencing features that are also found in various other works. As a result, it will often be the case that alternative works could have been chosen to form the basis of the discussion; however, in the interests of brevity the aim has not been to catalogue every work exhaustively, but rather to arm the reader with perspectives that may inform his or her own listening and investigations.

DEPARTURE LOUNGE

The main aim of *Inner Sound* is to provide an in-depth analysis of how time-based electronic music and audio-visual media may represent or induce ASCs, in order to develop the theoretical concept of ASC Simulations. The ways in which technologies shape the material form of artefacts is considered, and connections are drawn between these and the older traditions of shamanic art and music. Among the areas explored in the book, the representation of hallucinatory states in interactive video games and VJ culture is one that has so far received little attention from research. By giving this area the attention it deserves, it is intended to uncover the underlying structures, and in particular the concept of ASC Simulations, which will be of interest for audiences and practitioners alike.

With regards to the concept of ASC Simulations, there are several reasons why research in this area is worthwhile. ASC Simulations have already seen a practical application within the area of commercial video games, while we are also beginning to see their use as therapeutic tools. Perhaps most significantly, however, the generalization of research in this field may ultimately yield a set of systematic approaches for representing a variety of conscious human states. In providing virtual representations of human consciousness in all its forms, we may be better equipped to share and understand them. This could be useful for communications technologies, by enabling more human representations of our digital selves, in similar terms argued for by Rosalind Picard (1997) with regards to computers that can respond to or exhibit human emotions. Yet moreover, it also presents the possibility of gaining a better understanding of human consciousness.

As Turner (2008) has discussed, in the late twentieth century the twin forces of technological advancement and the threat of Cold War nuclear apocalypse led many to seek radical new digital utopias. For many the cybernetics of Norbert Weiner (1961) provided a new view of humans and technologies as information systems that could work together more effectively, providing pathways to a better world. Such theories promoted a progressive global outlook, in which the world is seen in terms of interconnected structures with many mutual concerns. Among the figures involved in this shift in thought, through his 'Gaia hypothesis'[16] James Lovelock (1979) argued that the most significant benefit of space travel came not from the possibility of visiting other planets, but from being able to see the earth from space. At this time the images of the earth viewed from space cropped up in many areas of popular culture as a powerful symbol of global communications, ecology, and society. Among these, the symbol is also found in the nexus of science fiction and psychedelic music, where space travel became a metaphor for travelling outside of one's usual conscious state. Just as seeing the earth from an outside perspective provided new ways of looking at society, these psychedelic cultures saw a similar potential in allowing consciousness to escape from the usual boundaries. Analogously then, the most compelling reason to investigate methods for simulating ASCs is ultimately to enable the exploration of consciousness from a position of alterity.

CHAPTER 1
Inner Worlds

[O]ur normal waking consciousness, rational consciousness as we call it, is but one special type of consciousness, whilst all about it, parted from it by the filmiest of screens, there lie potential forms of consciousness entirely different. We may go through life without suspecting their existence; but happy the requisite stimulus, and at a touch they are there in all their completeness, definite types of mentality which probably somewhere have their field of application and adaptation. No account of the universe in its totality can be final which leaves these other forms of consciousness quite disregarded.

—William James, *The Varieties of Religious Experience, 1902*

The term 'stream of consciousness' or 'stream of thought' as discussed by William James (1890), encapsulates the way in which our subjective experience seems to have a certain flowing continuity, like a river or stream. In normal waking consciousness, the contents of this stream may include sensory experiences such as visual images, sounds, smells, or tastes. They may also include experiences of hot or cold, pain, or other bodily sensations. Looking inwardly, we may experience mental images, thoughts, emotions, and a sense of self. We effortlessly record events to our memories, giving us a sense of past occurrences, supporting a smooth, continuous experience of time. Yet the stream may also change radically during heightened states of emotion, dreams, or hallucinations: 'altered states of consciousness' (ASCs). In these states the contents of our experiences may diverge significantly from the baseline of normal waking consciousness, to encompass all kinds of unusual perception that are more amplified or reduced in character.

In this book, I consider how ASCs can provide a basis for the design of music and art, that is, how time-based media such as sound or audio-visual artworks might be designed in such a way as to represent subjective experiences from a first-person perspective. Going beyond this I will consider how these media may also affect changes to the stream of consciousness, either through associative properties or by inducing heightened states of emotion for their audience. Since modern electronic technologies in particular have radically enhanced the capabilities for creating almost any sound or image imaginable, they are particularly well suited to both these tasks and are the main focus of this book.

In order to consider this area, this chapter begins by exploring in more detail what is meant by consciousness and how this changes during ASCs. Two models of consciousness are described, which conceptualize ASCs not as discrete states but as points on a continuum of possibilities. We then consider the effects of sound and music for the listener, such as elicited associations or induced emotions. This chapter therefore provides the necessary basis through which to consider how corresponding properties in the material design of electronic music and audio-visual media may allow ASCs to be represented or induced.

CONSCIOUSNESS

'Consciousness' describes the particular phenomenon of human awareness. Intuitively, we may presume that all humans have a conscious experience which is comparable with regards to its basic form. Probably apes, as the closest relative to humankind, have something we might also refer to as consciousness, with some (but not all) of the familiar features that we have. As we get further away from humans to consider other animals such as fish or bats, trying to imagine if these creatures are conscious in any way and if they are, what that would be like, becomes trickier. While animals may not have the complex reasoning abilities of humans, they nonetheless display behaviours and responses to their environment that may be accompanied by a form of awareness that we might term 'consciousness'. Yet if this is the case, then at what point down the evolutionary ladder does conscious awareness cease? Or is it everywhere? How and why does it occur?

These questions of how, why, and where consciousness occurs are the types of concerns that have troubled theorists. While the experience of conscious awareness is intuitively apparent, explaining precisely why we should have any experiences at all poses a serious problem for both philosophers and scientists alike. In humans, we know that the brain plays a critical role in controlling our bodies and exchanging information via neurons as electrical pulses, yet it is not fully understood why this should produce an experience of consciousness. Considering its material properties, the brain consists of neuron cells that exchange information between synapses via electrical pulses, and glial cells that hold the neurons in place and perform other supporting functions such as the supply of oxygen and removal of pathogens. Yet why should the interaction of these cells, which are made up of atoms and electrons like the inanimate objects that we presume are *not* conscious, actually produce experiences of awareness? For Chalmers (1996) this question of how physical processes give rise to subjective experience is the 'hard problem' of consciousness. This 'hard problem' is closely aligned with the notion that there are experiential qualities (or 'qualia') to subjective experience; that we do not only see or hear things, but there is also something that it is actually *like* to see or hear things. Thus while Chalmers acknowledges that physics can explain how material interactions within the brain take place, he remains unconvinced that our current models of physics are able to explain why the phenomenological experience of a subjective 'inner life' actually occurs. He therefore distinguishes this 'hard problem' of consciousness from the 'easy' problems addressed by cognitive psychology, such as how we process information in response to stimuli from an external environment, or how information is exchanged while performing particular behaviours.

Cognition

Before tackling the grander challenges of consciousness, it will be useful first to briefly consider some of the individual processes that are involved in the 'stream of consciousness' (the 'easy' problems). Over the last century cognitive psychology has developed our knowledge of how internal processes occur in relation to the external environment through participant studies, computational modelling, and neuroimaging. For example, Broadbent (1958) used 'dichotic listening tasks' in which participants were presented with different streams of audio in each ear, and asked to attend and report on one of these sources. This informed Broadbent's 'filter' model of attention, which describes how attended sources are passed for higher level processing while others are filtered out. In Treisman's (1960) revision of this theory, she suggested that unattended sources are 'attenuated', but may be passed for higher level processing less frequently. In the field of perception, Gibson (1950; 1966) and Marr (1982) are among those who have provided theories in which incoming visual stimuli provide a basis for internal representations that are constructed from the 'bottom up'. However, perception also involves 'top-down' processes in which the individual may internally generate 'perceptual hypotheses': predictions about visual stimuli, which are compared with incoming sensory information and used to fill in any gaps (Gregory, 1980). The latter effect goes some way to explaining why we are able to perceive patterns or faces in incomplete or noisy visual information such as Rorschach inkblots, and also shows that memory of existing forms has a role in perceptual processes.

Memory is a complex field in its own right, which subdivides into studies that explore specialized forms that are used in different situations. For example, Atkinson and Shiffrin (1971) discussed the distinctions of short-term memory (STM) and long-term memory (LTM). Our knowledge of these classifications has been further developed through other studies, such the models of 'working memory' provided by Baddeley and Hitch (1974; later expanded: see Baddeley, 2000). According to these models, 'working memory' is a component of STM that allows temporal processing of information, and is used in problem solving and language. Working memory consists of specialized units for processing visual and phonological information,[1] which are governed over by a 'central executive' that is linked to conscious awareness. Working memory also interacts with LTM systems, which similarly fractionate into various specializations. Among these LTM systems, 'episodic memory' deals with storage and recall of autobiographical events; 'semantic memory', by contrast, is a general store of information and factual knowledge (Schacter and Tulving, 1994).

Over the last few decades, emotion has also developed into an important field of cognitive psychology. Current theories consider that emotion involves a discourse between thoughts, behaviours, and physiological responses; hence thoughts may influence physiological responses and trigger corresponding behaviours.[2] Russell (1980) proposed a dimensional model of emotion, which plots the range of possible emotional states on two-dimensional coordinates. Valence (the x axis) ranges from positive states such as happiness to negative ones such as sadness. Arousal (the y axis) ranges from low-energy states such as relaxation, to high-energy states such as excitement. Arousal correlates with the sympathetic and parasympathetic autonomic nervous systems (ANS), which are associated with high-energy and restful states respectively. For example, the sympathetic ANS causes the release of adrenaline, increased heart rate, and pupil dilation; the parasympathetic ANS, by contrast, slows the heartbeat, stimulates the flow of saliva, and constricts the pupils. High-arousal states are associated with 'fight-or-flight' responses and sexual activity, while low-arousal responses are associated with relaxation. Physically engaging in high- or low-energy behaviours has an effect on arousal and thus the emotional state of an individual. Emotion also has an important role in many other cognitive processes: for example, studies by Bower (1981) and MacLeod et al. (1986) have shown that emotion plays a role in memory and attention respectively.

Global Workspace Theory

These are among those areas of enquiry that have enriched our understanding of cognition, but how do they come together to provide a sense of consciousness? In consideration of this question, Baars (1988; 1997) describes his Global Workspace (GW) theory of consciousness using a theatre metaphor. According to his description, the mind is a theatre with various conscious and unconscious processes occurring concurrently. Consciousness is like a spotlight, bringing certain elements into view, while other unconscious elements continue to work in the background like stagehands. Baars supported his theory of consciousness by pointing out that attention seems to correspond with conscious awareness. For example, if one attempts to calculate the solution to a complex crossword puzzle then the problem enters conscious awareness, while other routine tasks such as breathing often take place without awareness, almost as though they are automatic. In light of this correspondence, Baars discusses neuroimaging techniques that show the parts of the brain that are active during attention tasks. These, and studies regarding people with cognitive impairments, indicate the 'neural correlates of consciousness': neural states that correspond with conscious awareness. Of these, Baars cites the various cortices of the brain as particularly important, especially the visual cortex, which he sees as playing a role in consciousness by enabling the collaboration of different areas of the brain. Working memory also has a significant role in consciousness, since it is a central process that is involved from moment-to-moment, engaging various other repositories such as long-term memory (LTM), that are otherwise unconscious until their contents are brought into view. This view of consciousness leads to the theatre metaphor, where consciousness acts rather like a director by placing a spotlight on different information processes, bringing them into awareness and connecting them as required to carry out certain tasks.

Baars's (1988; 1997) concept of consciousness has not been without criticism; for example, Dennett (1993) attacked the use of theatre metaphors, proposing his own 'multiple drafts' concept that emphasizes the distributed nature of consciousness and the idea that there is no theatre in the brain 'where it all comes together'. Blackmore (2001) has supported this view; however, her argument does more to criticize the actual metaphor of the theatre, without exposing any actual flaws in the functionality of GW theory. It should also be noted that GW theory does not satisfy Chalmers's (1996) demands for a solution to the 'hard problem of consciousness', since he considers that such theories do not explain consciousness, but simply the cognitive processes that accompany it. Chalmers's argument presumes that the actual experience of consciousness involves something above and beyond these exchanges of information, in order to explain why there is a subjective, phenomenological experience. His own approach of Naturalistic Dualism aims to address this by proposing that experience is a pervasive property of the universe, even at the level of interactions between individual atoms. Although compelling, his conclusions point towards something that cannot be proven through our current models of science, and can only be justified in philosophical terms.

Taking a step back for a moment, all of the theorists discussed agree that consciousness is intuitively experienced in a way that can be described using the stream or theatre metaphors. The efficacy of this impression (even if it is viewed as something of an illusion, as Blackmore [2001] argues) is not disputed; what is at stake in these debates are the mechanisms of how and why this impression of consciousness occurs. As the purpose of this book is to explore the relationships between ASCs and electronic music and audio-visual media, it will not be necessary to comment in any further detail on how or why conscious experience occurs in the way that it does; for such discussions the reader is referred to those authors whose work I have briefly outlined. For our purposes, it will be sufficient for us to consider consciousness in accordance with how it is most commonly perceived. For this reason, the theatre metaphor will provide a useful conceptual basis to support our discussion.

Indeed, this metaphor will be particularly helpful to keep in mind as our discussion develops, since it lends itself easily to the possibility of representing conscious experience using video screens or loudspeakers. Thus, it will be possible to think about how first-person visual or auditory experiences might be used as a basis for corresponding sound or audio-visual media, and how the changes that occur to those sensory experiences might likewise indicate corresponding variations in the way sound or graphics are designed.

ALTERED STATES OF CONSCIOUSNESS

The term 'altered state of consciousness' came into use during the 1960s, most notably with Charles Tart's *Altered States of Consciousness* (1969). Within this volume, Ludwig's (1969, pp.9–10) definition of ASCs considers them to be any mental state induced by 'physiological, psychological, or pharmacological maneuvers ... representing a sufficient deviation in subjective experience from certain general norms [that an individual may experience during] alert, waking consciousness'. For our purposes here, we shall similarly consider ASCs as those states of consciousness such as dream, delirium, hallucination, and meditation that differ significantly from those we experience during normal, waking consciousness. Such states can be produced either voluntarily or involuntarily through various methods.[3] These include sensory deprivation, such as may occur due to solitary confinement; suspension in floatation tanks; or isolating environments such as long periods at sea. Conversely, ASCs may also be induced in situations of sensory overload, as found at Christian revival meetings; spirit possession rituals; or the rituals of Whirling Dervishes. They may also be caused by relaxed absorption into a repetitive task or heightened state of attention such as may occur through meditation. In addition, they may result from changes to body chemistry or neurophysiology, such as may be caused by fasting, dehydration, sleep deprivation, or various intoxicating substances such as psychedelic drugs. These states may produce a variety of changes to the stream of consciousness. For example, thought processes, attention, and awareness may be disrupted. Distortions to time perception may also occur, during which moments appear to pass much more quickly or slowly than usual. In some instances changes to one's sense of self may result, so that a person may feel as if he or she has been taken over by mystical or revelatory forces. Similarly, changes to body image such as feelings of weightlessness or 'out-of-body experiences' may occur. Heightened states of emotion, such as states of ecstasy or terror may also be associated with ASCs. Lastly, perceptual distortions may occur, resulting in hallucinations of the visual (sight), auditory (hearing), somatic (body), gustatory (taste), or olfactory (smell) senses. While this outlines in broad strokes the essential mechanisms and characteristics of ASCs, for the purposes of our discussion it will be useful to consider several specific varieties of ASC and their associated effects in further detail.

Psychosis

Psychosis is a broad category that describes a separation from reality, such as may be caused by psychological disorders such as schizophrenia, various medical conditions such as brain tumours, or substance abuse. Episodes of psychosis may include severe disruptions to thoughts and emotions; experiences of hallucination; delusions; or paranoia. A significant feature is that of 'auditory verbal hallucinations', during which an individual may perceive voices which seem to originate from the external environment around them, or as if inside their head (Wayne, 2012, p.87). Whilst these voices have no physical acoustic origin, they are perceived as if they are real, activating Heschl's gyrus (the auditory cortex), the same area of the brain that is activated when real sounds are heard (Dierks et al., 1999). In this regard they differ from the internal dialogue that most people experience as 'inner speech', though they may be a related process. Auditory hallucinations may also consist of hallucinated music (Kumar et al., 2014), bangs, or noises (Jones et al., 2012).

Psychedelic Experience

Hallucinogens such as mescaline, LSD, or psilocybin are sometimes referred to as 'psychomimetics', since the experience can be compared to a temporary psychotic episode, though others have found this term somewhat reductive and prefer 'psychedelics' (meaning 'mind manifesting'; see Adams, 1994). Among the most notable features is that of visual hallucinations. As Klüver (1971) discussed, these often assume typical 'form constants' such as lattice, cobweb, funnel, and spiral patterns of light, as seen in Figure 1.1. According to Klüver's study, during the earlier stages of hallucination these patterns may be perceived directly, while in later stages the participant may see forms abstracted from them. The view that visual hallucinations may consist of both pattern effects and figurative or narrative sequences was also supported by Strassman's (2001, p.147) DMT (*N,N*-dimethyltryptamine) studies.[4] Strassman's participants described geometric patterns that recalled Islamic, Mayan, or circuit-board designs and tunnels of light, while in the more intense stages of hallucination they saw fully formed figures such as strange beings, entities, and scenes.

Though less commonly reported than visual hallucinations, users of psychedelic drugs also report auditory hallucinations including music, noises, and voices (Weinel, Cunningham, and Griffiths, 2014). These experiences range in intensity; in subtle cases an individual may find their aural experience becomes more enjoyable or frightening than usual. As the effects intensify, the subjective perception of sounds from the external environment becomes significantly altered; sounds may appear to echo, distort, or appear more close or distant than usual. Some people also describe sounds appearing to slow down or speed up. Finally, in the most intense stages of hallucination sounds may be perceived that have no acoustic origin in the external environment. These may consist of hallucinated noises such as oscillations,

Figure 1.1. Visual patterns of hallucination or 'form constants', in (a) lattice, (b) cobweb, (c) funnel, and (d) spiral configurations. Reproduced from Bressloff et al. (2001), by permission of the Royal Society.

high-frequency tones, music, or voices. For example, one of Strassman's (2001, p.148) participants referred to 'high pitched', 'whining and whirring', 'chattering', 'crinkling and crunching' sounds.

Besides visual and auditory effects, psychedelic experiences may also produce perceptual distortions of other sensory faculties such as smells and tastes. These may occur in the context of 'synaesthesia' effects, in which different sensory modalities may become blurred (Cytowic, 1989). Although experiences of synaesthesia may occur across any of the senses, a commonly reported phenomenon is that of 'sound-to-image' visual hallucinations that appear to move or correspond with musical stimuli from the external environment (e.g. Bliss and Clark, 1962, p.97). Beyond sensory hallucinations, the psychedelic experience may also induce profound emotions and experiences of terror or euphoria. Sense of self and body image may also be disrupted, as in the cases of 'out-of-body experience' described by participants in Strassman's (2001) studies. During these episodes the individual perceives leaving their own body, sometimes hovering somewhere above it and looking down upon it. Similarly, dissolved ego boundaries or experiences of oneness with the universe are also typical.

Dreaming

Dreaming may also be considered as a form of ASC. During sleep, most people typically experience phases of NREM (non-rapid eye movement) and REM (rapid eye movement). Dreams usually occur during the REM stage. As Hobson (2009) discusses, dreaming may involve many of the features of waking consciousness, but differs in that sensory perceptions are internally generated within the brain, may be bizarre, and are often accompanied by a lack of self-reflection or access to memory. In these terms, dreams can be thought of as fundamentally similar to hallucinatory experiences that occur during sleep, and may entail sensory perceptions, bodily sensations, irrational thoughts, and heightened emotions. Hobson considers that dreams act as 'virtual reality pattern generators', which are involved in the development and maintenance of consciousness.

Hypnagogic Hallucinations

It is also possible to experience hallucinations on the threshold of sleep, such as when beginning to fall asleep (hypnagogic states) and when waking up (hypnopompic states), when one is neither fully asleep nor awake. A classic example of this is sleep paralysis, or the 'old hag' phenomenon, during which the individual perceives an old woman or creature sitting on their chest in a suffocating manner (Hufford, 1989). These experiences may involve both visual and auditory hallucinations. Those who experience sleep paralysis (or 'night terrors') commonly describe loud buzzing noises, vibrating sensations, and feelings of being suffocated and unable to move. Often the individual will see or feel the presence of ominous dark figures within their sleeping quarters such as daemons, creatures, or intruders.

Sensory Deprivation

Sensory deprivation induces experiences of hallucination by closing off the sensory inputs from the external environment. John Lilly (1972) carried out extensive research in this area through the use of specially designed sensory isolation tanks. These tanks remove all light and sound, and suspend the individual in water that is kept at a precise body temperature so that it feels neither hot nor cold. From his personal experiments, Lilly described 'awareness and increasing sensory experience … dreamlike sequences, [and] waking dreams' (p.42). Though subsequently he augmented these hallucinations through the use of LSD, even without the addition of drugs sensory isolation tanks are capable of producing strong experiences of hallucination.

Meditation

Meditation typically involves creating deeply passive states of awareness, and can also be considered as a form of ASC. While the religious context for meditation varies, Maupin (1969) highlights underlying similarities: usually meditation is seen as a way to suspend the busyness of daily thoughts to access a deeper level of awareness. Typical techniques involve seated positions and the focus of attention on breathing or an object. The main outcomes are a sense of improved relaxation and wellbeing. Though less common, meditation can also result in more dramatic ASCs. For example, hallucinations of 'celestial music' and visual experiences such as a 'faint glow around others' bodies' have been described (Hendlin, 1979). Despite Peleka's (1990) reservations about the reliability of such accounts, other reports of this nature can be found elsewhere. For instance, Lindahl et al. (2013) discuss 'light experiences' in Buddhist meditation traditions, which may be produced through comparable mechanisms to those of sensory deprivation.

Trance

Trance states are found in various religious contexts across the globe. As Rouget (1985) discussed in his classic study of trance in Bali and many other locations, these states typically occur in situations of sensory overload brought on by music, dancing, and the spraying of liquids. During these episodes, the individual may experience profound emotional and behavioural states. They may lose their sense of self or experience spirit possession, and may exhibit trembling, rigidity, or unusual physical faculties, such as the ability to withstand pain. In some cases the individual may be unable to recall the trance retrospectively. Musical characteristics such as repetitive drumming and quickening tempos are often associated with the production of trance[5]; however, research seems to suggest that these are not only physiological triggers but also serve partly as a means to structure events within a cultural context (Fachner, 2011). Becker (2004) has proposed a cross-cultural view that sees trance as a heightened emotional state to which some individuals, whom she terms 'deep listeners', are particularly susceptible.

Hypnosis

The American Psychological Association (APA) defines hypnosis as a procedure during which a hypnotist provides an introduction before guiding a subject with suggestions for using their imagination (Barnier and Nash, 2012). The procedure encourages the subject to respond to suggested changes to subjective experience and evaluate them. These changes in experience may relate to perception, sensation, thought, emotion, or behaviour. If the process of induction is successful, the inductee may display behaviour that appears almost delusional or compulsive in accordance with the suggestions of the hypnotist. However, such behaviours are also accompanied by an alteration in subjective experience for the subject, so that the individual may become absorbed in imaginative experiences such as mental images. For example, the subject may be informed that there is a fly buzzing around the room, and then will perceive this. Unlike mental images that are usually constructed voluntarily, the experience is involuntary, lending it a hallucinatory quality. Due to the changes in subjective experience that occur, hypnosis may be viewed as a type of ASC; though as Kihlstrom (2012) discusses, this distinction is still debated. As with trance, there is also some suggestion that some individuals are more susceptible to hypnosis, and comparisons have been drawn between the two states (Oakley, 2012).

Of those varieties of consciousness that have been outlined here, some have been a source of controversy. As was discussed in the Introduction, attitudes towards the possible benefits and consequences of ASCs vary substantially between different cultures. For example, some shamanic societies see psychedelic hallucinations as a form of healing, yet most countries outlaw their use. Experiences of psychosis are traumatic, though R.D. Laing (1967) argued that the labelling and treatment of schizophrenics by society was an important factor in making their experiences that much more negative. Sensory deprivation is found in the extremely different contexts of new-age therapies and torture. Even dreams, which are perhaps the most common and apparently benign of the ASCs may divide opinions with regards to their significance or lack thereof.[6] In some cases there are of course significant dangers that may be associated with ASCs, such as the risks of toxicity that are inherent with some drugs. For example, the naturally occurring hallucinogen datura is poisonous and can be extremely dangerous. ASCs are also highly problematic if they occur at the same time that one requires mental or physical dexterity, such as for the operation of motor vehicles or other machinery. Conversely, there have been some scientific studies that have suggested the benefits of ASCs in some circumstances. While the recreational use of psychedelic drugs and their subsequent prohibition has slowed down serious scientific research, in recent years organizations such as the Multidisciplinary Association for Psychedelic Studies (MAPS) have sought to drive forwards their medical and therapeutic use. Among the growing number of studies in this area, Mithoefer et al. (2010) showed positive effects for the use of MDMA in treating post-traumatic stress disorder (PTSD); while LSD and psilocybin have also shown some promise for treating addictions such as alcoholism (Bogenschutz and Johnson, 2016). Other ASCs such as meditation may also have potential health benefits; for example, Monk-Turner (2003) showed that young adults who meditated for fourteen weeks saw improvements to both psychological and physical health. Considering sensory isolation tanks as a form of therapy, Kjellgren, Lyden, and Norlander (2008) indicated that they might be useful for relaxation and pain reduction. Hypnosis has also been explored as a means for pain management (Montgomery, Duhamel, and Redd, 2000) or as a complement to the cognitive-behavioural therapies used for various conditions such as anxiety (Schoenberger, 2000). Perhaps in time then, just as the shamanic societies of old have found positive uses for ASCs, modern societies may also find ways in which to properly utilize them in order to achieve beneficial effects.

DIMENSIONAL MODELS

So far we have discussed ASCs primarily as if they were discrete states. However, this does not allow us to consider varying intensity, or the points between normal waking consciousness and ASC. It is possible to consider conscious states as a continuum ranging from normal waking consciousness to ASC. In these terms, ASCs can be considered as points that deviate substantially from normal waking consciousness on the continuum. Here we consider two possible dimensional models that will be useful for our discussion of ASCs as it develops.

Cartography of Ecstatic and Meditative States

Fischer's (1971) 'cartography of ecstatic and meditative states' describes various states of consciousness in relation to energy expenditure. The model provides a continuum ranging from 'trophotropic' to 'ergotropic' states. 'Trophotropic' describes states that promote energy conservation, such as relaxation and meditation. 'Ergotropic' states promote expenditure of energy, such as ecstatic hallucination. 'Normal' consciousness occupies a mid-point on this continuum, while ASCs are found with varying degrees of intensity at the ergotropic or trophotropic ends of the spectrum. The concept of energy expenditure used by this model relates to 'arousal', which as discussed earlier, describes the physiological and psychological states associated with energy levels. This function is also considered by valence and arousal models of emotion, such as Russell's (1980) 'circumplex model of affect', and corresponds with the functions of the ANS. In these terms arousal can be thought of as a dimension of emotion, and ASCs as particularly heightened states of emotion; though in considering this view we should not overlook the effects of ASCs across other systems.

Fischer's (1971) continuum will prove useful for our discussion as it unfolds, since it allows us to consider ASCs as related to states of high or low arousal. This view is consistent when considering the mechanisms that produce them, since as we have seen, ASCs such as trance states may be produced through mechanisms of sensory overload (or conversely, reduction of sensory input). Indeed, Rouget (1985) utilized Fischer's model in order to distinguish the concepts of 'ecstasy' and 'trance' as they occur in various shamanic and possession trance cultures. According to Rouget's definitions 'ecstasy' occurs with stillness, quiet contemplation and isolation; 'trance', by contrast, occurs with movement, loud noises, and social situations.[7] These definitions are especially useful for our purposes, since some forms of electronic music and audio-visual media are designed specifically to support the production of high arousal states and behaviours (e.g. fast techno music, which promotes energetic dancing) or low arousal states (e.g. ambient or 'chill-out' music, which promotes relaxation).

State Space

Hobson's (2003, pp.44–46) 'state-space' concept describes consciousness according to a three-dimensional system. This 'AIM' model of consciousness uses 'Activation', 'Input', and 'Modulation' axes to describe the range of possible states. In this model, 'Activation' indicates the level of brain activity; during states of normal waking consciousness activity will be high, while in states such as unconsciousness or dreamless sleep it will be low. 'Input' deals with the exchange of information between the individual and the external world; for example, during waking states visual information is received from the external environment via the senses, while during states such as dreaming or hallucination visual stimuli may arise via internal processes. 'Modulation' (or 'mode') deals with the way in which events are recorded to and recalled from memory; during waking states events are recorded to memory normally, while the contents of dreams are often unrecorded and cannot be recalled. Throughout a normal twenty-four hour cycle, a person will typically move through states of waking consciousness, NREM, and REM sleep states of dreaming. This cycle involves changes to the levels of activation, input, and modulation. ASCs such as hallucinations can then be considered as modifying the position of certain axes; for example, the input axis may be moved from 'external' towards an 'internal' position, resulting in the perception of sensory experiences produced internally within the brain. For Hobson dreams and hallucinations are of fundamental similarity, since both involve similar brain states that enable the perception of internally produced visions.

While critics have pointed out the limitations of Hobson's (2003) model in distinguishing between the qualities of different ASCs (Cardeña, 2011, p.7), it nonetheless provides a useful dimensional model of consciousness, which will inform our subsequent discussion. In particular, his definition of an Input axis will be of significance, since this allows us to distinguish the subjective perception of visual and auditory phenomena that originate in an external environment, from those perceptions that arise internally. As we have discussed already, experiences of visual or auditory hallucination are experienced subjectively during ASCs, and may consist of either distortions to the way the external environment is perceived, or experiences with no physical origin in the external environment. In cases of dreams, total hallucinations or psychosis, it is possible for experience to be completely engulfed by these internal phenomena, though often in waking states of hallucination the experience seems to blur the boundaries between the internal and the external. Thus experiences of hallucination could be considered as moving this Input parameter towards an internal channel of information. This concept of 'internal' experience can be viewed as broadly similar to the idea of an 'inner world', as discussed by R.D. Laing (1967) in relation to the experiences of schizophrenics, or the spirit worlds or underworlds of shamanic cultures.

Of course, this account of changes between internal and external experience may appear slightly reductive, since internal processes play an important role even in normal waking states of consciousness. While a normal waking state of consciousness may allow external sensory experiences of one's environment or bodily sensations, it may also include internal experiences such as mental images, inner speech, or imagined sounds. The reader may like to test this by briefly imagining a green teapot. If you did this and saw a teapot in your 'mind's eye', then you just experienced a mental image. Similarly, most people have an experience of inner speech and are able to imagine sounds or music ('aural imagery'; see Grimshaw and Garner, 2015, pp.143–145). As discussed earlier, perception also involves 'top-down' processes such as perceptual hypotheses. It is not so straightforward then to describe normal waking consciousness as arising entirely from external sensory perception, but certainly dreams and hallucinations appear to emphasize and promote a more vivid experience of internally generated images and sounds. For many of the ASCs described, internal perceptions seem to spill-out, colouring or distorting the sensory experience of the external world, as though distorted by a lens, or with internal images and sounds layered on top. Moreover, while typical hallucinations may combine the internal and the external, experiences of both dreams and total hallucinations (e.g. strong DMT experiences) appear to be almost wholly internal.

The dimensional models introduced in this section allow us to consider ASCs as points of significant divergence from the baseline of normal waking consciousness. Heightened emotional states may be thought of as a form of ASC, though as we see through Hobson's model, many types of ASC are also accompanied by changes in the operation of the brain that affect other cognitive systems such as memory, and turn attention towards internal sensory inputs.

ELECTRONIC MUSIC & AUDIO-VISUAL MEDIA

Having established a view of ASCs, we may now begin to consider some relationships with electronic music and audio-visual media. The effects of sound and music on conscious experience are interesting in their own right, and can be considered in terms of representational and affective responses. These two functions have received considerable attention from theorists, though they remain the source of much debate. In Ancient Greece, for example, Aristotle discussed the concepts of 'mimesis': the capability for dramatic works to imitate the world; and 'catharsis': the purifying emotional effects of a work. More recently in music, Meyer (1956) referred to the related concepts of 'referential' features that indicate non-musical properties, and 'absolute' or intrinsically musical properties of expression. Since these properties have important implications for the design of electronic music and audio-visual media, we shall examine each in more detail before considering how they may allow sound and music to represent or induce ASCs.

Representational Properties

In visual media, images and videos can be used to represent the physical world by recreating the patterns of light that enter the eye when we observe the environment around us. In electronic music and audio-visual media, sounds can be used to perform a similar function. For example, 'mimetic' sounds may reference real-world spaces, environments, or other aspects of culture.[8] One way these referential effects can be achieved is through the use of recorded sounds. For example, using a microphone we could record the sound of a dog barking or a babbling brook, which when reproduced with loudspeakers may invoke the listener's semantic and episodic memories, as they access their knowledge and past experiences of each. Through collaging of these materials (as used in forms of soundscape composition), composers may elicit rich tapestries of sound that represent the aural experience of a location.

Other representational techniques in sound that are more poetic or metaphorical are also possible, and these can be used to represent other non-aural aspects of culture. In classical music, for example, Vivaldi's *The Four Seasons* (1725) compositions elicit seasonal themes through features of the orchestral instrumentation. Here sound does not literally resemble the aural experience of pastoral landscapes, but metaphorically suggests such locations through evocative patterns of pitch, melodies, and dynamics. In electronic music, spectromorphological[9] properties of sound can be similarly used to imitate non-musical aspects of culture. Entertaining examples of this can be heard via Malcolm Clarke's (BBC Radiophonic Workshop) sounds on 'Splodges' (on Various Artists, *Play School*, 1972), in which characteristics of pitch, tremolo, and amplitude elicit the sounds of a variety of mythical 'splodge' creatures. The sounds are all actually created using analogue synthesis, but imitate characteristics of animals or objects in order to conjure the fictional creatures of the narrative. That the record is aimed at children is reflective of how effective and easily understood mimetic sonic materials can be, though we may also note that spoken dialogue supports the effect, providing a linguistic narrative that contextualizes the sounds and guides their interpretation.

Representational properties can be used to communicate aspects relating to the actual aural experience of ASCs, or the conceptual structures and ideologies of cultures that engage with them. Let us begin by considering the former case. Mimetic use of audio-visual materials can enable the aural and visual components of subjective experience to be represented. For example, if a video camera and microphones are mounted upon the head, they can be used to record audio-visual material that approximates that received externally via the senses of the person wearing the equipment. Using the approach described it is possible to represent the aural and visual components of first-person experience using sound and video equipment.[10] Indeed, we see this all the time in all kinds of media that use a first-person perspective, such as binaural recordings,[11] landscape paintings and 'first-person shooter' video games. However, media that uses a first-person point-of-view (POV) need not be limited to representations of normal waking consciousness, since it is also possible to represent aspects of ASCs such as hallucinations. Among their various effects, hallucinations cause a shift towards internal sensory inputs, producing distortions to auditory or visual perception. Of course, these internal inputs cannot be captured and recorded with microphones and cameras in the way that external inputs can, but this is where technology comes to our aid. Visual techniques provided by computer graphics may allow moving images to be created that represent the distorted perceptual experiences of hallucinations. Similarly, sound design techniques can be used to construct sounds based on auditory hallucinations. Combining both sound and video elements then allows audio-visual representations of ASCs, with regards to the aural and visual components of such experiences. Note that such audio-visual representations can be approached in a fairly accurate fashion with some equivalence, though stylized approaches that are more metaphorical or impressionistic are also possible. These methods have been used in some existing electronic artworks, such as video games that portray experiences of hallucination using first-person POV.

Affective Properties

Sound and music may also elicit affective responses, though the precise mechanisms through which this occurs have been a source of debate. In Kivy's (1990) work on music and emotion, he proposed the positions of 'cognitivist' and 'emotivist' to describe the respective views that musical emotions are represented and mentally perceived by listeners, or that they are actually 'felt' in a similar way to non-musical emotions. According to Kivy's cognitivist view, music does not act directly on the emotions, but instead provides a 'deep layer of representational qualities beneath its apparently abstract surface' (p.58). Kivy considered that the 'pure musical features' of pitch, harmony, melody, and rhythm provided this layer. In Gabrielsson and Lindstrom's (2012) meta-study of psychological research in this area, they found that high pitches, consonant harmonies, and major modes were often associated with emotions that have a positive valence such as happiness; low pitches, dissonant harmonies, and minor modes, by contrast, were more commonly related to emotions with negative valence such as sadness. Quick tempos and rhythms were the features most strongly associated with high activation or arousal properties of music. Although their study explored *perceived* emotions in music, there is also supporting evidence to suggest music can also *induce* emotional responses that have a physiological dimension. For example, Krumhansl (1997) showed that music could actually induce physiological changes that have some similarities to those of non-musical emotions; while Rickard (2004) reported a correspondence between listener accounts of musical intensity and arousal levels. Gabrielsson (2002) suggests that there is not always a 'positive relationship' in which the perceived emotions in music are equivalent to those that are induced, yet Evans and Schubert (2008) argue that this is most commonly the case. For our purposes then, it will be sufficient to presume that affective properties of music are strongly related to pitch, harmony, melody, and rhythm; and that these can often give rise to corresponding cognitive, physiological, and behavioural responses. As Sloboda and Juslin (2012) highlight, these responses are not absolute, and depend significantly on other factors such as the motivation and expectation of the listener.

Although research in music and emotion has tended to focus on abstract musical properties such as pitch, harmony, melody, and rhythm, we may also consider that representational sounds may also lead to emotional responses. Since representational sounds may invoke the semantic and episodic memories of an individual, they may also excite corresponding emotions that are linked to these recollections. For instance, a listener with a fear of dogs may experience a negative emotional reaction when listening to a sound recording of a dog barking, while conversely he or she may find the sound of a babbling brook relaxing. In this way sound effects and sonic art such as soundscape recordings that utilize representational sounds, may also give rise to affective responses, as Dean and Bailes (2010; 2011) have begun to explore for compositions such as Trevor Wishart's *Red Bird: A Political Prisoner's Dream* (1978).

If we consider consciousness in terms of arousal as indicated by Fischer's (1971) cartography, then it is possible to conceive of the affective properties of music as a contributing factor that may support the production of ASCs. The affective properties of music may also be used in combination with other techniques in order to produce heightened emotional states. For example, some listeners may use music alone to influence mood, while others may use it in combination with drugs or alcohol as a means to heighten or direct the experience. When used in a social context with other methods for increasing arousal such as vigorous dancing, it is possible for trance states to be produced. Conversely, solitary listening may provide states of relaxation comparable to those of meditation. These uses of the affective properties of music are pertinent when considering electronic music and audio-visual media, since the material design of the music may implicate its use for attaining high- or low-arousal states. For example, the rhythms of fast techno music may promote energetic states, while the pulse and gentle melodies of ambient house or 'chill-out' music may promote relaxation.

The representational and affective properties of sound and music may be viewed as related, since representations may indicate conceptual meanings that support the affective properties of the music and vice versa. For example, psychedelic music may have representational features that allow the listener to associate the music with the experience of ASCs or the concepts and ideologies of psychedelic culture. If the listener finds these features appealing, he or she may be sufficiently motivated to attend to the music and respond in an affective manner. In this way affective experiences may become framed by conceptual meaning, each reinforcing the other. Engagement by the listener through cognitive, behavioural, and emotional faculties indicates an agreement with the ethos expressed by the music; and thus as Becker (2012) discusses, listening is tied up with notions of personhood and identity, and implicates structures of knowledge and belief.

* * *

In this chapter I have provided an overview of consciousness and the way that various aspects of sensory experience, emotions, and bodily sensations may change during ASCs. As we have seen, there are various types of ASCs that may occur under different circumstances, and these can be thought of not as discrete states but as points of more radical divergence from normal waking consciousness. The use of these ASCs by different cultures varies widely, and in some cases both defines and reflects the ethos of the group. As a result much of the art and music that is related to ASCs can be considered in terms of the ethos it reflects, whether secular or religious. In the chapters that follow we shall see how the material design of electronic music and audio-visual media allows the representation of ASCs, and how this is related to the affective properties of the music. From psychedelic rock to rave, electroacoustic music, films, and video games, we shall see how various conceptual frameworks are constructed in accordance with different ideologies and aspirations. Yet while the technological methods are new, the fundamental mechanisms are old. Before looking forwards then, we must first look back to consider the art and music of an ancient form of cultural practice related to ASCs: shamanism.

CHAPTER 2

Ancient Ways

After Altamira, all is decadence.

—Pablo Picasso

In 1940 eighteen-year-old Marcel Ravidat discovered the entrance to a cave near Dordogne in the South of France. Returning to the cave with three friends, he found the inner walls covered with thousands of pictures of animals, human-like figures, and strange symbols. In the dark past of our species early *Homo sapiens* illuminated the cave with fire and carried out shamanic rituals using altered states of consciousness (ASCs). During these rituals the caves came alive with resonating sounds, as bright lattice and funnel patterns of light formed tunnels to the underworld. The rough surfaces of the cave walls became like Rorschach inkblots from which various animal hallucinations emerged: bison, horses, aurochs, woolly mammoths, deer, and felines. The caves were seen as a gateway to the underworld, a spiritual realm of profound importance that the shaman would mediate with for society. After the ceremonies, shamans would adorn the walls with images of the hallucinatory animals, creating lasting impressions of the sacred visions. It was the surviving traces of these ritual activities from over 17,000 years ago that the teenagers were seeing.

This is the hypothesized explanation for the Upper Palaeolithic rock art of sites such as Lascaux in France according to archaeologist Lewis-Williams (2004). While any account of artworks produced in prehistoric times will be subject to debate, if the theory is correct then some of the earliest forms of artistic practice in the history of our species may be closely aligned with ASCs. Moreover, in the ritual practices of surviving shamanic traditions, such as those of the Americas, we are able to gain a clearer impression of the relationship between ASCs, art, and music. An analysis of shamanic visual art reveals that the material artefacts frequently represent aspects of visionary experiences. This may occur by rendering the visual experience of ASCs, such as geometric or figurative hallucinations, using artistic materials, or otherwise representing them through stylized or metaphorical techniques. The resulting artefacts can be understood as invoking aspects of the spirit world within the everyday, making them concrete for those who may not be able to access the shamanic sensorium. The use of sound and music in shamanic traditions may similarly invoke the presence of supernatural forces within a ritual context. However, as we shall see, sound is also distinguished by its capability for inducing changes to consciousness at critical moments in time. By virtue of these two related functions, shamanic music may represent the contents of visionary experiences and/or induce them. These capabilities are fundamental, and later in this book I will argue that electronic techniques can be used to provide similar functions in distinct ways. The purpose of this chapter then is to establish underlying principles that will inform our subsequent discussion of ASCs in electronic music and audio-visual media. Towards this aim, the chapter begins with an overview of shamanism and visionary experiences, which is then followed by discussions of shamanic art and music.

SHAMANISM

Shamanic practices are found in many parts of the world, and may be among the earliest forms of human religion. As Vitebsky (1995, p.11) discusses, shamanism is 'scattered and fragmented', yet there are some striking similarities between many of the traditions. The term 'shaman' derives from the Tungus word meaning 'to know', in connection with the Siberian shamanism practiced by reindeer-herder tribes (Laufer, 1913). Among hunter-gatherer tribes of Siberia and Mongolia, the shaman plays an important role in mediating with the forces of nature, undergoing spirit flights in which he or she is believed to transform into an animal. In South and East Asia, many spiritual and religious traditions are found that may be considered to contain aspects of shamanism, such as the trance culture of Bali, where dancers are said to undergo spirit possession amidst percussive drumming. Traditions of possession trance are not exclusive to this area; the San people of South Africa, and the Haitian Vodou ceremonies of the Caribbean are just two other examples in which this type of practice occurs. In North America, Native American tribes such as the Kiowa follow a form of shamanism that is blended with aspects of Christianity, and utilize the hallucinogenic cactus peyote as a ritual sacrament to receive visions. In Mexico the Huichol also utilize peyote and worship various gods of nature; while the Mazatec use psilocybe mushrooms to invoke the spirits. Tracing further down the map into South America, indigenous peoples of the Amazon make extensive use of natural plants with psychoactive properties. For instance, both the Tukano of Colombia and the Shipibo-Conibo of Peru use the hallucinogenic brew yagé to induce powerful visions in which they contact the spirits of the forest. Though they have since perished, in Darwin's time shamanism was even known as far South as Patagonia, where Yámana shamans once lived upon the beaches of Tierra del Fuego.

The Role of a Shaman

In Eliade's (1964) classic text on the topic, he defined shamanism as a 'technique of ecstasy' and attempted to draw out the commonalities between practices of this kind across a range of global indigenous societies. Although subsequent scholars have pointed out the limitations of his study,[1] many of the essential comparisons he makes remain useful starting points when considering the nature of shamanism. Shamanic systems typically hold a tiered view of the universe, in which besides the regular world there is also a spirit realm above and/or an underworld below. In these societies, alternate planes of existence are perceived as having important consequences for many aspects of life and the wellbeing of individuals within the community. In Eliade's account, the process of becoming a shaman typically begins with selection or an initiation. This may involve a dream or vision in which the prospective shaman journeys into the spirit world, where he or she may be broken down and reassembled by the spirits. For example, one account from a Buryat shaman describes the initiate as being carried to the sky by ancestral spirits, who place him before an assembly that instructs him; the process includes cooking his flesh in a pot (pp.43–44). Following this initial calling to the vocation, the shaman learns how to transform into animals, speak their language, and traverse the boundaries of the spirit world. Once training is complete, the shaman becomes indispensible in matters of the soul; he or she can travel to the spirit world or underworld because he or she has been there already.

The need for shamanism arises due to the perceived efficacy that the spirit world has over the daily existence of the community. Shamanic societies are typically animist, and thus consider that all forces and entities within nature have a soul. Using ecstatic techniques to produce ASCs, the shaman is a figure who carries out rituals that enable him or her to mediate with the spirits of nature. Such techniques often involve the use of plant hallucinogens; however, the use of these within highly structured rituals has led some theorists to refer to them as 'Shamanic States of Consciousness' (SSCs), in distinction from other forms of ASC (Harner, 1990, pp.59–72). Through the use of these visionary states, the shaman is able to recognize the will of animal spirits, ancestors, or other natural elements upon which the community depends, and thereby promotes a harmonious existence in balance with nature. The shaman's work within the spirit world also assists the community by empowering them with a sense of control over unknown aspects of their destinies that they believe are affected by it, such as health, resources, and the weather. In the shamanic worldview, the spirit world is not separate from reality, but an integral and meaningful aspect of it. Nonetheless, a distinction between earthly and spiritual planes of existence is recognized, and shamanic societies may often use spiritual healing alongside herbalism or modern medicine.

Visionary Experiences

Visionary experiences are ASCs that are manifested within a shamanic context. They may include heightened states of emotion; hallucinations of the visual and auditory senses; and other perceptual distortions such as those discussed in the previous chapter. When we consider the form of these experiences, we find that some features are cross-cultural, while others are culturally dependent. In particular, Klüver's (1971) work on form constants, and other related studies such as Oster (1970), Siegel (1977), and Bressloff et al. (2001), suggests that tunnel and lattice patterns are produced by the visual system, and are experienced similarly by different people. In Klüver's account, these visual patterns are seen in the early stages of hallucination, while in more advanced stages the brain interprets them as iconic imagery, such as physical forms or objects. For example, in Siegel's (1977, p.134) study his participants saw 'recognizable complex scenes, people and objects, many in cartoon or caricature form, with some degree of depth of symmetry... often projected against a background of geometric forms'. In some instances these hallucinatory impressions were associated with childhood or strong emotional experiences 'elaborated and embellished into fantastic scenes' (p.136). Following Klüver, Siegel sees the iconic imagery as related to the form constants, but also asserts that they are dependent on memory, and hence vary according to the individual and his or her cultural background.

According to this view, visionary experiences may be understood as arising through a process of interaction between the sensory system under ASCs and culturally dependent memories. This view has been especially influential on the discourses regarding shamanic art. Notably, Lewis-Williams (2004) considers that the cross-cultural experience of form constants provides an explanation for the descriptions of tunnels to a spirit world or underworld in shamanic traditions; while the animals that emerge from his 'entopic phenomena' are culturally dependent manifestations. Extending this concept of hallucinations to other senses, he also considers that auditory hallucinations of cicadas, wind, trickling water, or swarming bees, may be derived from buzzing or tinnitus effects caused by increases in blood pressure during ASCs (p.153). Similarly, other recurring motifs related to bodily perception, such as weightlessness or flight, may be attributable to physiological changes during ASCs that are cross-cultural.

Looking beyond these typical effects, visionary experiences may also be shaped by sensory interventions conducted by the shaman. For example, shamanic rituals are often undertaken using a costume and various other accessories such as hanging metal objects, mirrors, animal parts, masks, and caps. These artefacts are imbued with magical significance or may embody spirits. For example, a shaman's costume may symbolize a bird in order to assist with his or her flight to the spirit world; or may resemble a human skeleton so that he or she may walk among the dead (Eliade, 1964, pp.158–165). In Siberia the shaman's drum is also considered to be an animal that the shaman 'rides' to the spirit world. These artefacts are not only symbolic, but are also multisensory instruments with visual, auditory, and tactile qualities. Hence the actual sound of the shaman's drum may signal the journey to the spirit world, while the rhythms may also elicit affective states of heightened arousal that assist with the production of ASCs. In this way the cultural products of shamanism including both visual and sonic art provide inputs into the ASC process that shape its construction.

This brief introduction to shamanism and the significance of the visionary experience allows us to begin unravelling the design of shamanic art and music. Visual arts may represent aspects of the ASC experience, such as the perception of form constants or iconic images derived from memory. Creating images of the spirit world may affirm its presence in the everyday existence of shamanic peoples. Sound and music provide a similar function, since they may be used to represent or embody aspects of the spirit world. However, as time-based media, they may be used at key moments within shamanic rituals, shaping the form of the visionary experience. This capability is not only representational but also affective, since music can be used to induce states of heightened arousal and actually contribute towards the production of ASCs. In these terms, shamanic art and music do not represent the spirit world in a passive or detached manner, but are intrinsically involved in its construction and maintenance. In order to explore how this occurs more specifically, we turn now to consider a variety of shamanic art and music.

SHAMANIC ART

While sound is the main focus of this book, the consideration of shamanic visual arts will also provide a useful precursor to our discussion. In this section we explore a variety of shamanic traditions and their associated visual artworks. The meta-analysis that follows will then allow us to begin to see in more detail how aspects of the visionary experience may be represented externally through a variety of methods. This discussion will reveal a range of possible approaches that may be characterized as somewhere between literal or accurate representations, and stylized approaches that may be more impressionistic, metaphorical, or symbolic in their depictions. Gaining a clearer understanding of these approaches will inform our subsequent discussion of sound, where an equivalent range of accurate and stylized approaches may be utilized to represent the contents of ASC experiences within the aural domain.

San Rock Art

The San people are the indigenous hunter-gatherer 'Bushmen' peoples of southern Africa, whose ancestry is believed to have a cultural continuity 30,000–40,000 years long.[2] Western knowledge regarding the traditions of the San people was significantly advanced through the ethnographic work of Lucy Lloyd and Wilhelm Bleek in the late nineteenth century (Skotnes, 2007). While prior to their work colonial attitudes considered the San to be a naive and simplistic people, the San culture was revealed as rich and complex. Among their traditions, the San believed in a tiered universe and utilized trance rituals that were brought about through concentration, music, dance, and hyperventilation.

Examples of San rock art range in date from approximately 300 to 26,000 years ago, and depict humans with bows and other implements, and animal figures in various postures.[3] Some of these images are rendered using pigments, while others are engravings. The images can be understood as depicting trance rituals and the interaction of the shaman with the spirit world (Lewis-Williams, 1996). For example, some images represent the organization of trance rituals, in which the women sit around a fire clapping and singing special medicine songs, while the men dance facing them (p.28). Other images seem to actually depict experiences of trance, including changes to bodily proportions and animal metamorphosis. For example, the artwork shown in Figure 2.1 indicates various humanoid characters that seem

Figure 2.1. Traced copy of a San rock painting at Ezeljagdspoort, Southern Cape, made by Thomas Dowson, 1988. Dark red; scale in cm. Reproduced with permission from Lewis-Williams, Dowson and Deacon (1993).

to have the tails of fish. This image can be interpreted as a metaphorical representation of the trance experience, and may be related to rainmaking rituals (pp.44–54). Although the shamanic interpretation of San rock art is not without criticism,[4] this narrative is widely supported and has also provided the basis for Lewis-Williams's theories of Upper Palaeolithic rock art in Europe.

Native American Art

Native American tribes such as the Kiowa, Comanche, and Tarahumara utilize peyote in their shamanic rituals (La Barre, 2011). In the Kiowa tradition, peyote meetings are held in order to pray for health or the successful delivery of a child; to express gratitude for recovery from an illness; or to mark a child's first four birthdays. Following preparations, which include taking a sweat bath and preparation of the tipi, the ritual commences. The ritual occurs over the course of the night in several defined stages, which include the use of cigarettes, eating of peyote, prayers, 'peyote songs', the use of rattles, drums, whistles, and other symbolic items. In the morning, a ritual breakfast is consumed in a more informal manner.

Designs are found on ritual artefacts, clothing, and musical instruments produced by the Kiowa and other Native American tribes (Swan, 1999). Many of these symbolize the sky spirits, such as the waterbird or 'peyote bird', which is represented through feathered headdresses, fans, and designs. Some designs also incorporate the crucifix, due to the influence of Christianity on Native American traditions (La Barre, 2011, pp.292–294). These motifs are also found amongst the brightly coloured bead patterns seen on the heads of ritual staffs, handles of gourd rattles, peyote pouches, and other accessories. The luminescent pinpoint style and zigzags of these designs may be related to peyote visions. Paintings on buffalo hide and paper also depict Native American life in the early twentieth century, and many show aspects of the peyote ritual such as the organization of participants and representations of the visionary experience. For example, Figure 2.2 is an Arapaho painting of a peyote vision on cloth, and shows bright flashes of light that may be attributable to visual patterns of hallucination, alongside the symbol of the peyote bird.

Huichol Art

Of the various indigenous peoples of Central America, it has been remarked that the rites of the Huichol (who refer to themselves as the Wixáritari, meaning 'the people') may bear the strongest resemblance to those of pre-Columbian Mexico (La Barre, 1970). Huichol religion is a deeply personal experience, described by Schaefer and Furst (1996, p.12) as essentially 'ecological', since it is primarily concerned with the spirits of nature. The Huichol have many gods, of which the Sun,

Figure 2.2. Arapaho painting of a 'peyote vision' on cloth, collected by James Mooney, *c.*1904. Courtesy of the Smithsonian Institution, item: E233093-0.

Deer, Maize, and Peyote are particularly notable. Shamanic activity is also based around the ritual use of peyote, which is used as a panacea for treating wounds and various other ailments.[5]

Huichol art and textiles frequently feature representations of peyote and other symbols from nature.[6] In the 1960s the Huichol began making 'yarn paintings', which include brightly coloured symbolic designs and patterns, the high level of craftsmanship of which has led them to become valuable commodities in Western culture (Miller, 1978). These yarn paintings are essentially symbolic in nature, typically consisting of natural figures such as the Deer, Peyote, or the Sun gods. Figure 2.3 is an example of an elaborate Huichol yarn painting by José Benítez Sánchez, which depicts a skeletal shaman at the centre of a detailed array of deer, peyote, and rain serpent spirits, while Huichol pilgrims look onwards. As Furst (2007, p.72) notes, the yarn paintings should not necessarily be taken as exact representations of the peyote experience, which come at such speeds that they would be difficult to retain or reproduce. However, the brightly coloured, high-contrast style of the designs nonetheless bear a strong resemblance to the quality of the peyote visions, such as might be perceived on the back of closed eyelids. This connection has also been acknowledged by several other authors (e.g. Siegel, 1977; Eger and Collings,

Figure 2.3. *Nierı́ka,* a Huichol yarn painting by José Benítez Sánchez, 2003. Courtesy of Penn Museum.

1978), who draw attention to the geometric patterns that are seen in Huichol textiles, which can similarly be seen as derivative of peyote visions.

Tukano Art

The Tukano people of the northwestern Amazon in Colombia believe in a creation myth, in which their ancestors had to undergo various trials, and were taught how to inhabit the earth by supernatural beings such as the Sun Father, the Moon, Thunder-Person, the Jaguar, Serpent Spirits, the Master of Animals, and others (Reichel-Dolmatoff, 1978). The mythology imparted to them via these spirits deals with issues such as procreation and fertility. In both these myths and their current life, the Tukano use yagé, a hallucinogenic brew containing the vine *Banisteriopsis caapi* and various admixtures, the precise combination of which is dependent on the specific shamanic need, since the plants themselves are considered to have symbolic significance. For the Tukano, yagé provides a means through which to contact supernatural entities, allowing them to live in harmony with nature. Yagé rituals require various preparations such as sexual abstinence and a special light diet, and are conducted after sunset amidst monotonous recitals, music and dancing with seed rattles, flutes, and a conch instrument that produces a croaking sound. According to the Tukano, yagé visions occur in three stages: in the first stage the individual flies upwards to the Milky Way, experiencing luminous sensations, yellow flashes of dancing dots, kaleidoscopic colours, and shapes; in the second stage the person is projected beyond the Milky Way, where dreamlike scenes unfold before him; while in the final stage the visions gradually subside amidst swirling colours, lights, waves of music, and contemplation.

In his ethnographic studies of the Tukano, Reichel-Dolmatoff (1978) discussed the artistic designs found on the walls of Tukano buildings, which he was informed were based upon yagé visions. In consideration of the zigzag, lattice, star, and spiral patterns, he notes that these are similar to the patterns produced by the visual system during hallucinations. However, through his interactions with the Tukano, he discovered that the symbols also have specific meanings related to the themes of fertility that are of central importance in their mythology. Reichel-Dolmatoff asked the Tukano to draw their yagé visions with colouring pencils, a task they were only too happy to undertake, which resulted in some interesting designs. Figure 2.4 is one of these images, and indicates what one sees after 'three cups of yagé'. The image resembles the densely packed geometric and dot-patterns of visual hallucinations, but also draws a symbolic interpretation from its author, who considers that it presents a vagina; drops of semen; and other gendered symbols. Thus from Reichel-Dolmatoff's assessment, we can also see Tukano art as arising from an interface between the typical forms seen in hallucinations and culturally specific interpretations that are consistent with the fertility themes present in their mythology.

Shipibo-Conibo Art

The Shipibo-Conibo are indigenous peoples of the Ucayali valley of the Peruvian Amazon rainforest (Eakin, Lauriault, and Boonstra, 1986). They speak a language of the Panoan family and subsist through hunting, fishing, slash and burn agriculture, and animal husbandry. Pottery also forms a major part of Shipibo manufacture for both domestic use and sale outside the community, and is decorated with a distinctive geometric design. Shipibo beliefs seem to be animist but also contain influences from Christianity. Their mythology holds that the sun was once closer to the ground and served for cooking, but later moved further away from the earth. Two boys who were makers and shooters of arrows shot many arrows into the sky, forming a connection that turned into a staircase the following day. Many animals ascended the staircase carrying food, but this enraged god, who broke the staircase, causing the animals to fall to the ground and be killed or transformed into

Figure 2.4. Tukano drawing of what one sees 'after three cups of yagé', by Biá. Reproduced from Reichel-Dolmatoff (1978), courtesy of the UCLA Latin American Institute.

armadillos. Today the staircase remains, beginning approximately two metres above the ground, but is accessible only to shamans during ayahuasca rituals. The staircase to the spirit world is believed to be jagged due to winds, and contains many villages of jungle spirits along its path. By ascending the staircase to visit the spirit world, the shaman sees spirits of animals and people in distorted, grotesque forms. When these spirits ask the shaman what he wants, he is able to make requests regarding the ailments of his patients. While shamanic healing is used for disorders of the spirit, use of herbal cures and Western medicines is also prevalent, and death is ultimately recognized as having both natural and supernatural causes.

The geometric art style of the Shipibo appears on their clothing, pottery, and skin, consisting of interlocking geometric motifs (shown in Figure 2.5). In Shipibo mythology the cosmic anaconda Ronin is the donor of the *ronin quene* (great boa design), '[combining] all conceivable designs in its skin pattern' (Gebhart-Sayer 1985, pp.149–150). The designs are mimetic of snakeskin; the form of the snake's body; and other living elements such as heads, wings, hands, and eyes. A specific sub-category of the designs, *vero-yushin-quene* (eye spirit design), is also related to death, since the 'eye spirit' of a person is believed to leave through the pupil of the eye upon death. It is believed that when used by a shaman, these designs entail

Figure 2.5. Example of a Shipibo *ronin quene* design. Jason Langley/Alamy Stock Photo.

various forms of spiritual power, and specific 'design medicines' can be used for healing purposes. In Gebhart-Sayer's assessment, shamans would have originally acquired these designs through visionary yagé experiences. Interestingly, Gebhart-Sayer also refers to a synaesthetic process whereby the visionary patterns perceived by the shaman are interpreted as shamanic songs. The songs are 'a direct transformation from the visual to the auditory', each containing hundreds of patterns that are seen and heard simultaneously by both the shaman and the attending spirits (p.162). Consequentially, Shipibo culture can be seen as making visionary experiences concrete through multiple modalities. Through both the *ronin quene* designs and shaman's songs, the other villagers are able to join in and connect to the spiritual planes of existence; the shaman acting as an 'acoustic hinge' between the ordinary and the spirit world (p.162).

The examples discussed reveal some typical mechanisms for the representation of ASCs. Firstly, we find that a distinction emerges between depictions of the 'real' and the 'unreal' (the spirit world). These categories can alternatively be described as 'external' or 'internal' sensory inputs (see Chapter 1, pp.25–26). For example, many of the San and Native American artworks discussed depict arrangements of people, artefacts, and the location of the ritual. These have a real, physical basis in the external environment that could by other means have been photographed. Conversely, many of the examples discussed render aspects of the visionary experience. These elements are 'unreal' in that they have no physical basis in the external environment. They can be understood as hallucinations that arise internally; they could not have been photographed. In accordance with the view of hallucinations as a multi-stage phenomenon, we can also further subcategorize representations of unreality, separating those that represent visual patterns of hallucination from iconic imagery.

Besides these categorizations of input, we may also observe significant variation in the artistic modes used for rendering ASCs in the visual arts. Some features of these designs seem to reflect the actual visual experience of hallucination with some degree of accuracy, while others are more symbolic or metaphorical. For example, the dense patterns of the Tukano and Shipibo-Conibo examples seem to reflect visual patterns of hallucination that one might see during a yagé experience in a fairly literal way. In contrast, Native American impressions of the peyote bird and San designs seem to be more metaphorical. However, in several of the examples both literal and metaphorical meanings may co-exist, as in the case of the Huichol yarn paintings that both resemble hallucinations in form and incorporate symbolic meanings in their contents. Style also varies: images may be rendered with different materials; and some may be presented with a sense of perspective and occlusion, while others may use a flat style of representation. Similarly, some images appear not unlike a snapshot of the visionary experience, while others condense the narrative of the ritual into a single frame, showing the trajectories of flights or metamorphoses that would span a longer duration.

These distinctions of internal/external and accurate/stylized material reveal general principles for representing hallucinations that are more broadly applicable. For example, this schema can be applied to a great deal of Western 'psychedelic art', such as the work of Alex Grey, which similarly combines geometric patterns of hallucination with symbolic meanings associated with the psychedelic experience. Since the focus of this book is on time-based media, further consideration of static visual arts will remain beyond the scope of our discussion[7]; however, I will return to these visual principles in Chapter 6 when exploring audio-visual representations of hallucination. Furthermore, they provide a useful background to consider when thinking about the ways in which sound may similarly be used to represent ASCs.

SHAMANIC SOUNDS

Music and sound play an important role in many shamanic and trance traditions that utilize ASCs. Some of these were hinted at in the previous section: the San people induce ASCs with the aid of clapping; Tukano shamanism occurs amidst chanting, percussion instruments, and flutes; and the curing songs of the Shipibo-Conibo are related to their visual pattern designs. The Huichol, Native Americans, and many more besides also use music.[8] While we must be careful not to excessively generalize regarding the use of music across different cultures, frequently sound is a vital element used to conduct the ritual. Sound may represent aspects of the spirit world, signal stages of the ritual, or invoke affective states. The following sub-sections review these uses of sound as they occur in various shamanic and trance traditions in more detail, in order to draw out the specific sonic functions. Where they are available, the discussion here refers to ethnographic sound recordings, since these are among the earliest artefacts that draw associations between electronic technologies and ASCs. These recordings are also significant since they capture practices that have since undergone transformations due to outside influences.[9]

Haitian Vodou Drums

Vodou is a religion of Haiti that has its roots in traditions such as West African Vodun, which were brought by slaves to the island up until the eighteenth century. Vodou is syncretic in that it fuses elements of multiple religions, including the Catholicism that actively sought to suppress it. Ceremonies are conducted by the *houngan* (priests) and *mambo* (priestesses) in order to invoke the *loa* (spirits). During these rituals, the *houngan* or *mambo* provides libations and recitations before drumming and ritual dancing begins. The ritual calls upon the *loa,* who may belong to different families, and have various personality attributes. Their presence is invoked through the possession of a host, who embodies the spirit through dance. The possessed dancer interacts with the group, providing its members with experiential knowledge of the *loa.* During the trance, the dancers are also sprayed with water and rum by the *mambo,* who directs the *loa* with a rattle.

The ritual practices of Haitian Vodou were documented by Maya Deren between 1947 and 1954, resulting in field recordings that were included on *Divine Horsemen: The Voodoo Gods of Haiti* (1980), and the documentary film *Divine Horsemen: The Living Gods of Haiti* (1985).[10] As presented on these recordings, different rhythms and songs are associated with various spirits, including Legba, the guardian of the sacred gate; Damballah, the sky god, who appears in the form of a snake; and others. Rhythm is considered as a means to invite the presence of the gods, while songs provide various prayers and invocations to the spirits. During the course of the ritual, percussive rhythms build in progressive layers as larger drums, rattles, and bells are introduced, providing increasing levels of rhythmic complexity. As a spirit begins to take hold, the dancer becomes more agitated and the drummers introduce the *kase* (from the French word *casser,* meaning 'to break'), a rhythmic attack that contradicts the main rhythm (Wilcken, 1992, pp.52–53).[11] Throughout these passages the tempo remains fairly constant, yet the *kase* ruptures the rhythmic intensity and complexity of the music during these phases. During spirit possession, the frenetic host enacts the dancing of the spirit, which reflects particular attributes; hence the serpentine characteristics of Damballah elicits a snake-like dance, while those in Ghede's grasp exhibit sexualized dancing. Rhythm maintains the presence of the spirit before departure, whereupon the dancer collapses. In Haiti, construction of Vodou drums also entails a ritual process, and both drum and drummer may be inhabited by *Outò,* the spirit of the drums (pp.44–45).

We may observe, then, that along with other techniques such as the spraying of liquids and ritual invocations, both the artefacts and music of Vodou play an essential role in structuring and inducing trance experiences. The sonic components of the music both represent spiritual meaning while also inducing it through the heightened states of arousal that the rhythmic drumming precipitates through mimetic dance. The resulting trances might reasonably be understood as potent experiential states that encompass cognitive, emotional, and behavioural configurations, and which are identified and personified as specific spirits in accordance with an animist worldview. These experiential states are manifested within individuals, but are experienced and understood socially by the group.

Amazonian Tukano Festivals

The musical instruments of the Tukano peoples of the Colombian Amazon (who were introduced in the previous section) consist of various panpipes, flutes, and seed rattles, the symbolic meanings of which are entwined with Tukano mythology. In Yakuna-Tukano mythology, for example, the heroic figure of Milomaki was an excellent singer who was burnt to death by his people. It is said that from his ashes grew a paxiuba palm tree that is used to make flutes, through which his voice lives on (Koch-Grünberg, 1909, cited in Tayler, 1972, p.34). Sexual meanings are also prevalent, in accordance with Tukano mythology. Hence flutes and panpipes are associated with birds, and are played in masculine and feminine pairs; while Reichel-Dolmatoff (1978, p.11) describes how the rubbing of a turtle shell instrument symbolizes the sexual stimulation of the Sun Daughter. In another account Reichel-Dolmatoff (1987, p.22) also describes the belief that the phallic handle of the rattle 'inseminates' the womb-like gourd when shaken. Although many instruments seem to have such symbolic meanings, in Tayler's (1972) account the actual presence of spirits is transitory, and some instruments have special significance while others are disposable.

In 1960 and 1961 Brian Moser and Donald Tayler collected field recordings of various indigenous tribes of Colombia, including the Tukano. These recordings were presented on the triple-LP *The Music of Some Indian Tribes of Colombia* (1972).[12] Among the Tukano excerpts, MC2.A.4d[13] captures the chanting of the elders whilst the hallucinogenic brew yagé is consumed. These chants consist of recitations of Tukano myths, but are not clearly enunciated and consist partly of humming sounds. They are delivered in a pitched form that Tayler refers to as 'song speech', lending both linguistic and musical qualities to the proceedings. As heard on the recording, these chants represent the spirit world through language, but also seem to invoke the numinous through patterns of pitch. When combined with the hallucinogenic properties of the yagé, both the linguistic and melodic qualities may assist with invoking the spirits and shaping the form of the visionary experience as a whole.

Side B of Record 2 (MC2.B) of the set documents a Makuna-Tukano festival. Tukano festivals are grand affairs in which 100–500 guests are invited to participate in musical performance and dance, whilst consuming large amounts of alcoholic chicha, coca, yagé, and long leaf-bound ceremonial cigars (Tayler, 1972, pp.41–44). The musical performances are participatory for those present, and include further chanting of origin myths by the elders (MC2.B.1); dances with maracas, singing, and ankle rattles (MC2.B.2); pan-pipe performances (MC2.B.3); and bamboo stave dances which involve ankle rattles and the conch flute (MC2.B.4). The rhythms of the dances are steady and uncomplicated, and a greater emphasis is placed upon the tonal subtleties of the group panpipes and flutes. These sounds may be seen as providing a convivial complement to the effects of the chicha, coca, and other intoxicants, while also supporting social interaction through dance. The Tukano believe that the spirits of the ancients are present at such events, and thus while the function of the festival is primarily social, it also entails a spiritual dimension that expresses the identity and ethos of its hosts through music.

Mazatec Mushroom Songs

In Mazatec shamanism, communication with the spirit world is achieved by *cuanderos* (shamans) through the use of hallucinogenic mushrooms and shamanic songs. Under Spanish rule shamanic practices involving the use of mushrooms (e.g. *Psilocybe mexicana*), *Salvia divinorum*[14], and other plant hallucinogens were considered idolatry, and were suppressed and forced underground (Wasson, 1972, p.192). Here they remained in relative secrecy until the 1950s, when ethnomycologist Robert Gordon Wasson undertook a series of expeditions to Mexico in order to learn about the 'divine mushroom'. Through these expeditions Wasson learned of *cuandera* María Sabina in Huautla de Jiménez (Oaxaca), with whom he was able to participate in four mushroom rituals during 1955 and 1956. His experiences were subsequently publicized in *Life* magazine (Wasson, 1957), bringing awareness of these practices into the sphere of Western culture. For our interests here, Wasson was also able to make field recordings of Sabina's rituals in 1956 and 1958, which can be heard respectively on the Folkways LP *Mushroom Ceremony of the Mazatec Indians of Mexico* (1957), and the four cassette tapes that accompany *María Sabina and her Mazatec Mushroom Velada* (Wasson et al., 1974). The latter of these is a more extensive documentation, and will form the basis of our discussion here.[15]

María Sabina and her Mazatec Mushroom Velada (Wasson et al., 1974) documents a ritual undertaken in order to enquire about the sickness of a boy, Perfeto José Garcia. On the recordings we hear Sabina's humming, singing, and clapping; the prayers and conversations of those present; the sick boy's coughing; and other background noises such as the sound of chickens outside. Sabina's vocalizations consist of humming and syllabic sounds (e.g. C1.A.2[16]; C1.A.3), which at times develop into melodic singing or vice versa (e.g. C1.A.1; C1.B.2). Throughout many parts of the ritual Sabina also claps by slapping the back of the right hand against the palm of the left hand. This occurs at lulls during the ritual (e.g. C1.A.2; C2.A.1), and elsewhere alongside the singing (e.g. C1.A.3). In Sabina's account, the clapping is similar to the humming and rhythmic use of syllabic sounds, all of which provide a means of sustaining activity when she is not moved to words (Wasson et al., 1974, p.4). When the words do come, the language Sabina uses reflects her communication with the mushroom spirits; at times she calls upon the spirits, whilst at other points they speak through her. For example, she declares her credentials as a shaman who is 'humble' and of 'clean spirit' (e.g. C1.B.2); and invokes the names and qualities of various spirits including Jesus Christ and the Catholic saints.[17] When the spirits arrive, they speak through Sabina, who adds the word *tso* (meaning 'the mushroom says') to the end of each line (e.g. C2.B.2; C4.B.1). Through her communications with the spirits it is revealed that Perfeto will not recover; a prognosis that unfortunately turned out to be correct a few weeks later. Although visions are described in the ritual, the recordings reveal a shamanic tradition that is primarily aural. The linguistic features of the ceremony are important (Munn, 1972), but so too are the melodic and rhythmic properties of the songs, syllabic repetitions, and clapping.

Kiowa Peyote Meetings

Among the peyote meetings of Kiowa Native Americans (whose customs were discussed in the previous section), peyote songs are sung in groups of four by each person. These songs may belong to individuals, who in some cases have been said to receive them through visions and peyote-induced auditory hallucinations (La Barre, 2011, p.20). In 1964, while being held in jail in Anadarko, Oklahoma, Harry Smith met members of the Kiowa, with whom he subsequently recorded a variety of the traditional songs that are sung in peyote meetings. These were presented on the Folkways album *The Kiowa Peyote Meeting* (1973). The peyote meeting consists of various stages during each of which certain types of songs will be sung from an available repertoire, thus marking the progression of the evening through to the early morning. The period of time between the 'Midnight Water Song' and the 'Morning Water Song' is of particular significance, as this is when visions are received. As heard on this record, peyote songs may consist of both words and non-lexical phonemes, and are accompanied by a rattle (a drum is also typically used). The linguistic content of the songs is significant, and consists mainly of prayers for good health, requests to the Almighty, and celebrations of the virtues of peyote. As with other forms of shamanic chanting, the musical qualities of the songs are undoubtedly significant; the melodies supporting a mood of uplifting spirituality, and the rhythms heightening arousal.

Mimetic Mayan Pyramids

In the noise of the modern world, it is easy to forget that pre-industrial societies were accompanied by a substantially different aural experience, which may have allowed for a greater sensitivity to acoustic subtleties. As a result, the acoustic properties and ecologies of ritual spaces may have important implications for their use, which in recent years have drawn the attention of archaeologists (Devereux, 2001; Eneix, 2016). Let us take a moment to imagine the caves of Palaeolithic shamanism, dimly lit by dancing flames illuminating the symbolic markings of the walls, with sounds echoing due to the acoustic properties of the cave. Now imagine the dramatic effects that the natural echoing and reverb might produce, when combined with the dark sensory deprivation of the caves and the use of shamanic techniques for altering consciousness. Considering such effects, Reznikoff and Dauvois (1988) suggested that the locations of cave art images at Grotte du Portel (near Loubens, Ariègemay, France) may have been selected to correspond with those areas of the cave that have the most dramatic resonant properties. Studies of Neolithic sites have similarly shown spaces that resonate within the range of the male voice, supporting the view that these sites may have been designed in accordance with acoustic properties that were perceived as spiritually significant (Devereux 2001, pp.75–104). Elsewhere, Gell (1995) suggests that the dense gloom of the Papua New Guinea rainforest privileges the aural senses of the Umeda people; while Tuzin (1984) also comments that the flickering darkness within which rituals are conducted places a special emphasis on sound.

Of particular interest in extending this line of enquiry is Lubman's (1998) theory regarding the acoustic properties of the Mayan pyramid of Kukulkan at Chichén Itzá. Lubman identifies that the pyramid produces a characteristic 'chirped echo', due to the periodic acoustic reflections produced by the step faces. According to Lubman, these echo sounds are similar to those produced by the Quetzal bird, which was sacred to the Mayans and is explicitly linked to the Kukulkan pyramid by a glyph in the Mayan's Dresden Codex. Kukulkan is known to have been used ritually by the Mayans, and also incorporates other mimetic features into its architectural design, such as the appearance of a snake shadow that occurs at the Spring and Autumn equinoxes. It is quite possible then that the design of the mimetic 'chirped echo' may have been a deliberate and sophisticated use of architectural features to provide symbolic acoustic properties.

Across these examples we find a variety of ways in which sound and music are used in relation to ASCs. As with shamanic art, aural practices may enable aspects of the spirit world to be represented. This may occur through symbolic meanings that are associated with the musical instruments as artefacts, as discussed with regards to the Tukano instruments and mythology. Representation of the spirit world may also occur through language, as in the case of María Sabina's songs, which call to the spirit world and allow the mushrooms to speak through her. Yet besides the words themselves, these songs also have musical and sonic properties that may be equally important. As we have seen, the use of sound to represent spirits can also be observed in the Vodou traditions of Haiti, where certain rhythms are associated with particular spirits. Tuzin's (1984) discussion of the Tambaran cult among the Ilahita Arapesh people of Papua New Guinea[18] is also of note here, since he describes the use of slit-gongs, bullroarers,[19] panpipes, whistles, trumpets, and flutes, in order to create mimetic sounds that resemble spirits such as birds. The suggested use of architecture at the Chichén Itzá site is fascinating as an extension of this premise, where the acoustics of Kukulkan create sounds that are mimetic of the spirit world. Through various means, then, shamanic musical practices may call to or invoke the spirit world through their representational properties.

While these representational properties are important, we may also consider the affective properties of these sonic practices. The latter may afford positive emotional responses through abstract musical qualities (Meyer, 1956; Juslin, 2008). From the uplifting melodies of Amazonian panpipes to the sensory overload of Haitian Vodou, music may elicit a variety of affective responses that are designed to complement the given situation. For instance, the music of the Makuna-Tukano festival may be understood as a means to lift the mood of the revellers as they imbibe various intoxicants, while fostering a sense of communal experience and identity. Where music is used alongside hallucinogens, affective properties may also provide a supporting emotional framework that reduces the risk of 'bad trips' (Dobkin de Rios and Katz, 1975). Indeed, it is well documented that hallucinogens such as ayahuasca or peyote may produce feelings of physical discomfort, nausea, vomiting, or intense fear; hence the melodic properties of the Tukano or Kiowa songs may provide an affective device that distracts from these effects and encourages a more positive mood. Yet these melodic properties may also go further in shaping the spiritual qualities of the experience. For instance, the singing of Kiowa prayers may enrich the religious aspects of the peyote meeting, while along similar lines, Gebhart-Sayer (1984, pp.12–13) describes the synaesthetic use of songs in order to actually shape the visionary experience and achieve the healing process.

Rhythm can be considered as an affective device that has special capabilities for raising arousal levels and eliciting corresponding behaviours such as dance. This may account for the use of syllabic reiterations in the Tukano elders' chants; the use of the rattles and drums in the Kiowa traditions; or María Sabina's clapping. Such effects may complement the effect of hallucinogens by raising arousal levels. In trance cultures such as Haitian Vodou, however, rhythm provides a means to actually induce ASCs without the use of drugs. Here the rapid drumming of complex rhythms creates the stimulus for the trance-dance behaviours, in combination with other techniques for inducing sensory overload such as the spraying of liquids and hyperventilation. Similar techniques can also be observed in other trance traditions such as those of the Ivory Coast, as seen in Jordi Esteva's ethnographic documentary *Komian* (2014), though the precise means through which trance states are elicited has been a source of debate. Neher (1961, 1962) suggested that the use of repetitive drumming in trance ceremonies functioned through rhythmic entrainment, in which brain waves became synchronized with the beats per minute (bpm) of drumming patterns; however, this explanation is not well supported.[20] Rouget (1985) emphasized instead the importance of cultural context and music as a means to communicate the structure of ritual events. Becker (2004) also recognizes the significance of context, while acknowledging the importance of rhythm and its effects on the body in producing heightened emotional experiences. Her own theory of trance describes 'deep listeners', individuals who are capable of strong emotional reactions to music. Seen in these terms, rhythm in the ritual context may support the production of peak emotional experiences,[21] inducing trance for some individuals.

In summary, sound plays a functional role in shamanic traditions, either by representing aspects of the spirit world, or by providing affective properties that complement or induce ASCs. Often these properties of sound are related, as in the case of shamanic songs, which include both linguistic representation and pitched contours that provide affective properties. In this way shamanic music may play an important role in invoking and shaping visionary experiences.

* * *

'Shamanism' is a construct that allows us to collectively consider a diverse range of global traditions in which visionary states are used in order to interact with a spirit world. Within these traditions, shamanic activity typically provides a means through which to establish a relationship between the community and the spirit world. This relationship can be seen in functional terms for tribal societies whose livelihoods are deeply entwined with the natural world. Through the shaman's activity, he or she is able to provide the community with a sense of meaningful connection with the spirits of nature, ultimately aiding survival. Visionary plants are frequently the means through which this connection is provided; however, as we have seen, artistic and musical practices are also significant. Considering these practices reveals some typical relationships between ASCs, music, and art that will be significant for our discussion as it develops.

Firstly, our discussion of shamanic art has shown how an image can represent both internal and external phenomena seen during ASCs. As we have seen, representations of unreality in shamanic art can also be sub-classified in terms of cross-cultural and culturally dependent elements such as visual patterns of hallucination, and iconic hallucinations, respectively. Images may also depict aspects of the visual experience in a fairly literal or accurate manner, or utilize more stylized approaches that make use of metaphorical or impressionistic techniques. These mechanisms for creating visual representations of ASCs are not only applicable for shamanic art, but can also be applied to other forms of art, such as psychedelic paintings or digital artworks. In Chapters 6 and 7 these principles will therefore allow us to consider the design of visual elements in audio-visual artworks, films, and video games that explore ASCs.

The examples of shamanic music also demonstrate some of the ways in which sound may be related to ASCs, which will be significant for subsequent chapters. For example, we have seen how musical practices may represent internal experiences of hallucination, either through symbolic meanings assigned to instruments, or through the sounds themselves. In the chapters that follow we will see how recorded sound similarly allows aspects of internal experience to be represented, and how the specific capabilities of electronic technologies assist this process. Thus, just as the design of Amazonian flutes invokes the sounds of the spirit world by imitating bird-calls, we shall see how electronic sound design techniques allow representations of internal experience to be created.

In this chapter we have also seen how the affective properties of shamanic music may complement experiences of ASCs, or even induce trance states without the use of drugs. These mechanisms will find parallels in Chapter 4, as we consider how various forms of electronic dance music provide complements to drug experiences, or even provide trance-like states without the use of drugs.

As we have seen in this chapter, shamanic art and musical practices also reflect the mythologies of the traditions from which they emerge. Indeed, since visionary arts shape the production of visionary experiences and vice versa, both emerge entwined in an almost recursive process. In these terms, the works discussed in this chapter not only reflect the experience of ASCs but also do so in a way that intrinsically reflects the ethos of the people. This connection between aesthetics and ethos will also be explored in later chapters, and will be significant in considering both similarities and differences between shamanic music and Western popular culture related to ASCs.

CHAPTER 3

Psychedelic Illusions

Music could be a bridge to potential, to the future; it's possible to paint pictures of infinity with music.

—John F. Szwed, *Space Is the Place*

Up a dusty track off the main highway that runs from Saint-Maxime toward Le Muy in the Provence region of southern France, lies the Musée du Phonographe et de la Musique Mécanique (Museum of Mechanical Music and Phonographs). This small museum houses a family's extensive collection of early sound recording and reproduction devices from the late nineteenth and twentieth centuries: a treasure trove of cabinet music boxes, wax cylinder phonographs, gramophones of all shapes and sizes, and various other antiques. These devices have an air of enchantment to them; when operated, they emit delicate fragile sounds from the past, transporting the listener to another time and place. Like the automatons that are also slumped among the dusty shelves of the museum, when activated these old devices elicit a kind of mechanical magic, conjuring illusory performances into life from wax, brass, and oak.

The manner in which sound recordings allow the listener to access sonic events from other times and places is of central interest in this chapter. Sound recordings can be used to present these sonic events with some degree of accuracy. However, as technologies advanced through the twentieth century, new ways to alter sound recordings using signal manipulation processes and magnetic tape were devised. These techniques were increasingly used in popular music in order to alter the perceived realities of sound recordings, and evoke various forms of conceptual meaning. This chapter begins by considering the illusory capabilities of audio technology, before exploring their use in various forms of popular music. First, we shall examine the rock 'n' roll music of 1950s America, where early forms of guitar distortion were used to express a raw energy and excitement that appealed to thrill-seeking teenagers. Next, we turn our attention towards 1960s surf rock, a specialized form of rock 'n' roll where reverberation provided the means to access a 'wet sound' that conjured up romantic visions of sun-kissed palm beaches and glittering waves. As the revolutionary spirit of the 1960s kicked into gear, interest in surf rock gave way to the more radical sounds of psychedelic rock. Here a variety of exotic effects and recording processes were among the techniques used to produce warped sounds that were suggestive of consciousness expansion; these too will be analysed. Lastly, this chapter delves into the cosmic fascinations of 1970s space rock and space jazz, which captivated audiences in the era of the space race and the atomic bomb, by exploring alternative views of humanity cast in the endless expanses of outer space. Here too, electronic sound processes and synthesizers provided an important means through which to communicate the concept of space technologies and alien worlds. Through the course of this chapter, then, we shall see how analogue signal processes allow the affective properties of music to become framed by various forms of conceptual meaning. In each case, these conceptual meanings can be seen to relate to a specific ethos, which audiences may find attractive to engage with. In addition, through the analysis of psychedelic music in this chapter, we shall also begin to see how technology can be used to represent the actual experience of hallucinations through sound.

SONIC ILLUSIONS

To expand our discussion regarding the representational properties of sound, we begin by considering how sound recordings can be used to conjure illusory impressions of environments and events from the past, or to fabricate ones that may never have existed. The concept of 'illusion' presented here could be considered as an auditory equivalent for the way in which paintings or photographic images provide a false sense of perspective, since sound recordings can similarly recreate the aural experience of scenes and spatial locations. This definition of 'illusion' should not be confused with that of 'auditory illusions', the aural equivalent of optical illusions, in which the ear is 'tricked' by stimuli such as Shepard tones.[1] Instead, just as a landscape painting may present scenes or fictional locations, so too can sound recordings construct an illusory sense of space. Let us consider in more detail how sound recordings enable this, and how they can be manipulated to present alternative or stylized versions of reality.

Sound Recordings

Sound recordings allow the reproduction of similar acoustic vibrations to those we would hear in the presence of the original acoustic event upon which the recording was based. On Thomas Edison's phonographs of the late nineteenth and early twentieth century, acoustic vibrations would be captured via a sound collecting horn containing a diaphragm.[2] When the diaphragm vibrated, it caused a needle to move, etching a groove into a rotating cylinder. These could then be replayed by rotating the cylinder with a playback stylus tracking the groove. The stylus would cause a diaphragm to vibrate, reproducing a sound that was then amplified by the horn. Subsequent developments in this technology led to the use of other media such as magnetic tape and electrical voltage (analogue audio), and later binary code (digital audio) to store and transport the audio signal, which would be propagated using a loudspeaker.[3] Even with later iterations, however, the basic premise remains the same: acoustic vibrations are captured, stored in some medium, and reproduced by causing mechanical vibration of a loudspeaker. Although various factors such as the quality or grain of the recording usually allow us to frame sound recordings as illusions, even with early devices such as those old wax cylinder phonographs at the Musée du Phonographe et de la Musique Mécanique, we can hear, comprehend, appreciate, and enjoy the sounds almost as if we were there. It is like looking through a misty window to the original sonic event, or conjuring up a faint spectre or trace of the original sound. The effect might analogously be compared with the experience of viewing an old silent movie; even with subtle speed variations, crackles, and pops, somehow the film takes you back into the past, while also giving you a sense of the age of the device.

The capability of sound recordings to provide an impression of another place or time occurs by allowing you to perceive the salient acoustic properties caused by the original acoustic event captured by the recording. However, when you hear a sound recording, you are hearing it from a secondary source that is removed from the original event, and this allows the perceived reality of the recording to be tampered with. 'Acousmatic' is the term popularized by Pierre Schaeffer (1966) for describing the experience of a sound for which the source is unseen. Schaeffer derived his view of acousmatic listening from the Greek word used by the mathematician and philosopher Pythagoras, who used it to describe the situation of instructing his students from behind a screen, so that they could not see him, and could thus pay more attention to his words.[4] Sound recordings can be thought of as acousmatic, since they typically represent the acoustic properties of a sonic event from another time or place that remains unseen (or more accurately, unheard). This acousmatic property is of significance to the illusory qualities of sound recordings, since the lack of experiential knowledge regarding the original object(s) of a recording allows the potential for disruption and alteration. What you hear on a sound recording might be a realistic representation of events, but equally the recording engineer may have edited or processed it to give an alternative version of events. From a technical point of view, these manipulations of reality rely on the ability of the recording engineer to alter the signal, as facilitated with the capabilities of audio electronics.

Multi-Tracking

In post–World War II America, magnetic tape opened up new worlds of possibility for recording sound. The main advantage of magnetic tape was the ease with which sound recordings could be edited and manipulated. This in turn created new opportunities to change the perceived reality entailed by a sound recording. For example, instead of presenting material live on radio, pre-recorded shows could be used, and mistakes or dead air could be edited out; the audience would not be able to tell the difference and would assume the show was live. Subsequently the convenience of magnetic tape also led to early forms of multi-tracking. Multi-tracking is the process of recording music on multiple parallel 'tracks', allowing various benefits such as the ability to record in multiple takes and combine the results. Les Paul and Mary Ford's 'How High the Moon' (1951) is an early example, on which Les Paul was able to layer multiple recordings to create a rich sonic effect (Kane, 2014a). By the 1960s multi-track tape recording was becoming available to artists such as The Beach Boys and The Beatles, enabling separate channels of sound to be combined and manipulated, allowing greater freedoms in sonic experimentation. This would ultimately allow sound recordings to become intricate tapestries of sound, still further removed from the notion of simply capturing a single live performance. Today multi-tracking remains the main method through which musicians record and mix audio. Software such as Pro Tools allows studio engineers to assemble recordings from sounds recorded at various points in time. Despite the origin of sound materials in events that are distributed over time, when mixed together the end result forms a cohesive whole, such that a recording can sound like a performance by a band that may never have even played in the same room together.

Effects Processes

With the invention of analogue signal processing devices such as echo and reverb, it also became possible to substantially modify the presentation of sounds. Echo and reverberation occur naturally in acoustic environments where sound waves reflect off walls or other surfaces, enabling the original sound source to propagate for an extended duration as it diffuses. Devices such as the spring reverb, oil can delay, tape echoes, the plate reverb, and their digital successors, would facilitate the convenient production of similar effects, which lend sound the illusion of space. In his discussion of echo and reverb in popular music, Doyle (2005) draws our attention to a variety of possible interpretations of these effects within popular music recordings, which range from realistic representations of space to non-realistic ones. For example, spatial effects can be used to indicate a physical space, such as the acoustic properties of a performance venue or concert hall. However these physical spaces need not actually exist, and studios regularly record in acoustically dampened environments, adding artificial reverb effects to 'dry' recordings as a means to give them a sense of 'presence' or authenticity, retrospectively.[5] Doyle also argues that some recordings use spatial effects such as echo and reverb in ways that could be considered more impressionistic or metaphorical. For example, Ennio Morricone's western soundtracks use reverb to suggest the desolate qualities of open spaces, while science fiction television programmes often use echo effects to convey a sense of the supernatural, or to suggest the internal spaces of the psyche. Indeed, Doyle comments that echo and reverb provide a particularly effective way to evoke the numinous, since they have historically been associated with sites of spiritual importance, such as shamanic caves, temples, and churches.[6]

As multi-tracking and signal processing devices became widespread in the popular music of the late twentieth century, their use on sound recordings to evoke a multitude of impressions for the listener markedly increased in complexity and sophistication. Other types of signal processes would include distortion, flangers, phasers, choruses, filters, wah-wah pedals, compressors, and later digital versions of these. Each of these processes modifies the sound in a different way, changing the impression for the listener. As we shall see, processes such as these would be among those that support the representation of conceptual meaning in various forms of popular music.

ROCK 'N' ROLL

Riding along in my automobile, my baby beside me at the wheel.

—Chuck Berry, 'No Particular Place to Go'

The 1950s were a time of economic affluence in post-war America; industry productivity increased, new technologies and consumer markets emerged, and these were met with enthusiasm by the post-war middle classes who were prospering in a period of low unemployment. With this newfound affluence came the emerging teenage culture; young people had a new desire for freedom, and the time and means through which to seek it through cars and music. The soundtrack for the new youth culture was rock 'n' roll music, and the transistor radio and records were key methods of propagation. Of course live performances were important too, but sound recordings meant that rock 'n' roll could be heard non-stop in cars, homes, and jukeboxes. Perhaps not surprisingly, then, the sound recording became an important artefact of rock 'n' roll in itself; for the artists, the recording would be the means to achieve fame if it became a radio hit, and for audiences the recording would often be heard before the real thing at live concerts. In the drive to distinguish the sounds of rock 'n' roll records, processes such as distortion began to see use as a means to enhance the abrasive and energetic qualities of the music.

Speed and Energy

Often credited as one of the earliest rock 'n' roll records, Ike Turner's Kings of Rhythm's (as Jackie Brenston and his Delta Cats') 'Rocket 88' (1951) encapsulates an enthusiasm for speed, girls, and technology through both its musical form and the theme as expressed through the lyrics. The Rocket 88 in question is an Oldsmobile V8 blacktop convertible, which is described as having a 'modern design' that allows its owner to 'ride in style' and impress women. The lyrics express the joys of speed, in terms of the car itself, the accelerated social lifestyle and sexual attractiveness it brings. This provides a conceptual representation that would be attractive for teenagers who were similarly motivated by the excitement of an accelerated youth culture. In 'Rocket 88', however, this theme is also matched by the affective properties of the music. The song consists of an up-tempo twelve-bar blues, delivered with a pumping energy that comes from the rhythm section. These rhythms provide the song with energetic properties, which for receptive teenage listeners may set pulses racing and heads nodding—physiological and behavioural manifestations of heightened arousal. In this way the song expresses speed and energy not only through the message of the lyrics, but also through the affective properties of the beat.

High-arousal themes would become pervasive in rock 'n' roll, as a few further examples will illustrate. Bill Haley and His Comets' 'Rock Around the Clock' (1954) expresses an urgency for perpetual partying, while on 'Whole Lot of Shakin' Going On' (1957) Jerry Lee Lewis encourages his baby to engage in abandoned physical dance. In 'Long Tall Sally' (1956) Little Richard describes a lady with a physique that is 'built for speed', while on 'Girls! Girls! Girls!' (1962) Elvis Presley describes one 'red-blooded boy['s]' almost obsessive sexual attraction towards girls 'in tight sweaters ... short dresses' and various other garments. Vehicular themes arise again memorably in Chuck Berry's 'No Particular Place to Go' (1964), where once again the car becomes a machine of attraction—at least until the protagonist finds himself unable to 'unfasten her safety belt!' In each of these cases, the aroused themes of the lyrics are backed by up-tempo rhythm and blues, and wild performance techniques, which underscore the energy of the music.

Distortion

Although rhythm and blues may be the main underlying mechanism that allows the production of energy in rock 'n' roll, there is another process that augments these qualities: distortion. Along with Joe Hill Louis's 'Boogie in the Park' (1950), Ike Turner's Kings of Rhythm's 'Rocket 88' (1951) is also frequently credited with being one of the earliest examples of guitar distortion on a sound recording. Early guitar distortion had arrived through the use of amplified electric guitars by blues artists, who were playing at high volumes that approached the limits of their equipment (Palmer, 1992). Technically speaking, the harsher and more abrasive sound is the result of pushing amplifier valves to their limit, which overdrives the audio signal causing it to 'clip'.[7] Although the effect may originally have been unintended, the visceral sonic qualities of distortion also became desirable in their own right. For example, on Link Wray & His Wray Men's 'Rumble' (1958), Wray reportedly achieved the effect by driving a pencil through his amplifier, in order to make his guitar sound like a gang brawl (or 'rumble'). A similar approach was used by Dave Davies of The Kinks, who slashed the speaker cone on his amplifier to record the harsh guitar sound on 'You Really Got Me' (1964). Later on, battery-powered 'fuzz-box' devices, such as Arbiter Electronics' Fuzz Face (famously used by Jimi Hendrix) and the Electro-Harmonix Big Muff π, would provide more convenient means through which guitarists could obtain an overdriven sound, simply by connecting a portable effects unit that was operated by a foot-switch.

The manner in which distortion produces an abrasive, aggressive, or energetic sound has been a source of debate (Hicks, 2000). For example, comparisons have been drawn between distortion and the sound of impassioned African American singing or saxophones. Hicks also discusses the view that distortion is a product of industrial processes, and as such embodies the violence and speed of industrialization, producing a sound that is fundamentally similar to the engines of cars and motorcycles. Yet another theory proposed by Palmer (1992, p.15) suggests that the added resonance and overtones of distortion make the guitar sound like a bell that 'ritually invoke[s] sonic space'. Each of these interpretations of distortion may have some validity, since the listener may acquire these associations through previous experiences of such sounds, and these may lead to common cultural interpretations. By delivering sonic qualities that are associated with high-arousal activities and mechanization then, distortion augments the high-energy representations and affective responses of rock 'n' roll music.

Rock 'n' roll music captured the speed, sex, and energy of teenage youth, and has since attracted comparisons with the orgiastic cult of Dionysus in Ancient Greece (e.g. Knowles, 2010). Energetic qualities were expressed in the music through rhythm and blues, which provided the high-energy affective properties that were needed to support dancing, while the lyrics delivered poetic descriptions of speed, excitement, and romance. Distortion effects fed into this process by producing abrasive, mechanized sounds that underscored the high-arousal themes of the music. These high-arousal sound qualities were wholly appropriate for the speed-driven culture of rock 'n' roll, and have also retained enduring popularity in a whole range of subsequent musical forms that are also associated with motorized speed, amphetamines, sex, and violence—from heavy metal to aggressive forms of electronic dance music. Yet distortion was not the only electronic process that would shape the associative and affective properties of popular music, and we now turn to consider another effect: reverberation.

SURF ROCK

We could ride the surf together, while our love would grow.
—The Beach Boys, 'Surfer Girl'

Californian surf music emerged in the early 1960s as a predominantly instrumental variety of rock 'n' roll characterized by relentless drumming and thunderous guitar sounds drenched in reverb. The core musical elements of surf music were similar to those of rock 'n' roll, providing high-energy music through the driving rhythm and blues. Yet surf music adapted the conceptual themes of rock 'n' roll in order to communicate the concept of surf culture. Just as rock 'n' roll had celebrated speed, cars, sex, and the occasional gang brawl, surf music appealed to teenagers by presenting a variation of that vision with a slightly different ethos. The surfer ethos revolved around the idealized thrills of surfing; travelling around the Californian coast and across the border to Tijuana; or romantic escapades on the beach. Although lyrics were sometimes used to indicate surfing culture, the original surf music was predominantly instrumental, with echo and reverb devices and recordings of non-musical sonic material playing a significant role in establishing the surfing connotations on the sound recordings. Through the expanded use of electronic processes to convey conceptual representations, surf music can also be seen as an important forerunner to the psychedelic music of the late 1960s.[8]

Wet Sounds

Dick Dale and His Del-Tones' *Surfers' Choice* (1962) opens with shouts and deep, reverberant guitar chords before breaking into the searing riffs and drums of 'Surf Beat'. Dick Dale's distinctive guitar sound was achieved through the use of high-gauge guitar strings, a rapid picking style, and reverb effects. While *Surfers' Choice* also includes many vocal songs such as 'Sloop John B', a traditional folk song from the Bahamas, it is the instrumental pieces such as 'Take It Off', 'Misirlou Twist', and 'Shake 'n' Stomp' that epitomize the surf rock style. The way in which *Surfers' Choice* evokes a sense of surfing culture can be attributed to several factors. For example, the packaging depicts Dick Dale riding a wave and the liner notes describe him as an 'avid surfer'. The Eastern tonality of 'Misirlou Twist', or the lyrics of 'Sloop John B' also suggest the exoticism of the sea and the boundaries of American culture. Yet while these factors are all significant, on *Surfers' Choice* and other records from this period such as The Impacts' *Wipe Out!* (1963), or The Lively Ones' *Surf Drums* (1963), it is the use of reverberation applied to guitars and saxophones that is especially important as a defining feature of the surf style.

In the early 1960s, Dick Dale was among the guitarists whom Leo Fender was directly supplying with new designs for guitars and amplifiers (Crowley 2011, pp.43–44). Fender would hand a few select musicians new devices to test out, and revise his designs based on their feedback. Rather than being used with the explicit intention of evoking gigantic waves, surfing, or a sense of physical space, the early oil can echo reverbs provided a way in which sustain could be achieved. In the days before distortion effects, this extra sustain allowed the guitar to provide a more prominent lead sound similar to instruments such as the saxophone, enabling newer players to create impressive riffs that had a big impact with only a few notes. Of course, the way in which this 'big' sound was created occurs by approximating the acoustic properties produced by a large physical space, but the aim was impact over spatial realism. While the big, reverberant sound of surf rock may not have originally been born out of any deliberate attempt to connect the sound with the water, it gradually acquired this association. Crowley refers to what became the desirable 'water sounds: the drips, pops, and drizzles' produced by the oil can echo reverbs and amplifiers as they began to heat up (p.149). Some bands would even kick the reverb unit to produce a sound effect reminiscent of a crashing wave, in substitution for the surfboard breaking sound effect heard at the beginning of The Surfaris' 'Wipe Out' (1963).

The way in which reverb effects suggest a 'wet sound' can be considered in terms of the mimetic properties of sound, which allow non-musical aspects of nature or culture to be referenced (Emmerson, 1986). For example, the crashing reverberation and tremolo[9] ripples that are closely associated with surf rock can be taken as mimetic of waves, which may suggest the activity of surfing. As it happens, the early oil can echo reverb units readily allow these mimetic sounds to be produced, because the device actually works by using the liquid properties of the oil; it literally produces a liquid sound.[10] When these liquid sounds are contextualized in surf music, they allow the listener to receive impressions of water and surfing culture. The way in which this is achieved can be considered in terms of DeNora's (2010, pp.21–45) discussion of the 'affordances' that music may provide. Although DeNora comments that we should be careful about ascribing any absolute effects to music, she suggests that music may 'afford' certain interpretations, which can be established and reinforced through patterns of use. In the case of surf music, we may consider that the mimetic use of reverb on the recordings may afford impressions of waves and surfing. These associations are also possible since surf rock as pioneered by Dick Dale and His Del-Tones on *Surfers Choice* (1962) did indeed grow out of the surfing communities of California, hence establishing patterns of association, which are then further reinforced through the packaging of the music.

Summer Dreams

The concept of surfing culture, and the exoticism and sense of freedom it encapsulated had widespread appeal for teenagers in the 1960s. Of all the groups who sought to capitalize on the appeal of surf-themed rock 'n' roll, The Beach Boys were the most successful. Their *Surfer Girl* (1963) album opens with the title track: a ballad in which the group's harmonized vocals describe the protagonist's yearning for a mysterious girl with whom he hopes to surf, romance, and take everywhere with him. The synthesis of yearning lyrics and the harmonized melodies provides the track with powerful affective properties of a more loved-up variety, which have a lower energy level in terms of arousal. These effects are also supported by the use of more gentle rhythms and smoother sounds. This approach is also used on several other songs on the album, such as 'Surfer Moon', a ballad about the moon as a symbol of romance and surfing; and 'Your Summer Dream', a song in which the yearning for—rather than the reality of—a surfing lifestyle is made explicit, as the group implores the listener to 'make it real your summer dream'.

While the original surfing music had an authentic connection with surfing culture, The Beach Boys' approach is markedly fictional, and forms something closer to a mirage of a romantic, idealized concept of surfing. Through the sound of reverberant rock 'n' roll music, harmonized lyrics, and poetic descriptions, the music offers a window to a fantasy of surfing that was desirable for many teenagers.[11] As it happens, the groundwork for this as a particularly enticing aspirational vision for teenagers had already been laid during the 1950s, as Hawaiian music was harnessed and stylized as a means to market the concept of Hawaii as an almost mythical, exotic, 'once in a lifetime' honeymoon destination (Doyle 2005, pp.120–127). Building upon these fantasies, The Beach Boys delivered highly desirable representations of an exotic and romantic surfing lifestyle through the sound recording medium. This was—and remains—an incredibly popular musical fantasy, though it is also of note that the smooth, romanticized vision of surfing culture expressed by The Beach Boys has been rejected by some surf music enthusiasts who see the music as inauthentic. This can be partly attributed to the fact that except for their drummer Dennis Wilson, The Beach Boys were not surfers, unlike originators of the style such as Dick Dale. Yet an important distinction can also be observed between the smooth, saccharine sound of The Beach Boys, and the raw, overdriven sound of Dick Dale. The ethos of the former is a dreamy, loved-up surfing fantasy, while the latter expresses something closer to an adrenaline soaked tube ride.

Hot-Rod Sounds

The roar of revving engines, vehicles passing at high speed, squealing tyres, and cheering crowds cut through the mix, before the steady up-beat pulse of the instrumental rock 'n' roll kicks in. This is the opening track 'Smooth Stick' from The Deuce Coupes' *Hotrodders' Choice* (1963) album of rock 'n' roll instrumentals thematically related to hot-rod culture. Throughout the song we hear guitar riffs overlaid with the vehicular sounds passing by in stereo. On 'Gear Masher' and 'Double-A-Fueler' the rock 'n' roll music is overlaid with engine sounds, while 'Hayburner' uses the sounds of car horns. The packaging reflects the car theme through photographs of customized machines, engines, and liner notes that frame the music in relation to hot-rod culture.

Hotrodders' Choice (1963) was among the records produced by Bob Keane's Del-Fi label as interest in surf music began to decline (Crowley, 2011, pp.109–112). The music substituted the surfing theme for one related to teenage hot-rod culture, which was seen as having a potentially broader appeal for inland American teenagers. As also exemplified on The Beach Boys' *Little Deuce Coupe* (1963), and Dick Dale and his Del-Tones' *Checkered Flag* (1963) and *Mr. Eliminator* (1964) albums, hot-rod culture could be seen as an adjunct to surfing culture that similarly expressed idealized notions of freedom and teenage thrills. The music on *Hotrodders' Choice* was similar to surf, but is distinguished through the use of a drier, cleaner, and more streamlined sound. Here the absence of reverb can be seen as a mimetic device; the 'dry' guitar sound more appropriately resembling the dry heat and dust of a race. Along with the packaging of the music, one of the key methods for evoking the idea of hot-rodding culture was the use of non-musical sound materials. Where surfing tracks such as The Tornadoes' 'Bustin' Surfboards' (1962) represented surfing by including the sound of ocean waves throughout the track, *Hotrodders' Choice* accomplished an analogous feat by using revving car engines at the beginning or during songs. The use of these materials creates the illusion of being roadside during a drag race, while the driving rhythms of the rock 'n' roll performance capture a sense of high-speed adrenaline.

Through surf and hot-rod music we begin to see the use of analogue electronic processes such as echo, reverb, and non-musical sound recordings as a significant means through which to adapt the conceptual themes of rock 'n' roll. These techniques allowed the affective properties of rhythm and blues music to be coupled with specific meanings, which in turn reflect variations in the ethos of the music. Yet as teenagers plunged into the revolutions of the 1960s, they would have more to think about than just surfing and hot-rods. Just as electronic processes were used to represent specific concepts in surf music, similar processes would also provide a means through which to create a further adaptation of rock 'n' roll that reflected a new cultural sphere: the psychedelic movement.

PSYCHEDELIA

Turn off your mind, relax, and float down stream.

—The Beatles, 'Tomorrow Never Knows'

The 1960s saw the advent of many cultural and social transformations: the civil rights movement, women's liberation, and the Vietnam War protests were among these. The hippy counter-culture of the era grew out of these transformations, as a rejection of the values that had sustained violence and inequality in America; after all, the post-war period had been one of prosperity, but this had not been enjoyed by everyone and had highlighted the injustice of society. This was the social context within which drugs such as LSD became popular among the hippies. More than just hedonistic escapism, psychedelic drugs were seen as a toolkit for reconfiguring the mind-set of a generation. The theory as espoused by key figures such as Timothy Leary was that LSD would enable the user to blow off the doors of perception, cleansing themselves of preconditioned thought structures, allowing new ways of living to emerge.

This historical period provided the backdrop for psychedelic music—fundamentally another variation of rock 'n' roll that connected the music with the concept of psychedelic culture. Psychedelic music was by turns an affirmation of revolutionary values of consciousness expansion, while also encapsulating the fantasy of psychedelic voyages. Like the surf rock that had come before, the music centred on a concept for the listener to climb aboard; it was part fantasy and part reality. Plenty of the musicians and audiences involved really were blowing their minds with acid on a regular basis, but there were also those who had never touched the stuff, and as Bell (1969) reported for the *New York Times*, 'you [didn't] have to be high'. Psychedelic rock really begins with garage rock bands such as the 13th Floor Elevators and The Beatles *Revolver* (1966) album in the mid 1960s, and continues into the 1970s where it evolves into what became known as progressive rock and others forms such as heavy metal. In this section we will consider several key examples in order to analyse the underlying mechanisms that associate psychedelic music with altered states of consciousness (ASCs) and the ethos of psychedelic culture.

Cosmic Themes

The discordant sound of piano keys crash at the onset of Kaleidoscope's 'Flight from Ashiya' (1967), as descending guitar chords and vocals lead into the regular drum thumps and bass notes of a psychedelic waltz. The theme of the song is developed through its lyrics and describes an impending aeroplane crash. As the protagonist looks out the window he sees 'puffs of white cotton passing the window', while chaos surrounds him as the 'captain sits and seems to be in a daze'. The aircraft descends from 'one minute high, [to] the next minute low'. Amidst the chaos 'visions of childhood rush past [his] eyes', thus the song gives us a window into the subjective experience of the individual in the face of impending doom. The descending pitch of the vocal lines matches the falling altitude of the aircraft, while the choral quality of these also provides an ethereal impression that suits the dazed sense of detachment indicated by the lyrics.

The above is a literal reading of 'Flight from Ashiya' (1967), but in the context of psychedelic culture, the song could also be understood as a metaphorical description of an LSD trip. In particular, the lyrics 'one minute high, the next minute low' as 'visions … rush past [his] eyes' are seemingly evocative of an ASC experience. Critically, the song interrogates matters regarding death, and internal subjective experience, which are aligned with the wider concerns of psychedelic culture. Just as Timothy Leary (1968) saw the psychedelic experience as a means of investigating the nature of the self, and its relationship with the universe, so too does the song articulate similar questions. In his discussion of lyrics in psychedelic rock, Larden (cited in Krippner, 2012, p.264) summarizes this point in his assessment that the era showed a general shift from the boy-meets-girl discourses that had come before to those of man-meets-cosmos. In fact, this shift is only partial, since the majority of psychedelic rock continued to explore relationship themes, albeit in times of changing sexual politics (Bovey, 2006). Yet this description certainly captures the shift towards introspection exhibited in 'Flight from Ashiya' and other psychedelic tracks such as The Byrds' 'Eight Miles High' (1966), Jefferson Airplane's 'White Rabbit' (1967), or The Amboy Dukes' 'Journey to the Center of the Mind' (1968). While these songs do not necessarily describe the psychedelic experience in explicit terms,[12] they describe metaphorical voyages through the internal spaces of the human psyche, and can be seen as a response to the counter-culture ethos of consciousness expansion. Yet as we shall now consider, in many cases this shift was explored not only through lyrics but also through aspects of sound design.

Warped Effects

A warped guitar chord sweeps across the speakers as tremolo chords ring out and the singer laments, 'last night your shadow fell upon my lonely room …'. The lyrics of The Electric Prunes' 'I Had Too Much to Dream (Last Night)' (1966) describe the protagonist's experiences of dreaming about an ex-lover. Yet 'too much to dream last night' is a play on 'too much to drink last night', alluding to dreaming as an intoxicating experience, not unlike an acid trip. The psychedelic or dream-like themes of the song are also indicated through the use of analogue effects processing on the guitar and vocal parts, which create a warped aural experience. For example, the piece uses electric guitar sounds that are heavily saturated with fuzz and tremolo, and reverse tape effects to present guitar parts backwards (Breznikar, 2011). In the lead-up to the chorus, the phrase 'gone, gone, gone …' fades into a haze of reverb, a production technique that is recapitulated at the end of the song. These production techniques on the sound recording support the evocation of the dreamy, acidic themes of the music; vocal lines become hazy and disappear into the distance; and guitar lines are strangely wobbly like the letters on a Haight-Ashbury concert poster, themselves an allusion to the melting visual perception experienced by LSD users.

In these terms, the mimetic use of sound processes on 'I Had Too Much to Dream (Last Night)' (1966) convey the perceptual distortions that occur during a dream or hallucination. For example, tremolo causes sustained notes to ripple by modulating signal amplitude, which can be considered to reflect the way in which colours appear to shimmer or pulsate during a psychedelic experience. The use of varying amounts of reverberation could be considered as an impressionistic representation of the perceptual distortions to aural experience that occur during hallucination, or as metaphorically suggesting the spaces of the inner psyche. Through the temporal use of such effects processing on 'I Had Too Much to Dream (Last Night)', the piece sonically represents the dissolution of the boundaries between fantasy and reality described in the lyrics, and expresses a way of seeing the world that emphasizes the subjectivity of conscious experience. This 'way of seeing' is consistent with the ethos of psychedelic culture, with its emphasis on challenging normal ways of thinking and behaving.

The use of studio production techniques to reflect dreamy psychedelic states is also present on various other psychedelic rock records from this era. For example, The Beatles' 'Blue Jay Way' (on *Magical Mystery Tour,* 1967) provides evolving, swirling textural effects through the use of flangers, rotary effects,[13] and tape sounds, reflecting the hazy psychedelic themes of the lyrics. Meanwhile, the 13th Floor Elevators' Tommy Hall used an 'electric jug' (a blown jug with a microphone attached to it, processed with effects) to create reverberant rippling sounds that could be seen as mimetic of LSD hallucinations (e.g. 'Roller Coaster', on *Psychedelic Sounds of the 13th Floor Elevators,* 1966).[14] Along similar lines, Ultimate Spinach's '(Ballad of the) Hip Death Goddess' (on *Ultimate Spinach,* 1968) and The Electric Prunes' 'Kyrie Eleison' (on *Mass in F Minor,* 1968) are further examples that utilize lead guitar sounds heavily saturated in tremolo and reverb effects, producing ethereal tones that evoke a ghostly sense of 'otherness'.

Time Distortions

One of the most iconic psychedelic compositions to make creative use of tape technology and multi-tracking during the 1960s was 'Tomorrow Never Knows', from The Beatles' *Revolver* (1966) album. The lyrics of the song were derived from *The Psychedelic Experience: A Manual Based on the Tibetan Book of the Dead* (Metzner, Alpert, and Leary, 1968), a book which itself interpreted principles derived from *The Tibetan Book of the Dead* (trans. Dorje, 2005) for the purposes of suggesting how to approach the psychedelic experience. The lyrics of 'Tomorrow Never Knows' can be seen as imparting wisdom derived from the Tibetan teachings, which could be taken as advice for anyone on LSD, or as a general evocation of a spiritual LSD experience. Looking beyond the lyrics, tape processes are used in combination with the musical arrangement to support this theme.

On 'Tomorrow Never Knows' the concept of cyclical existence and rebirth is encoded in the sonic properties of the music. Throughout most of the piece a

C-major chord is used with few changes, creating an effect similar to a drone. This allows comparisons to be drawn with the drones of traditional Indian sitar music. For Western audiences these sounds signal an exotic sense of otherness and point towards general notions of Eastern culture. The sustained evolving notes of the drone can also be understood as reflecting the theme of cyclical existence through the musical material. These cyclical notions of time are also embedded in the music through the use of saturated tape loops and reversed material. Throughout the piece these tape loops provide various bursts of sound that flow in the opposite direction to the music, as if to suggest past experiences and a dissolution of time on the threshold of death.

In these terms the use of drones and time manipulations can be considered as psychedelic, since these sonic materials are mimetic of the distortions to time perception that typically occur during ASCs. Manipulation of recorded material enables time to flow at a quicker or slower rate than the listener would normally expect. Elsewhere, speed manipulations and reverse effects are also used on The Jimi Hendrix Experience's '... And the Gods Made Love' (on *Electric Ladyland*, 1968), to create a rather woozy effect that he refers to as a 'sound painting of the heavens' (Noble, 1995, p.22). Here the tape manipulations do not suggest cyclical time, but suggest distortions to time perception such as those that might occur during the derangement of an ASC, lending the piece an impressionistic sense of otherness or the supernatural.

These examples show that electronic processes were among those methods that allowed the representation of psychedelic culture through the medium of the sound recording. As we have seen, the mimetic use of echo and reverb, tape processes, and flangers, can be used to represent various aspects of ASCs. The use of these effects could be characterized as impressionistic: in dreams or hallucinations we do not really hear voices as if they are especially reverberant, but the effect provides a means to metaphorically distinguish the otherness or unreality of certain sonic elements. Just as the use of reverberation in surf music allowed imaginary concepts of surfing to be constructed, in psychedelic rock these effects open up a hazy, dreamy space that is evocative of the interiors of the psyche. Of course, in most cases these do not replace the main representation—a rock 'n' roll band playing music—but they do allow this representation to be adapted. For the more effects-laden productions, the experience might be described as an aural equivalent of looking through a distorting camera lens; we hear a band playing rock 'n' roll music, but the sound is strange, warped, and supplemented with unreal, hallucinatory elements. Indeed, for live performances a similar effect was also produced in the visual domain, since psychedelic light projections gave a hallucinatory appearance to the stage performance (as, for example, in Figure 3.1), without the need for audiences to take drugs (Bell, 1969; see also Chapter 6, pp.129–130).

Figure 3.1. Psychedelic light projections by the Joshua Light Show, projected on to Frank Zappa and the Mothers of Invention at the Fillmore East, New York, 1967. Courtesy of Joshua White; photo: Herb Dreiwitz.

Through the presentation of the music with the addition of these visual and auditory effects, the music retains the energetic thrust of rock 'n' roll, with all the high-arousal effects that this entails; yet these affective properties are framed by the psychedelic concept. This 'psychedelic concept' may appeal to listeners who identify with the ethos of psychedelic culture; who find the music exotic; or perhaps, who find the colourful sensory explosions of the music as similarly appealing as the visual experiences of the drugs themselves. Both the representational and affective properties of the music may also make it especially appropriate as a complement for drug experiences, since the conceptual themes may provide a point of interest while the affective qualities may be used to direct the energetic mood of such experiences. However, it should be noted that not all examples advocate the psychedelic experience; songs such as Fapardokly's 'Gone to Pot' (on *Fapardokly,* 1966), Love's 'Red Telephone' (on *Forever Changes,* 1967), and C.A. Quintet's *Trip Thru Hell* (1969) are among those that express darker sides of psychedelic culture. It is also of note that acoustic psychedelic folk music provided a counterpoint to the acidic illusions of electronically enhanced rock. Folk records typically used less effects processes, and this could perhaps be seen as a more appropriate sonic expression of the earthly, naturalistic ethos that was prevalent among the hippies.[15] It would be incorrect, then, to presume that the warped sound of electrified acid rock stood for all of the counter-culture; yet through the use of effects processes we find various expressions of the psychedelic ethos through sound.

OUTER SPACE

I'm charged with cosmic energy, has the world gone mad or is it me?
—Hawkwind, 'Master of the Universe'

While 1960s psychedelic rock elicited a myriad of themes broadly related to the consciousness expansion of the times, one specific conceptual variation emerged which warrants closer attention: outer space. The possibility of space travel had sparked widespread public excitement, which peaked when the Apollo 11 mission made Neil Armstrong the first-person to walk on the moon. In tandem with this, science fiction became pervasive within popular culture, fuelling public desire for dreams and illusions of strange alien worlds. Films such as *Forbidden Planet* (Wilcox, 1956), *2001: A Space Odyssey* (Kubrick, 1968), and the original *Star Trek* (Roddenberry, 1966–1969) television series developed these interests on screen, while in music there was also a 'sci-fi/psychedelic nexus' (Hayward 2004, pp.15–29) in which the space theme was explored. Notably this theme was developed in the cosmic-jazz of Sun Ra, and John Coltrane's late 1960s output on records such as *Interstellar Space* (1974, recorded in 1967 during which time he had become interested in LSD); and in the psychedelic rock music of Pink Floyd, Gong, and Hawkwind. While the popularity of the space theme in mainstream culture can be seen on one level as an extension of teenage thrills of vehicular travel also explored in rock 'n' roll and surf music, the music of these groups reflects an ethos with more serious social implications.

Space Rock

The sound of a rising oscillator tone and sirens heralds the launch of Hawkwind's 'Master of the Universe' (on *X in Search of Space,* 1971), as the 'engines' of the driving rhythm section and distorted guitars power into action. The vocals of the track are presented from the perspective of a consciousness at 'the centre of the universe', and are delivered with a subtle reverse effect that lends a sense of unreality to their sound quality. Throughout the track the rock rhythms are accompanied by various sounds such as rising and falling oscillator tones that suggest the science fiction theme, while the guitar sounds are processed with wah-wah and flanger effects that enhance the psychedelic impression of the track.

'Master of the Universe' is an example of the 'space rock' music of Hawkwind, which melded the themes of psychedelia, outer space, and apocalypse. In space rock, the cosmic journeys into outer space became analogous to psychedelic voyages into the inner spaces of the mind. This was not pure escapism, as speculative science fiction provided an arena in which alternative notions of culture and society could be explored. Just as the otherness of the LSD trip enabled the user to crash and reboot their psychological system, hypothetical space voyages allowed society to be reimagined in alternative configurations. In this way, science fiction mythologies acquired the potential to symbolize various forms of transcendence and liberation. On albums such as *X in Search of Space* (1971), the concepts of outer space and the inner spaces of the mind become interchangeable, as tales of escaping concrete jungles in clouds of marijuana smoke merge with science fiction fantasy themes. Lyrics were provided for the band by science fiction writer Michael Moorcock, who also performed spoken word pieces with the band as documented on the *Space Ritual* (1973) live album (Delville, 1994). Among the more radical sonic departures of the band, the live version of 'Sonic Attack' featured on *Space Ritual*[16] uses electronic sound generation to create the apocalyptic siren sounds and warning message that might be heard in a dystopian future. The piece is fiction, but remains connected to the reality of life in the 1970s, where the very real threat of imminent nuclear annihilation was a feature of the Cold War (Ihde, 2015).[17]

The connection between synthesizers, electronic sounds, and science fiction exploited by Hawkwind and other groups such as Pink Floyd (e.g. *Dark Side of the Moon,* 1973) was possible because it had already been established in popular culture. Indeed as Braun (2002, pp.17–18) has argued, these new sound technologies afford a futuristic interpretation because they originate in military technologies that were the same as those used for space travel. Thus, in a very real sense these were the sounds of the future (or at least modernity), a point which was cemented in popular culture by the use of electronic sounds on Louis and Bebe Barron's pioneering soundtrack for the movie *Forbidden Planet* (1956). In many ways space rock can be seen as another permutation of psychedelic rock, but one that is centred specifically around science fiction themes. As with psychedelic rock, the conceptual meaning of the work is delivered partly through the use of electronic technologies, and could be readily explored due to the inherently futuristic properties of the new electronic instruments and effects.

Space Jazz

Sun Ra's 'There Are Other Worlds (They Have Not Told You Of)' (on *Lanquidity,* 1978) presents a drifting, cosmic mysticism through jazz. The sense of weightlessness is reflected mimetically through the use of synthesizer tones that have a gradual onset and decay; the destabilizing effects of tremolo; and the percussive strikes that loosely fall just after the beat. Reverb effects applied to the instrumentation also impressionistically represent the vastness of space. The piece includes spoken word elements that advise the listener there are other worlds that wish to make contact.

In the space jazz music of Sun Ra, space travel becomes a metaphor for escape from social and cultural restrictions imposed upon black people.[18] Through the concept of space, the dominant norms of society in the American South are marginalized and replaced by an idealized outer space in which the idea of society is revised. In these terms the music of Sun Ra forms a significant part of the canon of Afrofuturist culture, which explores revised concepts of race and society through media such as music, film, and literature.[19] As John Szwed (2000) explores in his biography of Sun Ra, the space concept was realized through many aspects of his music, performances, and the mythos that he created around his life. Considering the artefacts of Sun Ra's musical output, the theme was incorporated into his music through the use of chants about space themes, exotica influences, and the use of synthesizers to provide strange, new space-age sounds. Besides the music, by the 1970s Sun Ra's performances had become synaesthetic experiences that combined otherworldly costumes, lighting, and theatricalities built around the space concept—an experience of sensory overload that for some audiences was also heightened through the use of hallucinogenic drugs, even though Sun Ra himself was firmly opposed to them (p.339).

As with surf music and psychedelic rock, space rock and space jazz embrace a specific concept, which is represented through the music. The manner in which this representation is achieved is through a combination of factors, including album artwork; lyrics; aspects of the musical design such as rhythms; electronic instrumentation; and the use of effects processes. The latter processes specifically utilize the capabilities of analogue electronics, which enable aspects of space travel and the associated technologies of rocket ships to be represented impressionistically. As with surf music and psychedelia, the purpose of the outer space concept can be linked to a set of ethical principles: in various ways both Hawkwind and Sun Ra use space travel as a means for escapism in the face of social pressures in modern society. Rather than being apolitical, these forms of escapism highlight social issues and propose alternative ways of living through speculative fiction. Through the act of listening, the audience is able to engage with these concepts and draw upon the structures of knowledge they represent.

* * *

In this chapter we have discussed the capability of the sound recording for creating illusory representations. Sound recordings may be used to represent events in a realistic manner. However, by using the sound manipulation techniques afforded by new audio technologies during the latter half of the twentieth century, it also became possible to change the perceived reality of a sound recording. Using this capability, popular music records were able to deviate from realistic representations of performances with acoustic instruments towards stylized versions that incorporated artificial uses of space, non-musical sound materials, and other manipulations. Through these techniques, we have begun to see how sound could be used to provide several forms of conceptual adaptation. Each of these adaptations are connected to structures of knowledge or ways of seeing the world; they each express a particular ethos that their audience finds attractive.

In the case of psychedelic rock we also begin to see how music may represent aspects of the subjective experience of ASCs, through the use of effects processes to imitate the perceptual distortions that occur during hallucinations. However, psychedelic rock typically explores a variety of conceptual themes besides actual drug experiences. These themes broadly relate to the concerns of psychedelic culture, a point that was accurately summarized in Larden's observation that the era exhibited a shift towards man-cosmos discourses. Of course, music also does more than merely represent, and in the context of live performances, the evocation of conceptual themes works in combination with the affective properties of the music; the multi-sensory experience provided by light shows; and the social context. In the next chapter, then, we shall see how DJ culture allowed the full, illusory capabilities of the sound recording to be utilized in a live context to both represent and induce altered states.

CHAPTER 4
Trance Systems

The sun goes down, the moon comes up and you see the world spinning. My record is nine days without sleep. It's a shamanic thing.

—Mark Harrison

Glade Festival, 2005. The Bug's thunderous dancehall basslines pump out of the speakers on to the evening grass as dusk falls. Over the bass, abrasive industrial ambiences wash over the mix, while echo delays create repetitions, and stuttering spatial distortions to the sound of the MC's rhythmic chants. Fire jugglers, the smell of grass, and the sound of mobile vendors filling up balloons with nitrous oxide gas punctuate the scene. Behind the counters of the stalls, the vendors have portable refrigerators stocked with small brown psilocybin mushrooms and truffles, exploiting the final days of a loophole in the law that allows them to be legally traded provided that they are fresh (BBC News, 2005). With the euphoric enhancements of drugs and music, swathes of dancers move to the beat, as if caught in an invisible tractor beam or umbilical cord connecting their bodies to the bass bins. The rhythm is like an ancient tribal magic, and the dancers are locked into it—subservient to the bass, caught in its grasp. If trance states of the kind used in tribal traditions exist in modern Western culture, they are happening in this scene—right here, right now.

In the previous chapter we saw how sound recording and electronic audio manipulation technologies enabled rock groups to adapt their sounds in order to represent aspects of psychedelic culture and altered states of consciousness (ASCs). However, even as these bands began to experiment with effects processes and the capabilities of the sound recording, they remained constrained by the boundaries established by the group performance tradition, and many of the sound manipulations used in the studio could not be utilized in the live concert situation. In this chapter we begin by exploring how an alternative approach was forged through the use of the sound system as the primary vehicle for communal performances. Tracing the roots of sound system culture in Jamaica, we see how dub-reggae provided what Veal (2007) referred to as a form of 'psychedelic Caribbean music'. This sound system culture placed recorded sound at the heart of performances, and would prefigure the main approach of electronic dance music culture in the late 1980s and 1990s. Exploring the latter in more depth, we take a tour through the Chicago house and Detroit techno scenes, before moving across the Atlantic to the UK rave scene, where these influences collided with sound system culture, hip-hop, and dub-reggae. Through the course of the 1990s, the UK rave scene underwent a process of diversification to form a myriad of sub-genres, of which we shall explore just three: breakbeat hardcore, drum & bass, and ambient house. Looking beyond the United Kingdom, many innovations in electronic dance music were also taking place elsewhere in Europe and beyond. Among these the Goa trance scene was significant; it provided the seed for a 'technoshamanic' culture that continues to this day in the outdoor psy-trance parties that are held from Australia to Norway and beyond. Through analysis of key examples from each of these electronic dance music genres, in this chapter we shall see how the capabilities of studio electronics can be used to evoke conceptual meaning, while also providing energetic dance rhythms. Through this discussion, further approaches through which electronic sound can be used to represent ASCs will be uncovered, and we shall also see how the music affords the potential for eliciting experiences of trance through heightened sensory states that are framed by conceptual meaning.

SOUND SYSTEMS

The stylistic roots of The Bug's performance at Glade Festival were in the sound system culture of Jamaica, over fifty years earlier. In the 1940s proprietors of bars and shops in the island's capital of Kingston began to use open-air loudspeaker cabinets to play music and entice customers (Bradley, 2001, pp.4–8). At a time when few people had access to their own radios, this became the principal means through which many people were able to access professionally produced music. By the 1950s this practice gave rise to sound system culture, in which large sound systems were set up in halls and on lawns around Kingston. These events became social gatherings—a chance to relax, have a drink, dance, and meet people. Sound system dances would take place most nights of the week, and over the weekend would be all-night affairs. These dances brought in people from outside areas and made money through peripheral trading; but more than merely a commercial enterprise, the lawn dances also became a way of life and the voice of the community. In tandem with Jamaica's quest for independence from the United Kingdom there was a real thirst for music that was unique to the island, and before long the sound systems had progressed from playing American R&B to Jamaican ska, which was later followed by rocksteady, reggae, dub, and dancehall. As home-grown music gained momentum, then, sound system culture gave rise to a Jamaican recording industry that was not only a form of music for dancing to, but also became an expressive and empowering sound for Jamaican people in times of political turmoil and high levels of poverty.

Sound out the Box

One of the distinguishing features of the early Jamaican sound system culture was the way in which the sound recording was placed as the locus of performance. This approach avoids a long-standing problem faced by musicians using studio equipment to create popular music, where the music heard on the record cannot be properly reproduced in a live concert. Les Paul notably faced this problem in the 1950s, as he sought to perform hit songs such as 'How High the Moon' (with Mary Ford, 1951), which he had created with the use of his innovative multi-tracking techniques (Kane, 2014a). To perform these records in shows, he used various techniques such an additional singer off-stage, unknown to the audience, who would double the lines sung by Mary Ford. He also attached a mysterious black box to his guitar, which was actually a remote control used to trigger pre-recorded tape parts. Although Les Paul's approach provided entertaining and theatrical ways to showcase recorded sounds, sound systems circumvent the need for such stage-show trickery by simply embracing the use of pre-recorded sound as a means of performance. In the early Jamaican sound system culture records were specially made for performance by a DJ, and therefore acquired a primacy over the original asynchronous sessions used to create them.[1] In these terms, the proper realization of the music occurred when the needle hit the groove of a freshly cut acetate record and the basslines rattled out across the lawns. Placing the sound recording at the centre of communal performance experiences has significant implications, since it allows the full sonic capabilities of the recording studio to be enjoyed in a social context. Hence, just as we saw in the previous chapter how studio techniques provided a variety of representational capabilities in psychedelic rock, sound system cultures are also able to utilize these without restraint, and ultimately place them before a crowd.

Sonic Knowledge

Through his discussion of present day groups like Stone Love Movement, Henriques (2011) considers how the sound system communicates through various mechanisms. In particular, he describes the sound system as transmitting on what he terms the material, corporeal, and sociocultural 'wavebands'. In his discussion, the 'material waveband' describes the physical production of acoustic activity; the 'corporeal waveband' describes the movement of bodies; while the 'sociocultural waveband' deals with the social 'vibe' that propagates through the wider sphere of communicative activity. For Henriques, these three interrelated wavebands enable us to conceptually consider the way in which participation in sound system culture produces and transmits ways of 'thinking through sound'.

In Henriques's (2011) account, the material waveband is related to corporeal and sociocultural effects in an on-going process of negotiation between the audiences, musicians, producers, and sound system operators. To consider in more detail the role of the material sound recording in producing these effects, we may once again utilize the concepts of affective and representational properties of the previous chapters. As corporeal effects relate to physiological activity and behaviours, they can be associated with the affective properties of music. For sound system culture, this typically means the rhythm and bass, which through their transmission over loudspeakers are instrumental in raising pulses, setting feet moving, and promoting a positive mood. In contrast, sociocultural effects are more closely aligned with the communication of meanings and concepts in music, which engage cognitive processes. These effects can be elicited through various cultural artefacts, including records sleeves, concerts, and fashion; and also through the representational properties of sound. For example, music may communicate conceptual meaning through the linguistic messages provided by song lyrics or an MC's chants. As discussed in the previous chapter, music acquires representational capabilities through the use of recorded sound and electronic modifications, and these may reflect the ethos of the cultural group. When we consider both affective and representational properties together, musical materials may promote corporeal and sociocultural effects respectively. For the listener this supports the production of an affective response framed by conceptual meaning, contributing towards what Henriques and others such as St. John (2009) have referred to as 'the vibe'.[2] For the individual, 'vibe' has both cognitive and affective dimensions, and provides an experiential form of knowledge. Where such experiences are sufficiently powerful and aligned with a particular ethos, they may provide a form of transcendental *gnosis*, the term used in Ancient Greece to describe experiential knowledge.[3]

As sound system culture swept through popular music, it shaped the aesthetics in a multitude of musical scenes: from the hip-hop block parties of 1970s New York, to the rave music of the United Kingdom and beyond. In each of these permutations, the communicative power of electronic sounds created within the recording studio could be powerfully brought to bear on communal experiences of dance. As we shall see, the music of these various sound system movements was frequently psychedelic, combining hypnotic rhythms and bass with mind-melting textures and ambiences. In due course we will consider these, but first we begin by exploring the innovations of dub-reggae in more detail.

DUB-REGGAE

I never hear nothing like it in my whole life ... Tubby had him steel horns for the treble and he put them in the trees so it's like the sound is coming from all over. When the night was warm, the breeze is blowing and the music's playing, it's truly something to behold. King Tubby's sound system was definitely magical.

—Dennis Alcapone

Like many great inventions, dub music came about more or less as a happy accident, after a dubplate was mistakenly cut without a vocal track, producing an instrumental version which subsequently set the dance floors alight (Bradley, 2001, p.312). The approach of removing the vocal, and later, also removing other instrumental parts, emphasized the drums and the bass of the music. Studio engineers King Tubby, Lee 'Scratch' Perry, and Errol Thompson were among the first to pioneer this approach of creating what became known as 'dub versions'. The dub approach was also fuelled by economic factors, since creating alternative dub versions of a studio session enabled the producer to get more value out of the same recordings. However, in the hands of artists such as King Tubby these dub versions were much more than mere alternatives or B-sides; the pieces were new compositions in their own right, creatively resetting the production by dropping instruments in and out, and manipulating studio effects so that sounds seem to twist, turn, and drift off into the distance before popping back into the foreground. Just as surf and psychedelic music utilized effects such as these to evoke various forms of conceptual meaning, so too did dub integrate these sonic techniques as a means to express the ethos of the music; and in dub, the central ethos is a Rastafarian vision of African utopia.

Far East Sounds

We play music by feeling it. We call it the Far East Sound. 'Cause we play in minor chords. When you play those chords it's like a story without words.

—Augustus Pablo

Basslines pulse; snare drums crash with explosive reverberation; tom-tom fills rattle out and echo into the distance; cowbells pop through the mix. Meanwhile, the mournful sound of minor key trumpets and melodicas drift in and out of the mix and fragments of palm-muted guitar chords and pianos skitter across the stereo field. The complementary effects of the warm basslines and the drifting melodies creates a sound that is at once near and yet far, a vital presence in the room that transports the listener's mind to distant African lands. This is the sound of *King Tubby Meets Rockers Uptown* (Augustus Pablo, 1976), an album of instrumental performances reworked in the studio as dub versions. The record constructs an impressionistic sonic window into an idyllic African past, consistent with the Pan-Africanism of Rastafari.[4] Yet as the music is purely instrumental, it is not through lyrics that these themes are developed, but through the mournful minor-key notes of Augustus Pablo's melodica, which echo through the mix as if somehow emerging from a distant past. The effect is almost transcendental, and the echo chamber is integral to its delivery.

In his discussion of dub music, Veal (2007) considers how dub-reggae evokes a sense of African utopia. For Veal, the spatial effects of echo and reverb and the repetition of musical fragments enable an association between post-colonial Jamaica and the idealized notions of Africa that underpin Rastafarianism. His interpretation hears the fragmentary design of dub music, during which voices and instruments drop in and out amidst layers of effects processing, as reflecting the displacement of African people and the interruption of their historic legacy caused by slavery. Drawing upon Doyle's (2005) discussion, Veal argues that echo and reverb also lend qualities of supernatural otherworldliness to the music, so that voices are heard as if they are biblical echoes from the past, exulting Africans and redefining them in the present day. His argument is especially revealing when considering the instrumental 'far east' sounds of Augustus Pablo, as also heard on such records as *East of the River Nile* (1981), but can also be applied to other examples from the spectrum of dub-reggae. Seen in these terms, the echoing, fragmented sounds in the mid-high frequency range can be understood as a means through which to represent visions of African utopia. When coupled with the earthly physicality of the rhythm section, the representational qualities afford a cognitive impression that is coupled with the affective properties of the drums and bass.

Mystic Sounds

Dub acquires the fragrances of mysticism in the hands of Lee 'Scratch' Perry, who performs as a magician or shaman-like character with customized hats and shoes that are covered with mirrors and other totemic items. The sounds of The Upsetters' *Return of the Super Ape* (1978) glisten, rattle, and sparkle in a manner that recalls traditional shamanic rituals. For example, 'Crab Yars' is presented with a backdrop of shimmering bell sounds, while 'Jah Jah Ah Natty Dread' includes whistling tape sounds and percussive rattling. These collages of ornamental sounds are layered across the mix, as if Perry himself is dancing around it and conducting a ritual—the echo chamber reflecting sound fragments like the beams of light that emanate from his magic hats. The use of echo and reverb could also be considered as mimetic of the perceptual distortions that occur during marijuana-induced experiences of ASC, where distortions to time and spatial perception may occur.[5] For example, as metallic sounds bounce off into the distance on 'High Ranking Sally', they form an aural equivalent of the visual-trail effects that may be experienced in hallucinations. However, to interpret Perry's music only in these psychedelic terms would be reductive, as his work contains a rich and often humorous symbolic language that references visions of Africa, forces of nature, his libido, and a variety of personas drawn from film and TV.[6] On 'Return of the Super Ape' echoing flutes and Nyabinghi drumming[7] reference distant African lands, while the destructive energies of the 'Super Ape' character (depicted as a giant ape on the album cover tearing up trees while smoking an oversized spliff) are represented through machine gun fire and the sounds of smashing bottles. Through the use of studio effects and collaging of sonic materials then, Perry adapts dub to construct powerful new aural mythologies.

In Perry's craft, these symbolic approaches extend beyond the use of the sounds themselves, to an animistic approach in the studio, where the equipment used to create the sounds is treated ritualistically in order to affect perceived spiritual qualities within the music. As Katz (2006) has documented, Perry was known to bless the studio and utter incantations (p.176, p.319); connect a palm tree to the mixing desk; build a drum booth containing a pond in the shape of the Star of David (p.332); and engage in a variety of other seemingly eccentric rituals of his own devising. Famously, Perry's mysticism also extended to the extensive decoration of his Black Ark studio with talismans and obsessive 'X' markings that were intended to cancel out negative energies (pp.307–308). Such activities have led some to speculate on the influence of Obeah (a form of West Indies folk magic) in his work.[8] Indeed, Perry grew up around traditions of spirit possession and reportedly drew direct inspiration for his early single *People Funny Boy* (1968) from his observation of a Pocomania ritual.[9] However, Perry has denied any actual involvement with Obeah, and his mysticism is closely related to his various self-constructed personas, which also draw upon powerful figures from pop-culture and his unique sense of humour. In these terms Perry does not conform to any one established system of magical belief, but can be seen as a musical shaman on his own terms, who employs ritualistic musical techniques to create an affective state accompanied by mystical visions of African utopia, the elemental forces of nature and a cornucopia of superheroes and tricksters.

Future Sounds

Rising synthesizer tones proliferate over the punchy bass sounds on *Prince Jammy Destroys the Invaders …* (Prince Jammy, 1982). Throughout the record we hear pitched oscillations that are augmented with echo effects. As heard on 'Martian Encounter', the results closely resemble the sounds of sirens or radars that might be heard on the mission-control of the science fiction spaceships of the silver screen, or the coin-operated video games of *Space Invaders* (Taito, 1978) (which the album title references) and *Galaxian* (Namco, 1979). A related effect is also achieved by manipulating the filter cut-off point on the reverberating snare drums of 'Conspiracy on Neptune', causing the pitch to rise and fall in time with the rhythm. Here the futuristic qualities of the sounds produced by studio effects and synthesizers are emphasized, adapting the themes of dub by staging the show in outer space. The title also reflects the sound-clashes of dub-reggae culture, in which rival sound systems compete to impress audiences with the best sound; it says that Prince Jammy's sound can defeat anyone, whatever world they are from. This motif was a recurring one in dub-reggae at this time, as producers went head-to-head with a variety of otherworldly adversaries and emerged victorious.[10] The science fiction theme extends to the album artwork, which illustrates Prince Jammy cruising through outer space in his PJ1 craft, facing off against his 8-bit rivals.

Although the comic book and science fiction themes at this time could also be seen partly as a marketing technique, the space theme is especially recurrent in dub and could be seen as an extension of the Afrofuturist mythology of artists such as Sun Ra. The cover for the *I Wah Dub* (1980) record by Blackbeard (a pseudonym of Dennis Bovell), is especially revealing. The sleeve of the LP features the artist posturing in a kind of dub-reggae mission control, piloting a recording studio that is also a spaceship, with planet earth visible in its sights and the co-ordinates set for Africa. This image encapsulates the Afrofuturist idea of dub as a transcendental aural technology for reconnecting peoples of African descent with the cradle of humanity. This image is reflected sonically through the futuristic associations afforded by studio effects, as heard through the swirling filters, tape speed manipulations, and echoing pulses that are applied to the instrumental sounds of 'Electrocharge'. Yet simultaneously, the music is firmly grounded in a sense of biblical African history through the earthly basslines and distant melodicas (as heard on 'Blaubart'). Through the synthesis of future and past a particular Afrofuturist power emerges, and we might even go so far as to consider that Blackbeard's spaceship has traversed not only space but also time.

Through the examples discussed, we may observe how dub-reggae affords a variety of conceptual representations for the listener, and the role electronic studio processes play in facilitating these. As a predominantly instrumental form of music it is through not only lyrics but also the musical arrangement and electronic treatment of the sounds that these concepts are constructed. When these representations are coupled with the affective properties of the rhythm and bass, the music may induce powerful experiences that are aligned with the concept and ethos presented.

Veal (2007) characterizes these experiences in terms of Rouget's (1985, pp.200–204) definitions of 'ecstatic contemplation' and 'possession'. Comparing dub with African traditions of spirit possession, he invokes the visceral aspects of the Jamaican dances, in which audiences once fired gunshots into the air during moments of peak excitement. In his view, dub-reggae inherits this abandon from African trance traditions; however, he does not fully commit to the assessment of dub as eliciting trance, remarking that the dance style is actually 'cool, calm, graceful, and understated' (p.201). He then also draws upon the mystical or otherworldly effects of dub that are provided through subtle sonic properties such as reverberation, space, and texture. Although his discussion here is revealing with regards to the representational properties of dub, his claim that the sound system 'induce[s] pseudo-possession and/or contemplative ecstasy' is somewhat ambiguous with regards to the affective experiences of energy that the music elicits.[11] This ambiguity is easily diffused if we distinguish between different modes of listening, however. When listening to dub in relaxed, seated, solitary conditions, the filtering of instrumental parts may direct the attention of the listener towards certain sonic details, while the associative properties elicit conceptual visions. When combined with the slow tempos, the repetitive basslines may provide a state of relaxed, focused listening that is more meditative or hypnotic in form. Where it is used,[12] marijuana may complement the experience by promoting absorption into sonic details; eliciting mental images through sound via synaesthesia; and relaxing the individual. Contrast this, however, with the social situation of a sound system night, where basslines are projected at high volumes over walls of speakers, and are combined with dancing, cans of Red Stripe beer, and other intoxicants such as nicotine which have stimulant properties. The latter situation then clearly affords the possibility of high-arousal states. In accordance with the view of meditation and trance states as extreme, opposite points on a dimensional model of consciousness, it seems that either may indeed be possibilities. In either situation, the twin effects of representational and affective properties in sound create an imaginative and emotional space for the listener to engage with. For dub music, this enables the listener to identify with the powerful stance of righteous exultancy of the individual in the face of oppression and stress, and accounts for the music's power as a vehicle for communicating liberating mental and physiological states. The use of the sound system and the studio to provide such effects is an innovation that belongs to dub; however, as we shall see, similar approaches would subsequently also be exploited in a variety of other electronic dance music genres to communicate different forms of knowledge.

ACID REVELATIONS

The roots of all-night dance parties or 'raves' can be traced back to any number of scenes; the aforementioned Jamaican sound system culture and the northern soul scene in Britain are but two examples (St. John, 2009, pp.2–4). Modern rave culture as it exists today seemingly grew out of the basic human desire for night-time revelries, in combination with the facilitative potentials of electronic music equipment. In the gay, black, Chicago house scene of the 1980s artists such as Farley 'Jackmaster' Funk and Frankie Knuckles created music with drum machines, samplers, and massive sound systems that were designed to propel all night dance parties (Reynolds, 2008). With sweat dripping from the ceiling and significant levels of drug use, the club nights at The Warehouse, The Power Plant, and The Music Box saw dancers grooving to relentless hypnotic drum beats, which along with the

Detroit's techno and New York's Paradise Garage scenes would establish the blueprint for the burgeoning electronic dance music culture of the late 1980s and 1990s.

The presence of electronic music-making machines in these scenes was partly a matter of cost and convenience. As has been well documented (e.g. Homer, 2009), the availability of drum machines, synthesizers, digital samplers, and sequencers that used the Musical Instrument Digital Interface (MIDI) protocol effectively democratized music production, making it more accessible for musicians to create professional recordings without access to a fully equipped recording studio. However, the use of these electronic instruments also had an impact on the sonic aesthetics, allowing both an expanded sound palette, and the delivery of relentless dance rhythms with precise timing. In combination with the outputs of MDMA drug factories, these new sounds allowed the production of all-night dance parties on an unprecedented industrial scale.

Acid House

House music is a church for people who have fallen from grace.

—Frankie Knuckles

Marshall Jefferson's 'Move Your Body' (1986) is the quintessential Chicago house track: piano chords rain down over thumping $\frac{4}{4}$ drum machine kick drums, while the vocals cry out, 'Gimme that house music to set me free | Lost in house music is where I wanna be', and the endless refrains of 'Move your body | Rock your body'. As these lyrics reflect, above all Chicago house celebrates the ecstatic revelry and physicality of losing oneself in dance. In Reynolds's (2008, pp.22–23) account, the social scene of Chicago house was one in which gay black men were able to find liberating communal experiences of dance in response to their status as exiles from mainstream culture. The music defines these experiences in almost religious and transcendental terms, as heard on the Fingers Inc. song 'Can You Feel It' (1988), which pastiches a Christian sermon through the lyrics 'in the beginning there was Jack[13] ... and from this groove came the grooves of all grooves'. Through these biblical references, this piece and others such as Joe Smooth's 'Promised Land' (1988) extend a tradition of association between African American music and gospel that can also be found in rock 'n' roll performances such as those of Little Richard.[14] 'Can You Feel It' also plays on the religious pastiche by delivering these vocals through an echo effect, suggesting the acoustics of a church congregation space, or perhaps the voice of God echoing down from a mountain as the commandments of house are delivered from on high. Yet while the theme might be religious, the church of house music is hedonistic and explicitly sexual, as epitomized by the lustful lyrics of Jamie Principle's Prince-inspired 'Baby Wants to Ride' (1987).

These representational properties would probably mean little if they were not backed by uplifting soulful melodies and driving rhythms, which provide the main catalysts for emotion and dancing. As heard on Phuture's 'Acid Tracks' (1987), the rhythms of acid house[15] mechanized the $\frac{4}{4}$ beat of disco through the use of drum machines such as the Roland TR-707. The drum machine allows a relentless precision over longer durations than a human drummer could possibly provide, and is ideally suited for building tension and sustaining dancing over extended periods. On 'Acid Tracks' these rhythms are accompanied by the characteristic 'squelchy' or 'acidic' sounds of the Roland TB-303, which are created by manipulating various controls of the Bass Line synthesiser such as the filter cut-off and resonance parameters. As the track develops, these modifications create gradual sweeps and rhythmic twists that range from choppy percussive treble sounds to throbbing low-frequency pulses. As also heard on subsequent examples such as Humanoid's 'Stakker Humanoid' (1988) or Josh Wink's 'Higher State of Consciousness' (1995), these filter manipulations create contours of frequency which by turns provide wild sections of sonic spontaneity and crescendos in pitch. Vitos (2014) emphasizes the efficacy of these sounds for massaging and teasing the listeners' aural system, an effect he sees as particularly well suited to complement the heightened sensorium provided by dance drugs such as MDMA. In more general terms, however, the emotional effects these sounds produce are also consistent with Meyer's (1956) theories regarding the satisfaction produced through pitch contours and expectation in music.

Detroit Techno

> So the kids take a pill to feel the funk and the DJ takes a pill to feel the funk. I don't take a pill to feel the funk. Carl don't take a pill to feel the funk. Glenn Underground don't take a pill to feel the funk. Derrick Carter might take a pill for fun, but not to feel the funk.
>
> —Derrick May

Emerging in parallel with Chicago house, Detroit techno similarly utilized the energetic capabilities of drum machines and synthesizers. Yet where Chicago house expressed an ethos of abandoned dance, the Detroit techno scene carried one that was consciously styled on the futuristic technologies and 'techno rebels' of Alvin Toffler (1980) (for a futher discussion see also Sicko, 2010). Themes of technological empowerment and dystopia appealed to the aspirations of upwardly mobile GQ-reading, straight, black kids, living in a city that had fallen from the grace of a once proud automotive industry.[16] As heard on 'No UFOs' (1985) by Model 500 (Juan Atkins), Detroit techno emphasized electronic funk through synthesized instruments and robotic-sounding vocals, creating a technological sound that draws comparisons with the cyborg electronic pop music of Kraftwerk, or the Afrofuturist electro-boogie hip-hop of artists such as Afrika Bambaataa. As Trowell (2001) notes, this sound embraces the artificial characteristics of drum machines and synthesizers; it can be contrasted with the more soulful, organic sounds of Chicago house, which typically uses technology to recreate the sounds of acoustic instruments such as the piano. The high-tech sounds of Detroit can also be heard on the various works of Derrick May, Carl Craig, Juan Atkins, and James Pennington's (Suburban Knight) *Relics: A Transmat Compilation* (1992), which expresses a futuristic vision in sound using sublime synthesizer pads; science fiction pulses; and hypnotic rhythms that suggest industrial processes. For example, on Derrick May's 'A Relic' we hear rigidly quantized synthesized drums and pulses that evoke the blinking lights of high-tech instruments, or the digital pulses of satellite communications. Elsewhere on Carl Craig's 'Evolution' and Derrick May's 'MS 6', the rhythms incorporate pitched noise-based sounds, mimetically suggesting sophisticated robotic processes of manufacture. This sleek, futuristic concept is extended to the sleeve design of *Relics,* which portrays an image of the solar system. These motifs can be understood as representing the 'super-industrial societies' of Alvin Toffler's *Future Shock* (1970), in which information technologies and space travel are pervasive. Furthermore, just as Toffler's book described struggles of the human soul in the face of modernity, the music juxtaposes mechanical (dehumanized) and soulful (human) sounds, suggesting post-humanism. On Derrick May's 'A Relic' this effect is achieved specifically through the contrast of technological rhythms with majestic string sounds, and minor-key synthesizer pads with smooth time-varying filter envelopes.

For our purposes here, it is notable that the social scene of Detroit techno was reportedly not one heavily engaged with the use of drugs, and the ethos that the music reflects is one of intellectual sophistication and control. On other releases, the synthesis of philosophical concepts and mimetic sounds goes beyond Alvin Toffler to explore the terrain of other Afrofuturist narratives. For example, as documented in the liner notes for Drexciya's *The Quest* (1997), the group's music is based around the mythology of the Drexciyans: a race of mutant sea creatures descendent from pregnant Africans thrown overboard from slave ships crossing the Atlantic. As Williams (2001, p.168) discusses, this aquatic theme is elicited through sonic materials that sound like bubbles rising to the surface, 'tactile textures', and vocoded sound bites. These signature bubble sounds can be heard on tracks such as 'Hydro Theory' (on *The Journey Home,* 1995), 'Bubble Metropolis' (on *The Quest,* 1997), and 'Species of the Pod' (on *Neptune's Lair,* 1999), and are created not with actual bubble sounds but through manipulating the pitch and filter envelopes of synthesizers, resulting in sounds that are mimetic of air bubbles. On 'Andreaen Sand Dunes' (on *Neptune's Lair*) these sounds are blended with science fiction synthesizers, eliciting visions of the subterranean landscapes depicted on the album cover.

Along similar lines, music by The Martian on the Red Planet label develops an Afrofuturist concept based around the mythology of a sophisticated alien civilization of 'thought and spirit', which are at once tribal yet more advanced than humanity. As described in the liner notes of *LBH—6251876 (A Red Planet Compilation)* (1999), this race is attempting to contact humanity through music, in order to address the 'chaos and destruction that [H]umanity would cause to the Earth and later to the Solar System'. As heard on 'Comet LBH', the music of these extra-terrestrial tribes is represented using a collage of synthesized flutes, sounds that resemble birds, and electronic textures; 'Lost Transmission from Earth', meanwhile, uses high-frequency pulses to suggest advanced forms of trans-dimensional communication. The latter track also uses a sample from Black Panther co-founder Huey Newton's voice: 'the spirit of the people is greater than the man's technology', thus suggesting that the 'communication' is actually a reconstruction of signals originally from earth, which the Martians are alerting our attention towards. In this way the Red Planet mythology echoes the enlightened, ecological aliens of films such as *The Abyss* (Cameron, 1989), while also invoking a specifically African American voice in a manner that recalls the Afrofuturism of Sun Ra.

Through the examples of Chicago house and Detroit techno, we have seen how electronic technologies allowed the affective properties of the music to be developed, by creating relentless streams of percussion. In the hands of the DJ, multiple records are combined to form continuous streams of rhythmic stimulation for hours at a time, thus placing technology in the service of the all-night dance party. Although these affective properties of high energy are present in both genres, our discussion has revealed important distinctions of ethos between the respective subcultures, which are reflected through the representational properties of the music; thus Chicago house embraces intoxication, physicality, and sexual abandon, while Detroit techno follows a path that is more intellectual and politically conscious. Each of these imperatives may have their merits, and the aim here is not to promote one over the other, but simply to highlight the role of technology in defining each sound and ethos.

ACCELERATED CULTURE

In the late 1980s acid house reached the United Kingdom and intersected with a burgeoning ecstasy culture. In 1988 and 1989 a 'second summer of love' was born in the legendary Bacchanalian nightclubs of London's Shoom, Future, and Trip; Manchester's Haçienda; and the outdoor 'orbital' raves of the M25 (Collin, 1998; Reynolds, 2008). Fuelled by ecstasy (MDMA), it kick-started a rave culture which would continue to grow throughout the 1990s and beyond. As the culture developed in Britain, the music diversified into a myriad of sub-genres. Among these, styles such as breakbeat hardcore, drum & bass, and happy hardcore ramped up the tempos of the music, reflecting an ever-quicker frenzy of speed that corresponded with the high-energy states sought by ravers on stimulants. Yet while these styles emphasized speed and adrenaline, ambient house provided the relaxing flipside soundtrack for ravers coming down from drug highs. Ambient house artists absorbed influences from Brian Eno, minimalism, psychedelic rock, and dub music, creating a more laid-back experimental style that suited post-clubbing listening situations. Taken as a whole, then, the specializations of these different genres can be seen to reflect the needs of an accelerated culture, in which both drugs and music provide ways in which to reach emotional peaks and deal with the inevitable troughs.

Breakbeat Hardcore

The foundation of hardcore rave music was the breakbeat, a percussive section during which the drums are heard in isolation during bridge sections of funk and soul recordings.[17] As heard on Dance Conspiracy's 'Dub War' (1992), Egyptian Empire's 'The Horn Track' (1992), or Hyper-On Experience's 'Time Stretch' (1993), producers increased the speed of the breakbeats, thereby ramping up the energetic qualities of the music to suit the tastes of dancers under the influence of the euphoric stimulant MDMA (as illustrated in Figure 4.1). Typically production techniques emphasized the rhythmic qualities of the music by using more than one breakbeat, which may be alternated between, sliced, rearranged, layered, or used in combination with drum machines such as the Roland TR-909. These breakbeats were often underpinned by deep monophonic synthesizer basslines that would deliver a powerful low-end. The rhythmic qualities of the music were also emphasized through the use of syncopated synthesizer 'stabs', as heard on the jagged pianos of Bizarre Inc.'s 'Playing with Knives (Quadrant Mix)' (1991). Paralleling the effects of ecstasy, these melodic elements also provided uplifting

Figure 4.1. Intoxicated ravers move to the beat in a trance-like state at the London nightclub Megatripolis, 1990s. Pav Mxski/Photoshot.

and sometimes aching shades of euphoria, as heard on Adamski's 'Magik Piano' (on *Liveandirect*, 1989), Liquid's 'Sweet Harmony' (1992), Orca's '4AM' (1993), or Luna-C's 'Piano Progression' (1994). In combination, these rhythmic and melodic elements deliver the affective properties of kinetic, corporeal energy and emotion.

These affective properties were coupled with a representational approach that celebrated the mindless hedonism of ecstasy-fuelled raves, communicating something like a grotesque cavalcade of drug-induced delirium and spaced-out madness. The main linguistic signifiers were provided by samples, rapping or 'diva' vocals. A whole slew of tracks from this era sampled children's TV themes and dialogue to use as drug metaphors: The Prodigy's 'Charly' (1991), Urban Hype's 'A Trip to Trumpton' (1992), Smart E's 'Sesame's Treet' (1992), and Children's Stories' 'The Chocolate Factory' (1992) are four examples. Other tracks such as The Ragga Twins' 'Hooligan 69' (1990) and Rebel MC featuring Tenor Fly's 'The Wickedest Sound' (1991) incorporated aspects of the UK's hip-hop and dancehall culture, featuring MC performances which complement the music.[18] These samples mix together with a myriad of other sources drawn from music, film, TV, and popular culture, combining to create something of a psychedelic collage. For example, Acen's 'Trip II The Moon (Part 1)' (1992) blends such disparate samples as John Barry's 'Capsule in Space' (1967); a Jim Morrison vocal snippet 'back in my brain' (from The Doors' 'A Little Game', 1987); diva vocal snippets 'take me higher' and 'more than ever before' from British electro-pop group Tongue 'N' Cheek's 'Nobody (Can Love Me)' (1988); and the sample 'I get hype ... when I hear a drum roll' from Eric B. & Rakim's 'You Know I Got Soul' (1987).[19] These samples are all used in the service of an outer space theme, with space being used as a metaphor for getting out of one's head. The Acen track also displays the treatment of samples with incessant looping, repetition, and speed changes that were all *de rigueur* during this period, with the latter effect also producing the characteristic cartoon vocal sound that lends a carnivalesque character to the proceedings.

Drum & Bass

> All right London, do you want the energy? Do you want the *energy*?
>
> —Alpha Omega, 'MG's Chamber'

The breakbeat evolutions of jungle and drum & bass developed harder, faster versions of the music that emphasized dub-reggae, dancehall, and hip-hop elements. As heard on the Metalheadz label's *Platinum Breakz* (Various Artists, 1996), drum & bass increases the tempo of the breakbeats to around 165 bpm. The manipulation of these breakbeats had also become a highly sophisticated technical process, with each loop being divided into multiple samples that are then subjected to a myriad of digital manipulations, allowing a wide variety of permutations. The effect is highly syncopated and often unpredictable, giving a sense of perpetual excitement and surprise. Coupled with the deep, half-time, dub-influenced basslines, the music provides an accelerated form of high-energy funk music, which in the context of raves is augmented by the rhythmic chants of MCs and sustained for hours at a time.[20]

Kinetic energy is a constant in drum & bass, but the use of sampled materials and sonic manipulation also allows for considerable variation in conceptual meaning. For example, Doc Scott's 'The Unofficial Ghost' (on *Platinum Breakz,* 1996) uses samples of gangster rap group the Wu-Tang Clan and abrasive synthesizer sounds to produce a 'dark' sound; The Wax Doctor's 'The Spectrum', by contrast, uses synthesized strings, high-frequency pad sounds, and female vocal samples to provide a 'light' sound.[21] The titles of Peshay's 'Psychosis' and Photek's 'Consciousness', hint at the introspective evaluation of conscious states; this theme is reflected on the latter track through constant manipulations of space and frequency content, creating an intricate effect that draws attention to sonic detail in a manner that recalls dub (albeit with the crisp, cleaner sounds afforded by digital studio effects). Elsewhere futuristic dystopias are explicit, as on Dillinja's 'The Angels Fell', which samples dialogue from Ridley Scott's *Blade Runner* (1982) and the accompanying score by Vangelis; Hidden Agenda's 'The Flute Tune' and J Majik's 'Final Approach', by contrast, use instrumental samples to deliver high-tech beats with jazz-inflected sophistication. Taken as a whole *Platinum Breakz* and its sequel *Platinum Breakz II* (Various Artists, 1997) encapsulate themes of post-humanism that extend the high-tech futurescapes and dystopias of Detroit techno. However, these collections also exhibit a substantial diversity of conceptual representation, which would subsequently provide the basis for a host of sub-genres: from dark, futuristic techstep (e.g. Ed Rush and Optical, *Wormhole,* 1998; Kraken, *Dominion,* 2001) to Latin-infused liquid-funk grooves (e.g. DJ Marky, *The Brazilian Job,* 2001; Infrared V's Gil Felix, *Capoeira,* 2003).

Ambient House

While breakbeat hardcore ramped-up tempos to catalyse high-energy dance experiences, ambient house artists pulled the parachute chord, cultivating blissed-out soundscapes for depleted ravers in the morning afterglow. As the first rays of light carved beams through a haze of smoke, gentle beats and psychedelic sample collages provided the soundtrack for overflowing king-size rizlas and ashtrays. The KLF's *Chill Out* (1990) was a defining work of the genre, consisting of droning synthesizer sounds and pitch bends; fragments of radio commercials; and other sampled materials such as slide guitars, Tuvan throat singing, bird calls, ocean waves, trains, and jet planes. The KLF characterized the album as a mythical tour across the Southern states of America, a theme that was also developed in their unreleased road-movie *The White Room* (1991). The music provides the illusory sense of a journey through the associative properties of the various sampled materials, and the spatial movements of Doppler shift effects that rush across the stereo field. The sounds are frequently layered with effects (e.g. 'Lights of Baton Rogue Pass By'), and pitch distortions ('Rock Radio Into the Nineties and Beyond'), lending the aural experience a hazy, psychedelic, dream-like quality. Throughout the album, the musical properties of the sustained synthesizer pads and arpeggios reprise the rushing sounds of rave music in gentler doses, supporting an overall mood of escapism and positivity that acts as a crash-landing pad for chill-out tents (shown in Figure 4.2), and decelerating ravers experiencing bruxism (jaw clenching) and emotional deflation in the early-morning drug come-down.

Other works of the ambient house genre took the idea further, constructing sonic ejector seats that launch the listener into off-world colonies and alien environments. For example, The Orb's *Adventures Beyond the Ultraworld* (1991) elicits an outer space theme through the sounds of synthesizers, science fiction programmes ('Earth (Gaia)'), and NASA's mission control ('Supernova at the End of the Universe'). The record retains a sense of humour through both titles such as 'Back Side of the Moon' (a pastiche of Pink Floyd's *Dark Side of the Moon,* 1973), and irreverent use of samples. Underpinned by steady breakbeats and dub basslines, the overall effect is one of positivity and good-humoured psychedelia. Taking listeners further into outer space, The Future Sound of London's *Lifeforms* (1994) transports the listener to the ecosystem of an imaginary alien world. Here the use of sampling and synthesis gives the music a futuristic sheen, yet the use of hand-percussion sounds, bells (for example on 'Flak' and 'Cascade'), and other 'ethnic' or 'tribal' signifiers are suggestive of an earthly, organic past. The biological

Figure 4.2. Revellers at Boom festival relax to ambient music in the 'Chill Out Gardens', Portugal, 2016. Yumiya Saiki Photography.

concept is also developed through the use of synthesis techniques that produce sounds mimetic of organic life, such as those heard on 'Ill Flower', which resemble birdcalls through the use of fluctuating pitch. Elsewhere on 'Dead Skin Cells' we hear bubbling water sounds, while the rippling synthesizer arpeggios of 'Spineless Jelly' invite the listener to construct mental images of bioluminescent jellyfish. The overall impression is one of an alien ecosystem cast in synthetic technologies and artificial intelligence, a concept that was also rendered visually on the 3D computer graphics artwork of *Lifeforms,* the associated EPs (e.g. *Cascade,* 1993), and the *Lifeforms* (1994) music videos. This theme can be seen as part of a broader trend in ambient house that reflects an ethos of neo-tribalism, which seeks to reconnect society with ecological values and shamanistic techniques. This ethos extends the discourses of Gaia and 'spaceship earth' that are prevalent within the wider cultures of psychedelia, and were notably epitomized by Terence McKenna's monologue on The Shamen's *Re:Evolution* (1993).[22]

The examples discussed illustrate the way in which electronic production methods were used to provide affective properties that met the needs of the accelerated rave culture. Once again, we also see how both linguistic signifiers and sonic materials provide forms of representation that reflect the conceptual theme and ethos of the respective sub-cultures. However, rather than being entirely isolated entities, these genres also show emerging interrelationships, and suggest the use of music as a technology for manipulating consciousness. Whether the listener combines the effects of music with the use of drugs or otherwise, the experiences produced may be powerful or even transcendental. This has led some listeners to consider electronic dance music as a spiritual technology. Before we depart from the world of electronic beats then, we shall make one last stop to a place where this is the case: Goa.

TECHNOSHAMANISM

In the late 1960s, Goa saw increasing popularity as a destination for hippies seeking spiritual transformation abroad. As St. John (2011; 2012) discusses, the beach parties of once remote Anjuna gradually evolved from low-key affairs involving acoustic guitars and a few bongos around a campfire, into large parties powered by generators and tape decks. As the Goa party scene grew, DJs began to mix DAT tapes of electronic music, which eventually became the preferred music with which to propel all night electronic dance parties. Today this style of explicitly psychedelic electronic dance music is known as psy-trance, and is a popular among a global network of dance parties, including Hungary's O.Z.O.R.A., Portugal's Boom, and others.

Along with other outputs from the Dragonfly label such as the compilation *Order Odonata Vol.1* (1994), Pleiadians' *I.F.O. (Identified Flying Object)* (1997), and Shakta's *Silicon Trip* (1997); Hallucinogen's *Twisted* (1995) is a defining work of the genre. The tracks are driven by $\frac{4}{4}$ techno rhythms and basslines that are geared towards all-night dance experiences. The tracks utilize 16th notes in minor or phrygian modes in order to provide a 'mystical' Eastern exotic feeling to the music, while TB-303s and other synthesizer sounds with resonant filters are used to provide the characteristic 'acid' sound. On 'Snarling Black Metal' further morphing effects are provided using a digital frequency modulation effect. Elsewhere on 'LSD' these sounds are used in combination with gated[23] pads, synthetic organs, and choral sounds, providing a spiritual impression for the listener. In the breakdown sections of 'LSD' where the rhythms subside, dialogue snippets about drugs and spiritual transformation are used. However, just as significant are the pervasive spatial transformations, which allow the synthesizers and other whooshing sounds to dart back and forth across the stereo field on 'Orphic Trench' and others. The combined effect is one of driving trance rhythms accompanied by rich tapestries of exotic pulsating synthesizer sounds that weave spiral contours through the frequency and spatial domains—not unlike an aural equivalent to the form constants (Klüver, 1971) and sensory fireworks of the psychedelic experience itself.

As with other dance genres discussed, psy-trance DJ mixes are designed to take the audience on a journey. This concept is also built into the wider structure of events by programming different stylistic variations of the music in correspondence with the early evening, night-time, and morning phases of the event.[24] Besides these categories, a variety of other micro-genres exist within psy-trance, such as 'forest trance', which elicits an ecological concept. As heard on Derango's 'Deranged' (on *Tumult*, 2005), various mimetic sonic materials are used throughout that suggest forest sounds such as strange animal calls. These sounds and other organic or alien materials dart in and out of the stereo mix in a manner that is as disorientating as the title of the track suggests. The approach can be seen as an attempt to enhance or augment the forest settings in which psy-trance parties often take place (especially in Scandinavia where the group hail from). Used in such contexts, the design of the music may augment the environmental sounds of the real-world setting by adding an additional layer of artificial sound, dissolving the boundaries between the real sounds of the environment and those of the music. Notably, this concept is also similarly developed in the decor of psy-trance parties, where ultraviolet canopies and sculptures are constructed in the shape of mandalas, giant butterflies, and other organic forms (e.g. Figure 4.3; see also Chapter 6, p.131).[25] Used in conjunction with VJ performances that project psychedelic animations reminiscent of visual hallucinations onto these sculptures, sound and visuals modify the outdoor context towards the hallucinatory. The result is a psychedelic sensorium that either

Figure 4.3. Psychedelic UV decor and canopies at Mo:Dem festival, Croatia, 2013. ES Web Photography.

amplifies the effects of drugs, or simulates the experience so that they are no longer required.

Technoshamanism

As we have seen, electronic dance music utilizes the sound system in order to produce experiences of heightened emotion. The sensory overload of the music is often augmented through drugs, and visual elements such as lighting and projections. At the peak of the dance experience, some people describe the dissolution of the usual personal and social boundaries, producing collective experiences of unity. Such experiences may fit with the definition of trance provided by Rouget (1985), in which ASCs are produced in communal situations of loud music, bodily movement, and energy expenditure.

This potential for electronic dance music events to create ASCs experiences has led some theorists to apply the term 'technoshaman', in reference to the concept of the DJ as the conductor of a spiritual journey that the audience experiences through dance (Hutson 1999, pp.64–67).[26] This term has been applied especially in psy-trance music, where DJs such as Goa Gil have intentionally stylized their performances as spiritual or shamanic occasions (St. John, 2011; 2012). These 'dance rituals' extend the rhetoric of psychedelic rave culture discussed by McKenna on The Shamen's *Re:Evolution* (1993), in which experiences of collective trance-dance enable the individual to return to a more ancient form of knowledge and tribal unity with each other and the earth. When understood in these terms, the dance music experience may be considered to provide a form of spiritual healing; it becomes another tool in the pantheon of spiritual techniques adopted by hippies, along with yoga and meditation. This concept of 'DJ-as-shaman' can be considered in terms of Mayer's (2008) discussion of the concepts of shamanism that are most attractive for Westerners. In particular, it fits with the view of the shaman as 'healer', since spiritual healing is presumed to occur through the act of trance-dance; as 'master of ecstasy', since he or she conducts the dance ritual in order to facilitate trance ASCs; and as 'ecologist', since dancing reconnects the individual with McKenna's 'Gaian supermind'.

The musical design of psy-trance is particularly interesting for our discussion, since it includes features that represent the sensory experience of hallucination, besides those more broadly associated with the discourses and ethos of psychedelic culture. The concept of DJ-as-shaman is also readily applied to psy-trance culture, where DJs such as Goa Gil self-style themselves in this way. However, as our discussion has explored in this chapter, other genres of electronic music may also have similar capabilities for inducing powerful experiences of transcendental *gnosis*, whether they identify these experiences as shamanic and spiritual or not. What distinguishes psy-trance is that the culture actively venerates the psychedelic experience, and thus represents hallucinations extensively within the visual and aural design of the material culture.

* * *

Through the course of this chapter we have seen how the sound system places the sound recording at the centre of communal dance experiences. In doing so, the performances of DJs in dub, acid house, and various forms of electronic dance music were able to harness the full capabilities of the recording studio in social performance situations. We can consider the function of these musical forms in terms of affective and representational properties. The capabilities for dancing are delivered through the rhythm and bass, while other abstract materials such as pitch contours and melodic sequences also support the emotional impact of the music. Meanwhile, the use of sample collages, synthesizers, and various electronic processes supports the production of conceptual meaning, which corresponds with the ethos of the subcultural group. In communal dance situations, these properties may contribute towards the production of heightened emotional states that are framed by conceptual meaning. Here both the cognitive and affective faculties of the individual may become aligned with the group, producing experiential forms of knowledge or *gnosis*. Some individuals within these electronic dance music cultures may enhance this process with intoxicating substances, while for others the effects of music, dance, and the sensory overload of lighting and decor may be sufficiently stimulating in their own right. Indeed, the use of drugs is also more prevalent within some cultures than within others, and the experiences they offer are glorified in some cultures more than others. In correspondence with this, some genres such as psy-trance represent the actual sensory experience of hallucinations, while in other genres such as Detroit techno this is not the case.

Of course, the areas explored here have only been snap-shots from a much wider international culture, and the principles discussed could be extended to consider other strands of energetic dance music. For example, our attention could alternatively have been directed towards the anarchic free-party techno sounds of Spiral Tribe (e.g. *Spiral Tribe Sound System*, 1993); the pumped up grooves of hard dance (e.g. Tony De Vit, *The Dawn*, 2000); the rapid-fire drum machine blitzkriegs of Dutch gabber (e.g. Euromasters, *Alles Naar De Kl—te*, 1992); the cyberpunk dystopias of speedcore techno (e.g. Neurocore, *Starship Travellers*, 2009); and so on. Similarly, the more laid-back sounds of ambient house find parallels in the stoned-beats of Bristolian trip-hop artists (e.g. Massive Attack, *Protection*, 1994); or the experimental hip-hop soundscapes of New York's illbient scene (e.g. DJ Spooky That Subliminal Kid, *Songs of a Dead Dreamer*, 1996). In each of these cases we would find energetic qualities and conceptual representations that connect with the ethos of the subculture, sometimes as a complement to intoxicating substances, and other times as a stimulus by itself. Where ASCs—or the idea of ASCs—are celebrated as part of the ethos, we would expect to find sounds that represent them. The concept of representing the actual sensory experience of hallucinations is an important one for our discussion, and leads us to the following question: what would happen if the dance rhythms were dropped, and the representation of hallucination was taken as the main priority of the music? In the next chapter we shall explore this question as we consider another form of sound system: the electroacoustic diffusion rig.

CHAPTER 5
Shamanic Diffusions

High tech shamanism, why not?

—Gary Kendall

On the evening 18 September 2014 an audience eagerly awaits the performance of Jean-Claude Risset's *Elementa* (1998) at a special outdoor concert held at the National Observatory on top of Nymphs' Hill in Athens. The performance is to be of a twenty-two minute, four second piece of sonic art that will mark the climax of the annual International Computer Music Conference (ICMC). In four movements Risset conjures the elements of water, fire, air, and earth through the means of fixed-media[1] electroacoustic sound, incorporating various sonic and instrumental manipulations, diffused through a circular array of high-quality loudspeakers. 'Aqua' drips with otherworldly liquidity; 'Focus' ignites a crackle of flames that dance around the audience; 'Aer' disarmingly stirs the trees and insects with a mystical breeze that builds into engulfing wind; and 'Terra' buries the listener in unsettled grounds that heave and groan, as if communicating through the ancient language of the earth itself. The experience is almost hallucinatory; the synthetic sounds of the composition blending seamlessly with the cicadas and rustling leaves of the actual environmental setting of the concert, causing the boundaries between fantasy and reality to dissolve. Amidst the warm night breeze of this historic Athenian setting, the conjured aural circles of fire and elemental noises recall the rites of the Eleusinian Mysteries, at the climax of which it is said that Persephone revealed herself to the *mystai* (initiates) amidst a great fire (Eliade, 1978).

Describing his intentions with *Elementa* (1998), Risset remarked, 'I invite the listener to [take] a journey for the ear which, I hope, could be captivating'. This is a modest aim in which the piece admirably succeeds, providing the listener with an experience that one reviewer described as having 'an almost pagan sensuality encompassing the infinite and the mundane simultaneously' (Schedel, 2007).

Through its narrative qualities, *Elementa* can be seen as an example of a broader tradition of electroacoustic works that evoke spatial sonic environments that change in time, taking the listener on fantastical aural voyages. In order to consider the relationship of such works with altered states of consciousness (ASCs), this chapter will begin with an introduction to electroacoustic music, which establishes the 'language' communicated by various types of sonic material, and how this may be used to construct unreal journeys. Following this, we will explore a selection of compositions that provide such journeys, which are explicitly related to ASCs such as dreams, shamanic visions, and hallucinations. Some consideration will also be given to the type of affective response that electroacoustic music may provide, and I argue that the listener experience in concerts can be characterized as introspective and meditative, in contrast with the trance-like states afforded by electronic dance music. This exploration will then inform a conceptual model that describes how sonic materials may include properties that give rise to representational and affective responses. The 'representational component' of this model will allow us to consider how these sonic materials may correspond with internal or external sensory experiences; utilize various stylistic approaches; and be defined in different ways within the performance space. Meanwhile, the 'affective component' will describe how sounds may afford different responses with regards to emotional valence and the energetic qualities they communicate. The conceptual model as a whole will point towards the possibility of using sound to 'simulate' the subjective experience of ASCs, and will be expanded upon over the next two chapters as our discussion progresses into the realms of audio-visual and interactive media.

ELECTROACOUSTIC MUSIC

We must break at all cost from this restrictive circle of pure sounds and conquer the infinite variety of noise-sounds.

—Luigi Russolo, *The Art of Noises*, 1913

Elementa (1998) was commissioned to celebrate the fiftieth anniversary of musique concrète by the Groupe de Recherches Musicales (GRM), one of the collectives responsible for pioneering electroacoustic music during the 1950s. In the early twentieth century the Futurists are often credited as being among the first to call for an expanded musical language that went beyond the traditional timbres of orchestral instruments, to encompass a galaxy of noise-based sounds (Manning, 2004). The Futurists' early attempts at a noise-based music were famously facilitated with the 'Intonarumori', a collection of mechanical acoustic devices for creating noise-sounds through various configurations of strings, wheels, and drums. While these early noise-instruments were somewhat primitive, the 1920s would see a variety of new electronic instruments such as the Theremin (1922), Sphärophon (1926), Dynaphone (1927), Ondes Martenot (1928), and Trautonium (1930).[2] These instruments, together with new developments in optical sound,[3] and John Cage's use of oscillator test tones and amplified coils of wire on his *Imaginary Landscape* compositions (1939–1952), would broaden the horizons of musical possibility through electronic sound. However, it was not until the post–World War II period that the necessary conditions of economic prosperity, technological advancement, and a desire to initiate a radical break from existing artistic traditions would allow the proper realization of a new electronic music.

With the availability of magnetic tape technology, electronic music studios were established at Radiodiffusion-Télévision Française (RTF) in Paris and Westdeutscher Rundfunk (WDR) in Cologne. At the Paris studio Pierre Schaeffer pioneered musique concrète, while at the Cologne studio Karlheinz Stockhausen and colleagues created elektronische musik. Each studio explored different philosophical agendas: musique concrète relied on manipulation of material recorded to tape, while elektronische musik sought to create new sounds using electronic tones. Through the 1950s and 1960s these studios, along with those in Milan, America, and the BBC's Radiophonic Workshop in the United Kingdom, were instrumental in pioneering exciting new forms of electronic music composition. At these studios, philosophical compositional strategies were able to flourish in tandem with the newly available technologies for electronic sound synthesis and manipulation, such as voltage-controlled synthesizers and analogue effects. By the 1980s, the digital computer was widely available and would become one of the principal tools for creating 'electroacoustic music'. Today, in modern concerts of electroacoustic music, composers present works that use sophisticated computational processes that allow spectral (frequency) and spatial properties of digital audio to be manipulated with high levels of detail and accuracy. Works may be designed for performance ('diffusion') across multiple loudspeakers, using 8, 16, 24, or even 48 channels of sound. The contemporary repertoire includes pieces for live acoustic instrumentation and electronics, interactive 'real-time' digital performances, audio-visual pieces, and fixed-media 'acousmatic' works, the latter of which consist purely of electroacoustic sound, and will be our main focus here.

The Language of Sounds

Among those principles that underpin electroacoustic music, the premise that electronic methods afford a wider range of sonic possibilities for composers and audiences to explore is especially significant. Electronic techniques meant that composers of Western art music need no longer be constrained by the traditional sound pallet of the orchestra, and were able to directly manipulate the precise form of their musical compositions. The theoretical discourses that have developed in parallel with electroacoustic music have sought to unpack and classify the many sonic possibilities afforded by such approaches. For instance, Denis Smalley's (1986) concept of 'spectromorphology' allows us to consider how the spectrum of frequencies used in sounds changes over time. Meanwhile, Simon Emmerson's (1986) 'language grid' describes the communicative properties of electroacoustic music, and allows us to consider the type of 'discourse' and 'syntax' of sounds. Of particular relevance for our discussion in this chapter is Emmerson's continuum that ranges from 'aural' to 'mimetic' discourse. 'Aural discourse' describes sonic materials that communicate through conventional musical approaches, such as arrangements of pitched notes and rhythms. Emmerson refers to Karlheinz Stockhausen's *Studie 1* (1953) and *Studie 2* (1954) as examples of works that are 'aural discourse dominant', since they consist of abstract (non-referential) sounds such as sine waves. Works featuring 'mimetic discourse', in contrast, utilize sonic materials that reference nature or aspects of human culture. Trevor Wishart's *Red Bird: A Political Prisoner's Dream* (1978) is an example of such a 'mimetic discourse dominant' piece, since it forms a narrative through montaging of vocal and environmental sounds.

From Reality to Unreality

Emmerson's (1986) discussion of mimetic discourse is revealing, as it describes a class of sonic materials that can be used to represent the subjective aural experience of spaces and places. Such an approach is notably used in soundscape compositions and phonographies, which use sonic materials to construct aural impressions of environmental locations.[4] The sounds of an environment can be captured with a microphone, then manipulated and arranged using electronic techniques. When these are presented using multi-channel arrays of loudspeakers, the 'virtual acousmatic space'—the imaginary space created through the use of acousmatic sound (Wishart, 1985, pp.79–80)—provides an illusory impression that conjures a sense of spatial location. Journeys through these synthetic aural environments can be constructed, and high-quality loudspeakers allow them to be rendered with realistic levels of detail and accuracy. Yet as Kendall (2007; 2010) discusses, these journeys need not seek to replicate aural experiences of the everyday, since they can also be used to take the listener to places he or she 'should not be'. For example, Kendall refers to the use of spatial paths in Denis Smalley's *Empty Vessels* (1997), which take the listener through virtual acousmatic spaces that represent the aural experience of being inside garden pots—somewhere they could not physically be under normal circumstances. *Empty Vessels* therefore provides the listener with the type of aural experience they might have if they were shrunk, as if imitating the physical and perceptual changes that occur to Alice after she consumes the 'drink me' potion in Wonderland (Carroll, 1865–1871). Furthermore, compositions need not be limited to the use of sounds that imitate real acoustic activity, since as R. Murray Schafer (1994, p.144) comments in his classification of sounds, soundscapes may also consist of 'Mythological Sounds, the Sounds of Utopias, and the Psychogenic Sounds of Dreams and Hallucinations'. Though Schafer does not explore this category in further detail, his comment points towards the use of sonic materials that imitate the internal sounds of the psyche, such as those heard in dreams and hallucinations. Electroacoustic sound may enable not only realistic journeys, then, but also *unrealistic*[5] ones, and it is through this capability that the possibility to represent ASCs emerges.

This section has introduced the concept of electroacoustic music, and explored how works may use a range of sonic materials, including mimetic sounds that relate to aspects of nature or human culture. These mimetic sounds can be used to create compositions that provide synthetic journeys through virtual acousmatic space. While often these journeys resemble the acoustic environments of the real world, they are not limited to this, and may also construct aural journeys that imitate the unreal spaces of dreams or hallucinations. In the next section this capability will be further explored by considering a selection of electroacoustic compositions specifically related to ASCs.

UNREAL JOURNEYS

Journeys through abstract worlds and strange sonic landscapes of the unreal are pervasive in electroacoustic music, and were explored through the BEAST FEaST: Real/Unreal festival (University of Birmingham, 28–30 April 2016). This festival encompassed a wide range of performances and talks investigating the way in which electroacoustic music may engage with notions of reality and unreality. When 'unreal' is taken in fairly broad terms as it was here, it comes close to being a catch-all theme for much of the contemporary electroacoustic repertoire, since many compositions incorporate synthetic or heavily processed materials that lend their performances a sense of abstraction and dissociation from sounds we might usually hear in everyday acoustic environments. In these terms, the strange and illusory aspects of these electroacoustic compositions could be considered as inherently 'hallucinatory' in some respects (Weinel, 2014). However, there are also works that composers have specifically identified as being related to ASCs such as dreams, hallucinations, or shamanic visions, and it is these that shall be the main focus of our discussion in this section.

Synthetic Dreams

Dreamsong is a careful blend of synthesized sounds and recorded natural sounds that have been digitally processed or resynthesized. The result . . . is an expressive sonic continuum ranging from unaltered natural sounds to entirely new sounds—or, more poetically, from the real world to the realm of the imagination.

—Michael McNabb

The sounds of a crowd of people talking dissipates with a flanging effect and transforms into a vocal-sounding note, before this too morphs into synthetic tones as spatialized sounds rush past with a Doppler effect. Momentarily we are flung again into the sounds of ambiguous dialogue, before launching back into a dream-like sensorium that blurs the boundaries between recognizable acoustic voices and synthesized tones. These tensions between the recognizable and the strange—the real and the synthetic—are constantly at play throughout Michael McNabb's *Dreamsong* (1978), as the composer skilfully transports the listener in and out of a sonic dream-world, walking the razor's-edge at the borders of unreality.

Throughout *Dreamsong* (1978), McNabb uses two main categories of material, which can be considered in terms of the 'external' and 'internal' sensory inputs discussed by Hobson (2003) in his 'state-space' concept of consciousness. The sounds of people and crowds suggest a real-world 'external' environment, while the strange synthesizer tones depict the 'internal' world of dreams. By modulating between these sonic materials, McNabb moves the listener between representations of normal waking consciousness and dreams. Here the external sounds provide a fairly accurate or realistic impression of a real-world location, while the synthesized materials use a more metaphorical approach. This is achieved through the use of synthesizer tones in unusual modes such as myxolidian, which are arranged using Fibonacci sequences, creating an exotic impression for the listener that suggests the otherness of dreams.[6]

The concept of using electroacoustic sound to evoke a dream is not unique to *Dreamsong* (1978), and has also been used in the aforementioned Trevor Wishart composition *Red Bird: A Political Prisoner's Dream* (1978), where vocal and environmental sounds form a symbolic, surrealistic narrative. Elsewhere, a similar approach is also used on Adrian Moore's *Dreamarena* (1996), in which sonic materials provide 'fleeting images' that are suggestive of dreams; and on Åke Parmerud's *Dreaming in Darkness* (2005), which seeks to provide sounds on the boundaries of unreality, in order to 'create surrealistic fragments of a blind person's dreams'.

Mystical Soundscapes

> *The Shaman Ascending* evokes the imagery of a traditional shaman figure chanting in the quest for spiritual ecstasy . . . the listener is placed inside of a circle of loudspeakers with the vocal utterances swirling around at high rates of speed and timbral development. The work proceeds in increasing stages of complexity as the shaman ascends towards a higher spiritual state.
>
> —Barry Truax

Inspired by John Terriak's sculptures of Inuit shamanism, Barry Truax's *The Shaman Ascending* (2004–2005) utilizes electroacoustic sound to represent a ritual of shamanic ecstasy. Truax introduces *The Shaman Ascending* through the recognizable sounds of Inuit chanting. As the piece progresses, various granular time-stretching[7]; convolution processes[8]; and spatial rotations are applied to the sonic materials. These progressively transform the chanting into a rotating vortex of sound, which increases in speed and ascending pitch as the composition progresses towards a 'vibrating, dynamic layer of harmonics, [that symbolizes] the "ascent" of the shaman' (Truax, 2008). When performed on a 16-channel electroacoustic diffusion system, the spatial rotations of the composition are particularly effective, circling around the listener in a disorientating manner.

As with *Dreamsong* (1978), *The Shaman Ascending* (2004–2005) can be considered in terms of materials that correspond with external and internal sensory inputs. Due to their basis in the sounds of Inuit throat singing, the sonic materials retain some recognizable real-world characteristics that can be related to 'external' inputs. However, as the piece progresses these materials undergo various sonic adaptations to reflect the 'internal' experiences of a shaman's ecstasy and spirit flight. The digitally transformed sounds symbolize the shaman's ecstatic 'ascension' towards the spirit world above, through the use of rising pitch and accelerating spatial rotations. These materials may be understood as metaphorical since they do not reflect the type of sound one would actually expect to hear during a shamanic ritual (i.e. due to auditory hallucination), but rather they suggest the shaman's spirit flight symbolically through sound.

Shamanic themes have also been explored in the work of Gary Kendall, whose electroacoustic pieces *Wayda* (2002), *Unu* (2002), *Qosqo* (2006), and *Ikaro* (2009–2010) are based on the composer's spiritual practices and experiences studying with a Peruvian shaman (Kendall 2011a; 2011b). Recalling the aleatoric (chance-based) approaches of John Cage's *Music of Changes* (1951), for *Ikaro* Kendall used a crystal pendulum to divine 'answers' to certain compositional 'questions', such as the selection and duration of sounds, and synthesis parameters. Kendall also associates the overall structure of the composition with the three stages of an ayahuasca ceremony, and incorporates soundscape materials, giving an aural impression of a shamanic journey in the Peruvian Amazon.[9]

Journeys through such mystical or 'imaginary soundscapes' are also explored in several other more recent works by Barry Truax. For example, *Chalice Well* (2009) is based upon a myth regarding a water well situated at the foot of Glastonbury Tor, which according to Arthurian legend conceals a gate to the underworld (Truax, 2007). The composition begins with 'external' source materials that suggest the real location of the well, through environmental sounds such as running water. As the piece develops, the listener is then transported into the 'internal' mythological spaces of the underworld, which are depicted using demonic sounds and ethereal tones. More recently Truax's 48-channel piece *The Garden of Sonic Delights* (2016), showers the audience in synthetic droplet sounds, before revealing a rich imaginary soundscape of alien insects and wildlife.

In several of my own electroacoustic compositions, such as *Entoptic Phenomena* (Weinel, 2009) and *Nausea* (Weinel, 2011), I have used psychedelic hallucinations as a basis for composition. For example, drawing upon the movie *Altered States* (Russell, 1980), and Strassman's (2001) accounts of DMT (*N,N*-dimethyltryptamine) hallucinations, *Entoptic Phenomena* is based on an imagined hallucinatory experience that occurs in an isolation tank. In order to represent a hallucinatory narrative, *Entoptic Phenomena* incorporates the use of sonic materials that represent specific features of hallucination. As indicated in Figure 5.1, these are then arranged into a structure that follows three main phases of *onset, plateau,* and *termination,* reflecting corresponding stages that may occur during a psychedelic experience.

During the opening of the composition, the 'external' sounds of a snorkel indicate the real-world setting of an isolation tank. At the *onset* of the hallucinatory effects, rhythmic streams of percussive sound that rotate within the spatial field are heard with increasing density, which reflect the 'internal' experience of funnel and spiral patterns of hallucination, or 'entopic phenomena'.[10] Following this, a whooshing crescendo culminating in a booming sound is heard, signifying the 'breakthrough' to the *plateau* phase. During this phase we hear 'strange voices' based on auditory hallucinations of the entities described in Strassman's (2001, p.214) study; and droning sounds that indicate the sense of 'timelessness' that may occur during such experiences. Following this, as the peak effects of the ASC begin to lessen, a transition occurs back to the 'entoptic phenomena' of before—once again represented through the use of rotating streams of percussive sounds that symbolically represent visual funnel patterns of dots. Finally during the *termination* phase, the hallucinations subside, and the listener is returned to the 'external' sounds of the isolation tank.

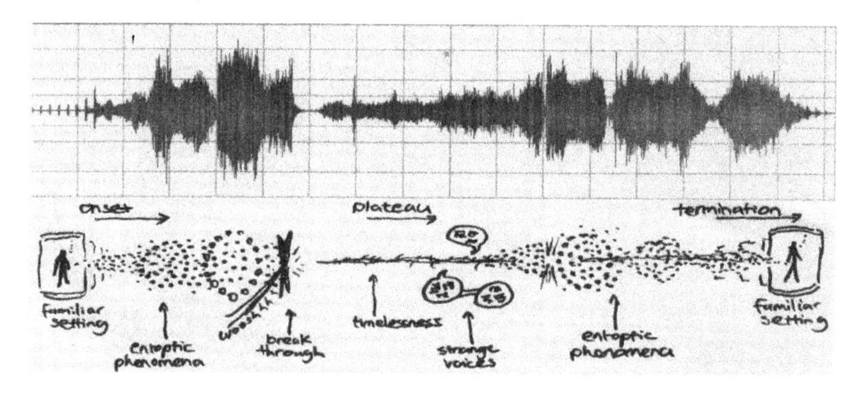

Figure 5.1. Graphic score illustrating the structure of Jon Weinel's *Entoptic Phenomena* (2009) composition.

Entoptic Phenomena (2009) exemplifies one of several possible compositional strategies, through its use of sound in relation to the 'arena space', the term used by Smalley (2007, p.55) to describe 'the whole public space inhabited by performers and listeners'.[11] In particular, *Entoptic Phenomena* transports the listener into a hallucinatory sonic narrative, by constructing a synthetic virtual acousmatic space through the use of electroacoustic sound, which is distinct from the one that occurs naturally within the arena space. In order to sustain this illusion, all other sounds from the arena space must be suppressed as far as possible when the piece is performed. However, for some electroacoustic compositions, sounds may be overlaid on to the arena space, so that they fortuitously blend with those of the virtual acousmatic space. For example, on Rajmil Fischman's composition *No Me Quedo* (2000), the composer explores the 'convergence'[12] of live percussion, with synthetic conga drums and abstract electroacoustic textures. This approach allows the boundaries between real acoustic sounds and synthetically produced electroacoustic material to dissolve, rendering performances with an almost hallucinatory quality. This effect can also be observed in live performances, such as the outdoor presentation of Risset's *Elementa* (1998) at the National Observatory in Athens that was described in the opening of this chapter. For this performance of *Elementa,* the naturalistic qualities of the composition blended with the sounds of real cicadas and leaves rustling in the wind, providing points of convergence. With the added benefit of a sensuous warm evening breeze, and the sense of history elicited through the architecture of such a historical site, this melting at the boundaries of the acousmatic illusion lent the performance an air of magic and mystery.

Through the electroacoustic compositions explored, we may observe the use of narrative journeys through sound to reflect various forms of ASC. Sonic materials allow the construction of unreal dreamlike or hallucinatory sonic environments, which the listener is aurally transported through. These aural voyages reflect an ethos of sonic exploration, directing the attention of the listener towards intricate and poetic tapestries in sound. These listening experiences may enrich our awareness of acoustic worlds, which occur not only outside of us, but also within the internal spaces of the psyche. Such works may be technically constructed by using sonic materials that correspond with both external and internal sensory inputs, and these may be rendered in ways that are more accurate and authentic; or they may be stylized, impressionistic, and metaphorical. In addition, as we have seen, the use of arena space in relation to virtual acousmatic space also provides various possible compositional strategies. These approaches will shortly be used to provide a conceptual model that describes how sounds may represent ASCs. First, however, we turn to consider the affective properties of electroacoustic music.

SONIC MEDITATIONS

How surprising . . . that when we come to the role of feeling and emotion in electroacoustic music, professional discourse has been so aloof. Its historic literature is dominated by technical discussions and inclined toward abstract theories of sound that preference a detached intellect over feeling and emotion.

—Gary Kendall

In previous chapters, the affective properties of music were considered as strongly related to the abstract musical properties of pitch, melody, harmony, and rhythm. This was justified, since the rhythm section of music plays an integral role in raising the pulse, while melodies and harmonies help to convey a sense of emotional valence. In a study by Robinson and Hirsch (1972) these features were distinguished as the 'beat' or 'sound', in contrast with the 'message' delivered by lyrical content. Electroacoustic music may not have a regular 'beat' in the way that rock music or electronic dance music does; yet tonal and rhythmic properties are present through the 'aural discourse' of noise-based sounds, and may also provide affective properties. Similarly, mimetic sounds may also provide representations that trigger emotional responses, albeit in ways that are perhaps more subtle. In what follows, I explore how these mechanisms may allow electroacoustic music to elicit affective responses that can be characterized as more meditative and introspective than those high-energy examples of sound system music discussed in the previous chapter.

Electroacoustic Affect

As Gabrielsson and Lindstrom (2012) reveal in their meta-study of music and emotion, pitch, melody, and harmony are among the musical features that contribute towards perceived emotional valence. For example, high pitches, consonant harmonies, and major modes may often be associated with emotions that have a positive valence such as happiness; low pitches, dissonance, and minor modes, on the other hand, are more commonly related to emotions with negative valence such as sadness.[13] In many of the pieces discussed, these features are used to communicate the emotional component of the ASC they describe. For example, McNabb's *Dreamsong* (1978) utilizes high-frequency harmonic choral sounds to lend a dream-like ethereal impression in some sections; elsewhere, dissonant tones elicit a sense of uneasiness. These materials provide positive and negative fluctuations in emotional valence, which reflect the turbulent emotions associated with dream states. Elsewhere in Truax's *The Shaman Ascending* (2004–2005), harmonic pitched materials are used to elicit positive emotional valence, in order to give an impression of light or spiritual feelings, reflecting the ecstatic state of the shaman.

Gabrielsson and Lindstrom's (2012) meta-study also highlights that tempo and rhythm are features strongly associated with the activation properties of music. Quick rhythms often suggest a sense of excitement, while slower rhythms provide more tranquil states of low energy. Electroacoustic compositions may also use these properties to suggest different energy levels within an ASC. For instance, McNabb's *Dreamsong* (1978) has few percussive elements, and consists mainly of gradually evolving tones with long attack and decay times. These provide a low level of kinetic energy that is suitable for articulating a dream-state. Meanwhile, in Truax's *The Shaman Ascending* (2004–2005), the rapid spatial movement of sounds creates accelerating circular rhythms, reflecting the increasing arousal levels of the shaman's ecstasy. Similarly, my own piece *Entoptic Phenomena* (2009) uses highly kinetic distorted pulsing sounds, which are similar to the bass drums of hardcore techno music.[14] Through these rhythms, the piece suggests a more energetic and visceral experience of hallucination.

Musical features of pitch, harmony, melody, and rhythm are particularly important in defining the affective properties of a composition. However, as discussed in Chapter 1, mimetic sounds may also elicit associations that give rise to affective responses. This is the case since representations may invoke semantic and episodic memories, and excite corresponding emotions. Indeed, R. Murray Schafer (1994, pp.148–150) unpacks some of these effects in his discussion of 'sound contexts', proposing that sounds such as alarm bells may trigger recollections, leading to frightened responses. Considering this function in Truax's *Chalice Well* (2009), the sounds of running water may evoke a pleasing sense of relaxation for some listeners, as the materials elicit the sights and smells of damp caves that one may have experienced in the past. Yet later in the piece this mood gives way to one that is claustrophobic and foreboding in character, as we hear demonic sounds that have animalistic associations. In this way the representational properties of sounds may afford affective responses, and as the narrative of a piece unfolds this may take the listener on an emotional journey.

Ecstatic Introspection

While electroacoustic music may afford a range of affective responses, in general the typical listening experience that electroacoustic concerts promote is one of low arousal compared to the high-energy raves of the previous chapter. When considering this distinction, we may find some interesting parallels with Rouget's (1985) definitions of 'ecstasy' and 'trance',[15] which we shall briefly recapitulate here. Rouget defines 'ecstasy' as an introspective condition that occurs in stillness, quiet, darkness, and solitude; 'trance', in contrast, is related to sensory overload, with bodily motion, loud noises, and social interaction in effect. His classification of these states was derived from Fischer's (1971) 'cartography of ecstatic and meditative states', and thus his definition of 'ecstasy' is a low-arousal state

Figure 5.2. An audience contemplates the virtual acousmatic space at an electroacoustic concert, Bangor University, Wales, 2009. Photo: Andrew Lewis.

similar to meditation, while 'trance' is a high-arousal state (see also Penman and Becker, 2009).

As illustrated in Figure 5.2, audiences at electroacoustic concerts typically experience the music in a congregation of stillness, with each individual remaining in a quiet and attentive seated position. The concert hall is dimmed in order to privilege the aural over the visual senses, increasing immersion into the virtual acousmatic space and the associative mental imagery that this may conjure for the listener. These images are acquired across the sensory modalities, as the listener pays attention to their internal experience of sound, and the recollections it evokes. Although the experience is communal, members of the audience do not interact with each other during performances, and the listener experience has a significantly solitary, introspective dimension, not unlike a group meditation session.

Now if we contrast this with a typical electronic dance music event, we find the latter more closely resembles Rouget's (1985) definition of trance. The experience at raves is one of communal dance; as Hutson (1999) has noted, ravers often describe peak experiences of collective unity at the height of events. These experiences occur in situations of sensory overload, with high volume levels (usually much higher than electroacoustic music), physical contact, and exchanges of sweat. Visual projections, lasers, fog machines, strobe lights, and unusual costumes further intensify the sensory experience, as do various drugs such as ecstasy and alcohol. The electronic dance music milieu therefore more closely resembles that of trance rituals, and it is quite likely that at least some individuals at these events may experience a secular equivalent of spirit possession. As the rhythm takes over their bodies and minds during peak moments, the effect is similar to Ghede entering the bodies of Vodou trancers, albeit with the distinction that ravers tend not to anthropomorphize the experience, and use words like 'vibe' to articulate the feeling instead.

The differences between the respective forms are related to the material properties of the music, as well as the cultural norms surrounding their presentation. Electroacoustic music often utilizes detailed spatial mimetic sounds that transport the listener into the virtual acousmatic space, through seated attentive listening. Conversely, electronic dance music prioritizes the beat, which allows audiences to engage through dance, forming part of the spectacle in the 'here and now' of the arena space. In this way, electroacoustic concerts promote introspective states of absorption that we might consider meditative, while electronic dance music provides high-energy corporeal states of trance. These distinctions are not arbitrary, and also reflect a difference in the underlying ethos, since electroacoustic music prioritizes awareness of detailed spatial listening experiences, which contrasts with the abandoned dance hedonism of rave culture.[16]

In the previous section we saw how electroacoustic compositions may represent aspects of ASCs using a variety of approaches. By additionally considering the affective properties of electroacoustic music here, we have seen how these may also provide a means through which to communicate the moods and emotions that accompany ASCs. While musical features may suggest these emotions, in general I have proposed that the typical mode of listening in electroacoustic concerts may provide a form of meditative introspection that might reasonably be considered as a form of ASC. This analysis will now be used to inform a conceptual model that describes the function of sound with regards to both the representational and affective properties of the medium.

A CONCEPTUAL MODEL

In this section I present a conceptual model, which will allow us to consider how the material properties of sound may represent or induce ASCs. First, I propose a 'general model' that describes how sound may elicit representational and affective properties. This model will describe how sound may afford corresponding cognitive, physiological, and behavioural responses. Following this, I provide individual components for this model, which expand upon the ways in which sonic materials may represent or induce ASCs using a variety of possible approaches, such as those demonstrated through the analyses of work so far.

General Model

The left-hand section of the general model illustrated in Figure 5.3 shows how the material properties of sound may include both representational and affective properties. 'Representational properties' encompasses features that represent spaces, places,

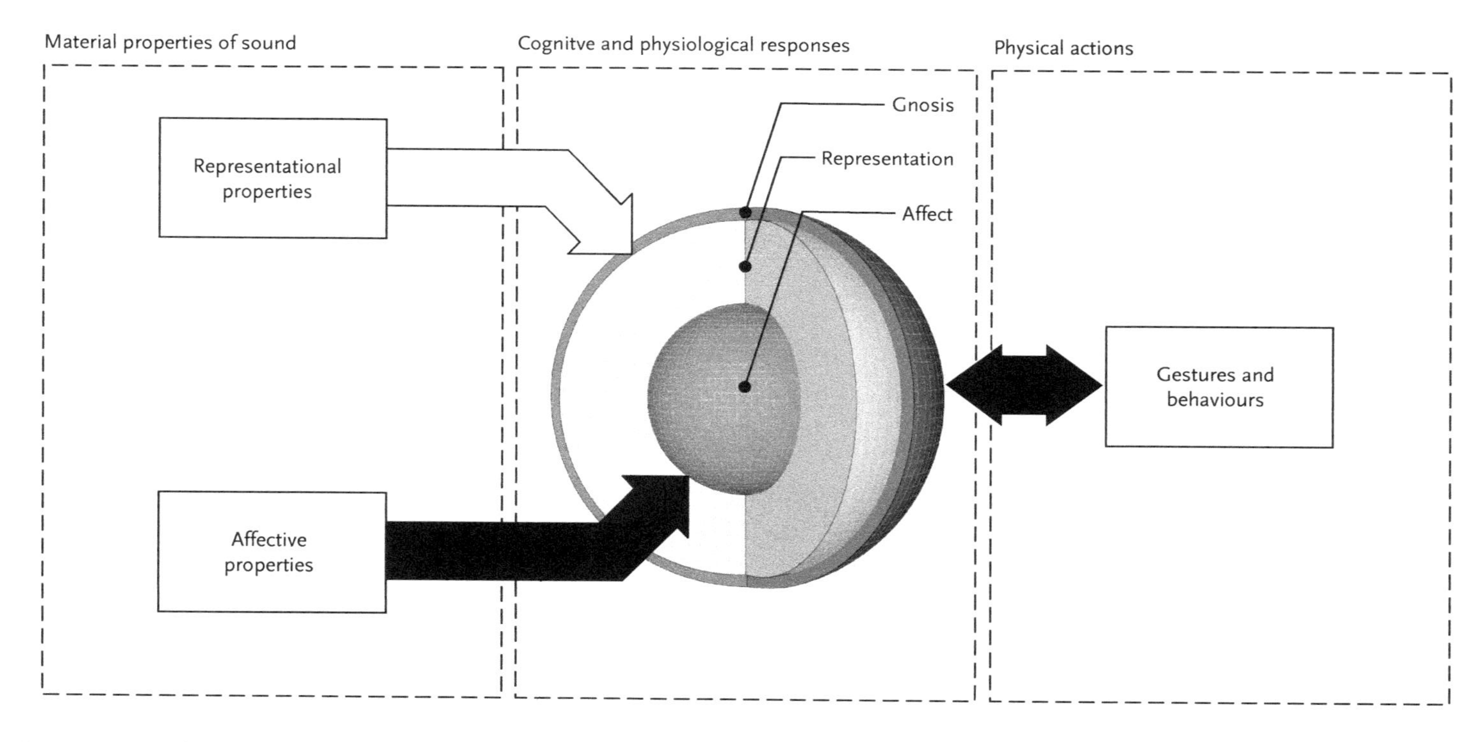

Figure 5.3. General model, showing how material properties of sound give rise to corresponding listener responses and behaviours.

events, or concepts. Meanwhile, 'affective properties' describes those features such as pitch, melody, harmony, and rhythm that are related to mood and emotion. As noted in Chapter 1 (pp.26–30), there is some overlap between these categories, since the latter may be considered as a 'deep layer of representation' (Kivy, 1990, p.58).

The central section of the general model indicates the response of the listener. For suitably attentive listeners, representational properties may afford a corresponding cognitive response, while affective properties may give rise to an emotional response that includes both cognitive and physiological dimensions. Although these responses are distinct, they may also be viewed as related, since representations may invoke memories, producing recollections that trigger emotions and vice versa. Representational responses allow the affective response to the music to be framed by conceptual meaning, leading to a form of experiential knowledge or *gnosis,* as indicated by the outer layer in Figure 5.3. Since *gnosis* encompasses both the meaning of music and the feelings that it stirs within the listener, it may relate to what authors such as St. John (2009) and Henriques (2011) and have referred to as 'the vibe', and is closely linked with the ethos of the music. This in turn is significant in defining the extent to which the listener finds the music appealing, and is therefore involved in the motivational processes that promote listener attention.

As the right-hand section of the general model indicates, listening may also lead to certain types of physical activity. For engaged, attentive listeners, affective properties may also suggest corresponding energetic behaviours such as dancing or relaxation. By engaging in these the listener affirms the affective response, since these behaviours have an effect on the arousal system, raising or lowering the heart-rate and precipitating the release of stress hormones. Although Figure 5.3 focuses on the processes involved for an individual listener, in social situations physical behaviours and gestures also provide additional nodes of communication that may transmit further representational and affective properties, and confer agreement between members of a group.[17]

Representational Component

The 'representational properties' of the general model can be expanded to provide the 'representational component' shown in Figure 5.4. Through the analysis of music discussed in previous chapters, we have seen a progression from works that use analogue instruments and effects, to those that utilize digital synthesis and sample manipulation, in order to represent ASCs. Within this progression, we find a range of possible approaches, and a general trend towards the construction of accurate depictions of hallucinations with the aid of technology. For example, psychedelic rock music uses analogue electronics to subtly warp or colour the sounds of an instrumental performance, so that it is heard as if under the influence of psychedelic drugs. Yet in psy-trance music, or the imaginary soundscapes of electroacoustic music, digital sounds are used to construct detailed spatial representations of

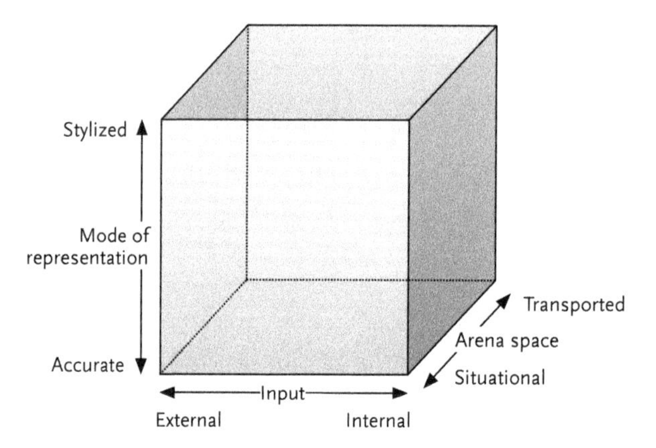

Figure 5.4. Representational component, showing possible approaches for representing ASCs through sound.

hallucinatory sound-worlds. The latter works suggest the use of sound to accurately represent, or even 'simulate' the subjective experience of ASCs such as dreams and hallucinations. However, there remains various dynamic possibilities for the design of sonic materials, and it is these that the representational component addresses. The section below considers the three axes of the component:

- Input
- Mode of Representation
- Arena Space

The 'input' (x) axis describes the use of sonic materials that relate to subjective experiences that arise either 'externally' or 'internally' (Hobson, 2003). 'External' materials correspond with sensory perception that is caused by external stimuli such as acoustic phenomena in a real physical environment. In contrast, 'internal' materials represent sensory perceptions that do not originate in the external environment, such as auditory hallucinations. The input axis therefore describes the range of possible internal and external materials, with the mid-point representing sounds that are partially distorted or altered by internal experience. These may occur during hallucinations where sounds with a real acoustic origin are experienced as perceptually altered, and may be designed through the use of various digital effects processes applied to external source materials.[18]

The 'mode of representation' (y) axis describes the use of approaches ranging from 'accurate' to 'stylized' representations of subjective experience. 'Accurate' representations provide sounds that correspond with the subjective aural experience as closely as possible. For example, the design of internal sounds such as auditory hallucinations in an accurate manner would require the use of sounds that recreate a similar aural experience as would be perceived subjectively during the hallucination. For instance, if a deep voice were heard during a hallucination, then a corresponding voice may be designed using vocal sounds in the low-frequency range. In contrast, 'stylized' sounds may present materials using a variety of artistic techniques that provide more impressionistic, symbolic, or metaphorical effects. Works may incorporate techniques that are partially realistic or stylized.

The 'arena space' (z) axis describes the conceptual approach used with regards to the environment in which the performance and audience are located, and its relationship with virtual acousmatic space. Various strategies may be used ranging from 'situational' to 'transported'. 'Situational' approaches utilize the natural sounds of the arena space and work cooperatively with them, overlaying the virtual acousmatic space on top of the sounds of the real, physical space. For such works, no attempt is made to suppress the natural sounds of the arena space, which may be desirable and form an important part of the composition when it is performed. In contrast, 'transported' approaches seek to dislocate the listener from the natural sounds of the arena space, by suppressing unwanted sound from the physical space, and replacing it with the synthetic sounds of the virtual acousmatic space. In some cases a composition may modulate between situational and transported approaches, providing points of convergence and divergence between layers.

Using the representational component, the axes of input, mode of representation, and arena space can be used to distinguish various possible approaches for representing ASCs through sound. In some instances, a composition may occupy a fairly small region on these axes, while in others dynamic transitions may occur between states. For example, a composition may traverse representations of external and internal sound; change between accurate and stylized representations; or move from situational to transported approaches during its course.

Affective Component

In order to discuss affective properties, it is not necessary to devise a new conceptual model since we may select one that already exists: Russell's (1980) 'circumplex model of affect'. Indeed, various studies have already sought to classify music according to this model.[19] As Figure 5.5 indicates, this model can be used to provide an 'affective component', which allows us to consider the dimensions of mood and emotion that are provided through the material properties of a piece. Here I shall recapitulate the axes of this model:

- Valence
- Arousal

The (x) axis plots emotional valence, which ranges from negative or unpleasant emotions, to positive or pleasant emotions. Sonic materials may relate to emotional valence through the use of features such as pitch, melody, and harmony. For example, high pitches, consonant harmonies, and major modes may often

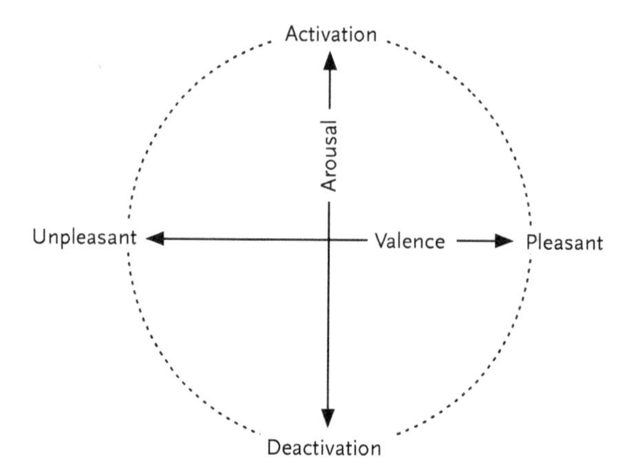

Figure 5.5. Affective component, showing affective properties of sound according to the dimensions of valence and arousal.

be associated with emotions that have a positive valence such as happiness; low pitches, dissonance, and minor modes, in contrast, are more commonly related to emotions with negative valence such as sadness.

The (y) axis plots energy states from low arousal to high arousal. For example, rhythmic, percussive, or highly kinetic sonic materials may provide highly energetic properties. Conversely, compositions with few percussive elements or gradually evolving sonic materials with long attack and decay times may provide relatively lower levels of energy activation.

Using the affective component allows us to define the properties of mood and emotion within a work, which may change dynamically during its course. Although listener responses to these may vary, and may also be effected by other factors such as behaviours, these features can be instructive in defining the type of affective response and corresponding behaviours that a piece of music may afford for the listener.

The conceptual model presented allows us to consider the material properties of sound, and the corresponding representational and affective responses that these may give rise to. Through the individual components for each of these functions, we can consider the range of possibilities that may be used by a given work, and how these fluctuate and undergo transitions between various states over time. These components can be used either as tools for analysing existing work, or as a means through which to conceptualize sonic materials when creating new works. Although the conceptual model here has characterized representational and affective properties as distinct features, an overlap between the two has been noted, and the combined response leads to an integrated form of experiential knowledge or *gnosis*.

* * *

In this chapter we have seen how electroacoustic music provides specific capabilities for representing or inducing ASCs. Acousmatic works such as those discussed use high-quality loudspeakers and spatialization tools to provide the audience with journeys through narrative representations of unreality in virtual acousmatic space. By exploiting the illusory capabilities of these technologies, these works are able to represent external and internal inputs. This can be achieved using accurate or stylized modes of representation, and situational or transported approaches in the arena space. I have also argued that the affective response that accompanies these representations may vary in valence and arousal, but in the seated concert situation it is usually more introspective and meditative in character than the high-energy trances of electronic dance music. When both representational and affective responses are considered together, electroacoustic music may afford experiential forms of knowledge or *gnosis*, which are related to the ethos of the music.

The conceptual model presented in this chapter, and its respective components, provide a means through which to consider possible variations in the design of sonic materials, which may fluctuate during the course of a composition. Besides being a useful tool through which to consider electroacoustic sound, the conceptual model has also been presented in some detail, since it will be of use in the next two chapters when considering time-based audio-visual and interactive media. While allowing us to consider the use of sound in these media, the model also has some relevance for visual elements, since these may be considered according to the dimensions discussed. Just as electroacoustic music may elicit meditative experiences through sound, then, in the next chapter we shall begin to explore how the design of audio-visual media may also provide such technoshamanic capabilities.

CHAPTER 6
Synaesthetic Overdrive

Your body lies in the darkness, heavy as lead, but your spirit seems to soar and leave the hut, and with the speed of thought to travel where it listeth, in time and space, accompanied by the shaman's singing and by the ejaculations of her percussive chant. What you are seeing and what you are hearing appear as one: the music assumes harmonious shapes, giving visual form to its harmonies, and what you are seeing takes on the modalities of music—the music of the spheres.

—R. Gordon Wasson

The pulse quickens with the onset of racing high-hats, synthesizer arpeggios, and echoing sound effects of Pink Floyd's 'On the Run' (on *Dark Side of the Moon*, 1973). A pitch-black void is punctuated by strobe lights that are emitted through a matrix of spinning windows, casting rays of light through a haze of smoke. The vortex of spinning geometry, fractals, and 3D imagery pulls the audience into its illusory perspective, causing disorientation of the senses. As 'On the Run' gives way to the searing guitar solos of 'Time', this panic-inducing high-speed rush through mazes of tunnels gives way, as the visual field opens out to reveal a fully formed 3D scene of a room filled with clocks, which engulfs the field of vision.

This is not a synaesthetic experience of closed-eye visual hallucinations brought on by an acid-trip at a Pink Floyd concert—though the description might be equally suggestive of this—but rather a psychedelic audio-visual experience created using immersive projections. In the hallway of the Old Library at the Custard Factory in Birmingham, *Pink Floyd 360: Dark Side of the Moon* (McEuen, 2013) event curator Mario DiMaggio can barely contain his excitement as he prepares his next audience for what they are about to experience in a black igloo-shaped inflatable dome. The low-key setting of the hall with its creaky floorboards and folding metal chairs recalls the scene from David Cronenberg's movie *eXistenZ* (1999), in which Allegra Geller is about to demonstrate a new virtual reality game for a group of unwitting participants. Indeed, as DiMaggio's audience enters the womb-like dome structure, their prone bodies lie awaiting technological stimulation upon the cushioned floor, forming an orgiastic scene that is not far from the clandestine virtual reality *eXistenZ* describes. Inside the dome a high-resolution digital projector focuses light on a parabolic mirror that reflects animated images across the ceiling of the dome, opening up an illusory visual field above the audience. While the technology was originally designed for planetarium shows, here the audience are taken on an after-hours voyage of computer-graphics, surrealistic 3D impressions, and Pink Floyd-driven psychedelia designed by Aaron McEuen, which shows what the tech is *really* capable of.

Pink Floyd 360: Dark Side of the Moon (McEuen, 2013) is just one example from a much larger constellation of work that shows immersive audio-visual technology being used to create synthetic dreamlike or hallucinatory experiences. In order to consider the design of these works, this chapter begins with an overview of film sound, and the effects of combining sound and image. Following this, we begin to explore early examples of audio-visual media that take dreams or hallucinations as their subject matter, including avant-garde films from the surrealist movement and the 'trance film' genre. While such films typically prioritize visual techniques over sound as a means to communicate altered state of consciousness (ASC) experiences, a number of Hollywood feature films would later develop these approaches with the aid of digital audio and computer graphics; here we will analyse several key examples. Meanwhile, an alternative strand of 'expanded cinema' sought to actively engage and transform the consciousness of its audiences through synaesthetic audio-visual forms. Exploring work in this area, we shall consider examples of 'visual music' films, psychedelic lightshows of the 1960s, and VJ (video-jockey) culture of the 1990s and beyond. Through these examples, in this chapter we shall see how the conceptual model of the previous chapter can also be used to analyse audio-visual media. In doing so, we find the model allows us to identify a number of distinct approaches, while technology also allows artists to push ever-closer towards 'accurate' simulations of ASCs.

SOUND AND MOVING IMAGES

Today the combination of sound and moving image is pervasive in film, television, and online videos; yet prior to the 1920s, films did not have an audio-track, and music had to be provided by live performers. With the advent of the sound film, the ability to combine audio and moving images synchronously had a transformative effect on filmmaking practices, as works began to incorporate longer shots to accommodate dialogue, and background music to support theatrical mood (Buhler and Neumeyer, 2013). This led to the development of several distinct types of audio that are used in films, including sound effects, dialogue, environmental ambiences, and background music. Here we begin by considering these typical classifications of sound, before examining in further detail how they may combine with images to provide affective or representational properties.

Categories of Film Sound

Film sound can be classified using the terms diegetic and non-diegetic (Sonnenschein, 2001, pp.152–153). Diegetic sounds consist of those that occur in relation to the narrative world of the production. For example, dialogue may be presented to accompany characters speaking, while sound effects may be heard in relation to the interactions of physical objects. In contrast, non-diegetic sounds consist of those that do not exist within the narrative world that is presented on screen. For instance, Hollywood films often use orchestral music to provide a soundtrack; unless an orchestra is actually depicted in the story, this accompaniment exists outside the narrative world and is therefore non-diegetic.

Although musical soundtracks are typically non-diegetic, diegetic music can also occur in some situations where these sounds are emitted from within the narrative world. This may occur in any scene where music has a source within the story: a character switching on a car radio, or going to a bar where a live band is performing are just two possibilities. In such cases, where music can be directly attributed to the acoustic environment within the scene, it is diegetic. However, the boundaries between diegetic sound effects and non-diegetic music are not always clearly defined, and sound designers may even seek such ambiguity. For instance, for the movie *THX 1138* (Lucas, 1971), George Lucas stated that the explicit intention was to create 'music [that] would operate like sound effects and ... sound effects [that] would operate like music' (Ondaatje, 2002, p.19). In such cases it is not always possible to categorize sound as diegetic or non-diegetic; however, these terms nonetheless provide an essential starting point when considering sound within audio-visual media.

Functions of Film Sound

Utilizing the terms used throughout this book, diegetic sounds in films provide 'representational properties', since they enable the construction of spatial environments, events, and narratives. Yet for audio-visual media, these representations are also guided by the visual images on screen, and vice versa. In psychology the associations that occur between sound and image were demonstrated by the 'McGurk effect' (McGurk and Macdonald, 1976). The 'McGurk effect' showed that changing the movement of a person's mouth alters the vowel sounds that are perceived by an observer, and thus showed that visual perception influences auditory perception.

More recently, neuroimaging studies such as those by Calvert et al. (1997) and Callan et al. (2003) have also shown that visual stimuli can increase activity in the auditory cortex.[1] This natural tendency to integrate sounds and images has also been described by Michel Chion (1994), who uses the term 'synchresis'. Synchresis allows audio designers to make use of techniques such as 'automated dialogue replacement' (ADR) and foley to construct parts of the soundtrack retrospectively. New sound materials can be placed in synchronization with visual footage, and the two will form an illusory impression of cohesion. This can be effective even when sound effects have no obvious relationship with what is actually seen on screen. For example, it is well known that foley artists may smash watermelons or chop fruit and vegetables as a means to create the sound effects that accompany scenes of violence in horror films. Despite the seemingly tenuous relationship of these sources with the events they depict, when we see the heads of zombies being crushed and hear these sounds, we perceive a single, cohesive entity. More generally, then, when diegetic sounds and moving images are placed together, they work in combination to provide representational properties, forging a sense of spatial location, physical interactions, and events.

'Affective properties' may arise from these representational properties, since they allow us to perceive characters within environments, and these in turn allow the development of narratives that may have an emotional impact. However, music can also play a pivotal role in defining the emotions of a film sequence. For example, using up-tempo breakbeats in an action film may afford an aroused or exited audience response, while the same scene with melancholic strings may yield a response with lower arousal and negative valence. The powerful emotionality of music allows directors to promote certain affective responses, then, and these can also provide a means through which to communicate the emotions of characters, or other 'unseen' qualities.

This section has provided a brief introduction to the concepts of diegetic and non-diegetic sound, and how they may be used in films. Our discussion has highlighted the multi-modal effects that arise when sounds and images are used together in audio-visual media. Sound guides the interpretation of moving images and vice versa, allowing cohesive spatial representations of diegetic environments, characters, and events to be formed. These representations are often supported through the use of non-diegetic music as a means to enhance the affective response of a sequence. Building upon our discussion of the conceptual model presented in the previous chapter, then, we may consider that audio-visual media provides both representational and affective properties, which lead to representational and affective responses for the audience. Since these essential properties remain present, in the analyses that follow we may continue to use the conceptual model and its components, in order to consider how audio-visual media may represent or induce ASCs in a variety of ways.

AVANT-GARDE VISIONS

The cinema, then, constitutes a conscious hallucination ...

—Jean Goudal, 'Surrealism and Cinema', 1925

Narrative cinema exploits the illusory capability of the medium to transport the audience into another time and place. Within these places, films may describe situations in which fictional characters become intoxicated, enter into trance states, or otherwise enact scenarios related to ASCs. Significant early examples of this can be seen in avant-garde films. For instance, films of the surrealist movement used the medium to invoke the irrationality of dreams or the unconscious according to the Freudian view. These films influenced the development of what Sitney (1979, p.21) referred to as the 'trance film', a genre that explores the lives of somnambulists, ritual initiates, or the possessed.[2] Indeed, according to his view, the representation of internal experience through film would become a major preoccupation of American avant-garde cinema throughout the mid-twentieth century. In what follows we shall consider several key examples from this area, which demonstrate the use of innovative techniques to represent ASCs in the visual domain, with the support of a musical soundtrack.

Surrealist Cinema

A man sharpens a razor blade and raises it to the face of a woman who is poised as if to receive a haircut. The shot cuts to the moon as a thin cloud slices across it, and then returns to show the slicing of an eyeball. If not one of the most visceral scenes in cinema, this opening sequence from Luis Buñuel and Salvador Dali's *Un Chien Andalou* (1929) is certainly one of the most notorious. As the film continues, the viewer is presented with various irrational juxtapositions: the film cuts from a handful of ants to the hair of an armpit; a man dispassionately pokes a severed hand on the street, while a couple gaze sedately onwards from their apartment window; and hands fondle a woman's breasts, which fade into a pair of buttocks. We witness heightened emotional states of anger and lust; a man hauls a bizarre wreckage of junk and people; another is shot with a gun; and a woman fixes her anxious gaze over a death's-head hawk-moth. These scenes are connected by a skilful editing process that plays upon the viewer's expectation of visual continuity, while denying any logical narrative: as the razor slices the eye, it is the moon that we see sliced; where we expect to see one individual, another is often substituted in the next shot; and in the closing sequence a woman exits a room, only to immediately step out onto a beach.

It was not the explicit intention of the filmmakers to represent a specific dream in *Un Chien Andalou* (Buñuel, 1929), but rather to induce an experience of heightened emotion and irrationality that mirrors that of the unconscious. Buñuel (1947, p.101) qualifies this, stating: '[*Un Chien Andalou*] does not attempt to recount a dream, although it profits by a mechanism analogous to that of dreams'. This 'mechanism' involved the use of an automatic process to generate ideas, and the rejection of any ideas that the filmmakers considered were rational. Those that remained were used to design the irrational montage of juxtapositions, which reflect the fantasies of wish fulfilment, unrestrained passion, and sexual desire described by Freud (1899) in his theories of dreams and the unconscious. Although some theorists have attempted to draw out specific meanings from these scenes,[3] for the purposes of our discussion these are less important than the essential mechanism, whereby the montaging of non-sequitur images, sometimes with the aid of unusual props and costumes, induces a visceral experience of irrationality that is analogous to that of dreams and the unconscious.

Un Chien Andalou (Buñuel, 1929) did not have a soundtrack in its original form, but was performed with excerpts from Wagner's *Liebestod* (1859) and two Argentinian tangos on a gramophone, which have since been restored for modern prints of the film. Although the juxtapositions these create may be suggestive of the irrational, the visual montaging of *Un Chien Andalou* is relatively more powerful and innovative. These surreal techniques can also be observed in Buñuel and Dali's *L'Age d'Or* (Buñuel, 1930), and were highly influential on a great many subsequent films that drew inspiration from the surrealist movement. For instance, while Richardson (2006, p.73) has remarked that Hollywood directors such as David Lynch (e.g. *Blue Velvet,* 1986) often draw superficially from the 'visual style' of surrealism, he finds meaningful extensions of the movement in the anthropomorphic objects of Jan Švankmajer's animations (e.g. *Alice,* 1987, based on Carroll, 1865–1871; *Faust,* 1994), or the complete dissolution of boundaries between the real and the unreal in Alejandro Jodorowsky's films (e.g. *El Topo,* 1970; *Holy Mountain,* 1973).

The Trance Film

For a time the dream generated a form of its own, occurring simultaneously in the films of several independent artists. I have called this the trance film.

—P. Adams Sitney, *Visionary Film*

A hand lowers a flower onto the road. Moments later we see the shadow of a woman who picks it up as the darkly cloaked figure who left it disappears out of sight. As the woman returns home, her key slips from her hand and bounces down the steps. Entering the house she surveys various configurations of objects throughout the rooms before falling asleep in a chair. As she drifts into slumber we observe her dreams, which involve multiple reiterations of earlier events and confrontations with malevolent reflections of herself. In the climax of the film the woman seems poised to cut the throat of her sleeping self, but in the next moment she awakens from the dream to see the face of her partner as he returns home. All seems well, yet in the final scene we see her throat cut, implicating her suicide.

According to Deren's (1965, p.1) explanation of the film: '[*Meshes of the Afternoon*] reproduces the way in which the sub-conscious of an individual will develop, interpret and elaborate an apparently simple and casual incident into a critical emotional experience', while also drawing out the 'malevolent vitality [of] inanimate objects'. Of particular interest for our discussion, these themes are explored through the form of a dream-narrative. This dream-narrative is presented using a mixture of first-person and third-person perspectives, with the aid of props, costumes, and editing to elicit a sense of unreality. For example, at points the camera follows the protagonist's eye-view, as swaying camera angles indicate her disorientation within the dream-experience. Elsewhere, manipulation of footage causes props to impossibly disappear and reappear, while the cloaked figure recalls the dark apparitions seen during episodes of sleep paralysis.

In its original form *Meshes of the Afternoon* (Deren and Hammid, 1943) was a silent movie, though a musical score by Teiji Ito was subsequently added in 1959, which appears on current distributions of the film. Ito's score was specifically composed for the movie and incorporates elements of Japanese gagaku music, utilizing flute, koto, a bamboo mouth organ, a drum, and metallic percussion (Deren, 2005, p.253). Drawing comparison with exotica film soundtracks, Deren points towards a sense of otherness that is achieved through the music. For some audiences the score may also recall such suicidal tragedies of Kabuki theatre as 'Yamashina Kankyo': the ninth act of *Kanadehon Chûshingura* (1748). Specific scenes are closely synchronized with the music, so where we see the darkly cloaked figure or a knife appearing on the bed, we hear a recurring hummed drone (Robertson, 2015). Elsewhere percussion adds tension, accentuating and punctuating the rhythm of events as they unfold. In this way Ito's score underlines the malevolence and otherness of the dream through non-diegetic music.

In Sitney's (1979, p.21) account of American avant-garde films, *Meshes of the Afternoon* (Deren and Hammid, 1943) is an essential example of the 'trance film', the origins of which he finds in the somnambulists of *Das Cabinet des Dr. Caligari* (Wiene, 1920) or *Le Sang d'un Poète* (Cocteau, 1930). Among the 'pure' examples that he counts within this category, Curtis Harrington's *Fragment of Seeking* (1946) and *Picnic* (1948), and Kenneth Anger's *Fireworks* (1947), are other films that contain dream-like sequences, as a means to explore themes of sexuality.[4] For our purposes here, we may note that these early examples were all made as silent films that rely on visuals, with music added retrospectively; hence they do not benefit from the use of diegetic sound to assist with constructing the world of dreams.

Occult Visions

Kenneth Anger was an important figure in the development of the trance film, whose early work *Fireworks* (1947) depicts a violent homoerotic dream. In his subsequent film *Inauguration of the Pleasure Dome* (1954), Anger would include direct references to drug use, and utilize innovative techniques to represent visual hallucinations. Drawing its title from Samuel Taylor Coleridge's 'Kubla Khan' (1797), a poem about an opium-induced dream of a 'pleasure dome', *Inauguration of the Pleasure Dome* is a 38-minute narrative that describes an occult ritual based on Aleister Crowley's Thelema religion. In the opening scenes we see a ritual unfolding in exquisite detail, until mid-way through, when a ceremonial joint is smoked and a chalice containing a hallucinogenic brew is passed between members of the congregation. In the chaotic scenes that follow, brightly coloured symbols flash on screen, creating the impression of the characters receiving visual hallucinations associated with the occult.

The majority of *Inauguration of the Pleasure Dome* (Anger, 1954) is presented from a third-person perspective, and contextualizes the scenes of hallucination through the use of props such as the joint and the chalice. However, the main innovation for reflecting ASCs is the use of a 'vertical montage' technique, whereby images are superimposed to suggest derangement of the senses and iconic visual hallucinations. During these sequences, the images that flash on screen may be understood as the hallucinatory visions of the ritual participants, presented from a first-person perspective. Alternatively, since Anger has stated his desire to 'project ... images directly into people's heads' (Sitney, 1979, p.133), we might view these images as a form of synthetic hallucination that Anger aims to induce in us directly, through the representational properties of film.

Inauguration of the Pleasure Dome (Anger, 1954) was presented with a variety of re-appropriated musical soundtracks such as Leoš Janáček's *Glagolitic Mass* (1926).[5] This piece provides a powerful musical support, lending the grandeur of a Catholic ritual to the proceedings. The use of a Catholic Mass as a soundtrack for an occult ritual with homoerotic undertones is subversive and provocative, not unlike the use of seemingly innocent rock 'n' roll music to underscore a motorcycle gang's acts of violence and brutality on Anger's later film *Scorpio Rising* (1963) (Hutchison, 2011, p.129). As with the other avant-garde films discussed in this section, however, we may note that the film does not provide any diegetic representations of auditory hallucination.

Across these examples, we begin to see how innovative techniques allow the visual components of hallucination to be represented. Visual impressions of unreality can be constructed through the use of props, costumes, camera angles, editing techniques, and superimpositions. These techniques allow the subjective experience of hallucinations—otherwise unobservable phenomena that cannot be filmed with a camera—to be synthetically created from subjective first-person or third-person perspectives.[6] Such techniques could be seen as an early form of 'special effects' for creating visual impressions similar to those that may occur during ASCs. However, at this time it is notable that there is no diegetic equivalent for these visual effects within the auditory domain. This can be seen partly as a technological limitation, though since visual aspects of ASCs are more commonly reported, they may also have been seen as more important. While sound effects are not provided, non-diegetic music is typically used to underscore the mood of these sequences.

PSYCHEDELIC FEATURE FILMS

While the avant-garde paved the way for the representation of ASCs on screen, in the 1960s mainstream feature films such as those of the 'hippy exploitation' genre began to incorporate scenes of psychedelic drug use. These films often took tales of sex and drugs among the counter-culture as alluring subject matter, portraying hippies in a negative light of wild excess and debauched immorality. The drug sequences of these films often relied on special effects techniques for compositing sound and image, and as the technology for creating these developed they gradually became more sophisticated. By the 1990s, computer-generated imagery (CGI) could be used as a means to articulate detailed visual hallucinations, while digital audio techniques allowed auditory hallucinations to be described. These technological advances led to more accurate representations of ASCs, which we shall explore in this section through consideration of several key feature films.

Hippy Exploitation Films

Billy: Just shut up and take it.
Wyatt: Put it on your tongue.

—*Easy Rider*

Roger Corman's *The Trip* (1967) describes advertising man Paul Groves's (Peter Fonda's) first experience of LSD, following the divorce of his wife. As Paul embarks upon his trip while wearing an eye-mask, we hear a heartbeat, see kaleidoscopes, pulsating coloured lights, and funnel dot patterns, presenting a first-person view of hallucination. The camera then shifts to a third-person view of Paul walking across a hallucinatory beach scene. Later on as he makes love to a new female acquaintance, abstract ripple patterns that are suggestive of synaesthesia are projected onto their bodies. On the soundtrack, a pulsing drumbeat, oscillating Moog tones and sustained electric guitar notes quicken in tempo as the writhing bodies approach orgasm. As the film progresses, the figurative hallucinations begin to incorporate fantasy elements that recall *Lord of the Rings* (Tolkien, 1954–1955), as the protagonist is chased and attacked by dark medieval figures on horseback, cultists, and dwarves. Finally, as Paul begins to lose his mind, these sequences grow ever more chaotic—the camera rapidly cutting between different scenes and hallucinatory patterns that recall those of *Inauguration of the Pleasure Dome* (Anger, 1954).

The use of sound in *The Trip* (Corman, 1967) consists mainly of a non-diegetic musical accompaniment provided by The Electric Flag, which ranges from eerie oscillator tones to psychedelic pop music, and loosely underscores the mood of the hallucinations, while also associating the film with the hippy counter-culture of the time. A small number of diegetic sounds related to the hallucination sequences are also used, however. For example, the heartbeat sound that we hear as Paul enters his first hallucination provides a diegetic means through which to reflect the physiological state of heightened arousal brought on by the drug, and the shift of attention towards internal sensory inputs. During some of the fantasy sequences, we also hear occasional sound effects that accompany the events on screen, such as the sound of crackling flames when Paul sees hallucinations of fire. In this way *The Trip* begins to exhibit some limited use of diegetic sounds to suggest auditory hallucinations.

A similar approach to sound can also be found in *Psych-Out* (Rush, 1968), another example of the so-called 'hippy exploitation' genre. *Psych-Out* tells the story of Jenny, a deaf runaway who arrives in the San Francisco Haight Ashbury scene looking for her brother in debauched hippy dens of iniquity. At the climax of the film, Jenny finds herself tripping hard on STP (DOM: 2,5-Dimethoxy-4-methylamphetamine, a psychedelic drug), and hallucinates various spontaneous eruptions of flame. Here hallucinations are described through pyrotechnics, while crackling sound effects provide a diegetic aural accompaniment.

Relatively more sophisticated is the LSD sequence in *Easy Rider* (Hopper, 1969), seen as the protagonists stumble off the streets of the New Orleans Mardi Gras festival into St. Louis Cemetery. Here director Dennis Hopper uses a clever editing technique to disperse fragmented scenes of the protagonists on acid, providing a non-linear montage that reflects the dissolution of time caused by the LSD. The soundtrack of this scene eschews the psychedelic rock music used throughout the rest of the movie in favour of a sound collage, which includes a repeated chiming effect from an oil pump; dialogue of the characters' manic ramblings; fragments of the Lord's Prayer; and environmental sounds such as traffic and birdsong. Here parts of the soundtrack are asynchronous with the footage, contributing to the fragmented, non-linear impression of the visuals.

Psychedelic Metamorphoses

We were somewhere around Barstow on the edge of the desert when the drugs began to take hold.
—Hunter S. Thompson, *Fear and Loathing in Las Vegas*

Flash forwards to 1980, and Ken Russell's *Altered States* is released, a dramatic film that is loosely based on the sensory deprivation experiments of John C. Lilly (1972). In the film, the ASC experiments of a university professor begin to spill over into reality and cause him to undergo a shocking form of biological devolution. To portray hallucinations, *Altered States* developed many of the techniques that had come before, providing elaborate special-effects-driven sequences through rapid cuts between footage; pyrotechnics; surrealistic symbolism and juxtapositions; animated patterns of moving lights; and magnified images of coloured oils and organic cellular forms. On the soundtrack, John Corigliano's score supports the dramatic urgency of the hallucination sequences, contrasting orchestral sounds with abstract electronic music consisting of tape manipulations and synthesizer tones (similar to musique concrète). As the film progresses, this contrast yields a dialectic in which orchestral sounds accompany scenes of normal consciousness, while the weird electronic sounds form a synaesthetic accompaniment to the protagonist's increasingly bizarre hallucinations.

In *Altered States* (Russell, 1980) we find the usefulness of special effects such as mattes, animations, and electronic sound techniques clearly in evidence as a means to construct ASC sequences. By the 1990s, the widespread availability of CGI and digital audio techniques would further expand these possibilities, as most effectively demonstrated in Terry Gilliam's (1998) carnivalesque adaptation of Hunter S. Thompson's *Fear and Loathing in Las Vegas: A Savage Journey to the Heart of the American Dream* (1971). For example, as Hunter S. Thompson and Raoul Duke arrive at their hotel in Las Vegas, CGI is used to distort faces, while the vine designs on the carpet creep up the walls. Thompson turns his attention to focus on a telephone conversation across the room, where a reverb effect causes the speaker's voice to momentarily fill the sound stage, suggesting Thompson's heightened sense of awareness as he is drawn into the sound. He stumbles to approach the receptionist, who we see with a reduced frame-rate that reflects the cognitive impairment caused by his intoxicated state. As he reaches the desk, the receptionist metamorphoses into a snake, while a corresponding pitch transposition drops her voice into a demonic low-frequency rumble, layered with a hissing sound. These digital techniques are combined with more traditional approaches, such as the use of costumes, mirrors, and multiple camera passes, which allow Gilliam to construct Thompson's hallucination of a bloody 'reptile zoo' in the lounge area (Gilliam and Christie, 1999, p.250).

In this way, *Fear and Loathing in Las Vegas* (Gilliam, 1998) builds upon previous approaches, but relies on diegetic sound effects more than music, as a means to construct impressions of hallucination. The results are strikingly effective, providing a stylized form that engages with the satirical themes of the novel, where hallucinations provide one of the means through which Thompson conducts his vicious dissection of the American dream.[7] At the same time, though Terry Gilliam has no personal experience of LSD (Gilliam and Christie, 1999, pp.258–259), these techniques begin to accurately resemble what participants in LSD studies describe, and thus hint at the possibility of 'simulating' ASCs through digital technology.

Digital Unrealities

While *Fear and Loathing in Las Vegas* (Gilliam, 1998) hinted at the potential for accurate representations of ASCs through means of digital technology, Gaspar

Noé's *Enter the Void* (2009) would push significantly further towards this capability. *Enter the Void* tells the story of Oscar, a small-time American drug dealer living in Tokyo, who is killed, and whose soul subsequently flies across the city. The story is predominantly told from the subjective, first-person perspective of the protagonist, by using the camera to display his eye-view. We see what he sees, including periodic flickering when he blinks, while the soundtrack allows us to hear what he hears. Sound is used not only to describe external sensory inputs, but also to reflect his internal thoughts through the monologue of his inner speech. This inner speech is distinguished through the use of a reverberation effect to metaphorically suggest the internal spaces of his psyche.

During the opening sequence, Oscar smokes a glass pipe containing DMT (*N,N*-dimethyltryptamine). The onset of the drug is represented by blurring the image and heightening the contrast, while spots flicker across the visual field. As the protagonist leans back and closes his eyes, the external environment is switched off, and the audience sees his internal visual hallucinations of organic fibre networks and fractal patterns (constructed with CGI). The camera then drifts into a spinning third-person view of the protagonist, suggesting a brief out-of-body experience.[8] The soundtrack reflects these experiences through sounds of the external environment, distorted versions of these, and internal sounds of hallucination. For example, as Oscar heats the glass pipe, we hear the external sound of his cigarette lighter. Then, as the hallucinations set in, ambiguous textural sounds constructed using dialogue can be heard, suggesting his scrambled thoughts. We hear street noise from below his balcony, but this is processed using digital effects such as flanger, reflecting sensory derangement. As his mobile phone rings, Oscar is startled out of his hallucination, though some residual effects persist, which are described through the use of background sonic textures and visual effects.

Although *Enter the Void* (Noé, 2009) is one of the most technically impressive first-person perspective representations of hallucination to date, the increasing sophistication and decreasing cost of CGI technologies have yielded many other ASC sequences in films and TV programmes. These typically use variations of the approaches discussed so far. For instance, in *Blueberry* (also known as *Renegade*) (Kounen, 2004), an elaborate sequence of ayahuasca intoxication uses electroacoustic sound design techniques and CGI to create unreal scenes of hallucination involving insects, snakes, geometric patterns, and fractal geometry. The following year, Hollywood blockbuster *Batman Begins* (Nolan, 2005) also utilized extensive audio-visual post-processing techniques to produce the Scarecrow's terrifying hallucinations. More recently in the finale of *Embrace of the Serpent* (Guerra, 2015), minimal music is used alongside aerial shots of the Amazon and colourful symbolic animations (based on Tukano designs, see Chapter 2 pp.39–40), to illustrate the yakruna-induced hallucinations of ethnobotanist Richard Evans Schultes.[9]

Over time the decreasing cost and increased power of computer graphics and digital audio effects has allowed filmmakers to incorporate sophisticated representations of ASCs. Where before they were absent, diegetic sounds to represent auditory hallucinations could now be provided, alongside funnel patterns and other visual forms of hallucination. In terms of the 'representational component' of the conceptual model, both sound and image were now being used to describe 'external' and 'internal' inputs. At the same time, the increasing sophistication and availability of technological tools enabled a gradual progression from 'stylized' towards more 'accurate' modes of representation.

EXPANDED CINEMA

The works discussed so far all provide representations of ASCs through the use of narrative forms, and were conceived for presentation within the confines of the cinema. Yet in the late 1960s other forms of audio-visual media began to emerge, which avoided narrative conventions and sought to actively engage audiences in other ways. The term 'expanded cinema' was coined by Stan VanDerBeek to describe this emerging field of work, and was subsequently developed in Gene Youngblood's (1970) seminal book of the same title. Developing McLuhan's (1964) theories, Youngblood saw television and video as extensions of the nervous system, and expanded cinema as a means to usher in a new form of synaesthetic global consciousness. Within this area, the 'visual music' films of Jordan Belson and others are of particular interest, since they provide synaesthetic explorations of light and sound that reflect internal aspects of consciousness. These films also find parallels in the psychedelic lights shows of 1960s rock concerts, where oil projections turned stage shows into dazzling sensoriums. In turn, these light shows would anticipate the subsequent development of VJ culture in the 1990s and beyond, where digital technologies provided new ways to integrate sound and image. In what follows we shall undertake an exploration of this alternate trajectory in audio-visual media, in order to consider how these synaesthetic artworks represent internal states, or transform the consciousness of their audiences.

Visual Music

I reached the point that what I was able to produce externally, with the equipment, was what I was seeing internally. I could close my eyes and see these images within my own being, and I could look out at the sky and see the same thing happening there, too.

—Jordan Belson

'Visual music' describes works that explore musical forms and structures through visual imagery. The origins of visual music can be found in early 'colour organ' devices that displayed coloured lights in correspondence with sounds, or the paintings of Kandinsky that incorporate music-like forms and structures. This term was also subsequently used to describe the work of filmmakers such as Len Lye, Norman McLaren, Oskar Fischinger, and John Whitney (Moritz, 1997; Brougher and Mattis, 2005). Although these works are not necessarily related specifically to ASCs,[10] as Wees (1992) discusses, a branch of this work provides films of the 'inner eye' that externalize internal processes such as those associated with hallucinations or states of meditation, and it is these that are of particular interest for our discussion here.

Harry Smith was a member of the Beat Generation, known also for producing the *Anthology of American Folk Music* (1952), and whose field recordings of ritual peyote music we encountered previously in Chapter 2. Though many of his films were lost or destroyed, surviving examples were collected on *Early Abstractions* (Smith, 1939–1957). These films were created utilizing techniques such as direct animation, where paint and stencils are painstakingly applied to individual frames of film, in order to create explosions of colour and moving shapes. Harry Smith's approaches were informed by those of the pioneering visual music filmmaker Oskar Fischinger, and he also cites sleep deprivation and intoxicated hallucinations among his sources of inspiration (Sitney, 1979, p.233). In particular, he refers to a Dizzy Gillespie concert, during which marijuana seems to have precipitated a synaesthetic experience of 'all kinds of [coloured] flashes' in relation to jazz music (Sitney, 1965, p.270). Such experiences of synaesthesia provided the basis for his paintings, and also inform many of the *Early Abstractions* films. Harry Smith projected these films alongside live jazz performances, and cut fixed-media versions with various soundtracks including The Beatles' *Meet The Beatles!* (1964) (Singh, 2010, pp.24, 34–36).

Filmmaker James Whitney also provided notable investigations into internal aspects of consciousness in his films *Yantra* (1957) and *Lapis* (1966). *Yantra* draws its title from a sanskrit word meaning 'instrument', and describes a meditational device similar to a mandala that balances or focuses the mind. The film consists of flickering colour changes and various expanding and contracting clouds, fountains, and geometrical dot formations, which Whitney saw as providing a means through which to communicate concepts of meditation that are otherwise resistant to verbal explanation (Moritz, 1985). Dutch composer Henk Badings's *Electronic Ballet Music 'Cain and Abel'* (1958) was added retrospectively as a soundtrack, and complements the visual imagery through accelerating crescendos of synthesizer tones with rising pitches, which seem to fit with the expanding clouds of particles in *Yantra* (Moritz, 1977).

The use of electronic music on *Yantra* (Whitney, 1957) lends the piece a futuristic quality, recalling the outer space/inner space themes discussed in Chapter 3. However, such dichotomies are more explicitly addressed in the films of Jordan Belson (a contemporary of Harry Smith), which provide introspective meditations on consciousness and the universe. For example, in *Allures* (Belson, 1961) and other works such as the unfinished film *LSD* (Belson, 1962), we see funnel patterns that are suggestive of internal visual patterns of hallucination, which also hint at the external forms of cosmic radiation, magnetism, or celestial activity. Using such imagery, Belson draws our attention to similarities in form between the inner psyche and outer space.[11] On *Allures*, an original electronic soundtrack composed using synthesizer tones and tape delay effects complements this imagery and underscores the futuristic mood of mysticism and otherness. Notably, these films were informed by Belson's personal experiences with LSD, peyote, and yogic meditation (Youngblood, 1970, pp.169–171, 174). Yet as with James Whitney's *Yantra*, his films do not only seek to represent past experiences, but actually strive to induce a form of meditation for the audience through the audio-visual medium.[12]

Psychedelic Light Shows

Harry Smith's projection of visual music accompanied by live jazz can be seen as an early form of audio-visual performance, pre-dating the VJ culture of today by several decades. During the 1960s performances of this kind would see a significant growth, as artists began to explore multimedia approaches within the sphere of popular culture. For example, Andy Warhol's notorious *Exploding Plastic Inevitable* (1966–1967) shows provided multisensory experiences involving projections, strobe lights, dancers, and live music by the Velvet Underground (Joseph, 2002). These performances were highly kinetic, bombarding the senses to induce trance-like states of heightened arousal through sensory overload.[13] Similar approaches were also explored in multimedia artworks of the USCO collective, which sought to transform consciousness by overloading the senses through light and sound (Oren, 2010). For instance, Jud Yalkut's *Turn, Turn, Turn* (1968) presents footage of kinetic sculpture and light, set to looping, overdriven fragments from The Byrds' (1965) song of the same title. Here the dizzying whirlwind of imagery seeks to alter consciousness through rotation, recalling the practices of Whirling Dervishes who overload their senses by spinning.[14]

Around the same time, artists such as The Joshua Light Show provided psychedelic visual projections to accompany rock concerts at venues such as the Fillmore East in New York (Signore, 2007; Zinman, 2008). Elsewhere Mark Boyle and Joan Hills provided projections for the UFO club in London (Boyle and Robertson, 2000; Robinson, 2007). Among the various techniques used, these 'liquid light shows' were created using coloured oils, which were mixed above an overhead projector, throwing multi-coloured patterns of light on to the walls of the venue, audience, and performers. As seen on The Joshua Light Show's *Liquid Loops* (1969; see also Figure 3.1), amoebic blobs of oil expand, contract, and subdivide, producing an organic quality that recalls the hallucinations of 'cellular level energy consciousness' discussed by Timothy Leary (1968). In other examples we also see funnel patterns reminiscent of Klüver's (1971) form constants. For instance, Figure 6.1

Figure 6.1. Light show by 'Humble' Ben Van Meter at the Avalon, as part of an event welcoming Swami Bhaktivedanta, founder of the Krishna Consciousness (Hare Krishna) movement to San Francisco, 1967. Swami Bhaktivedanta, Allen Ginsberg, Gary Snyder, and others are on stage. Photo: Ben Van Meter.

documents a light show by 'Humble' Ben Van Meter,[15] which displays a funnel pattern that was created using a crystal cookie dish (Van Meter, 2016). These light shows were often manipulated by multiple individuals, allowing correspondences with the music to emerge through synchresis. In this way, the imagery is suggestive of synaesthetic experiences of sound-to-image hallucination, not unlike those that may occur through the use of psychedelic drugs such as LSD. Yet here such experiences are made concrete through the use of projection technologies, and are perceptible to audience members who are not on drugs, while also augmenting the sense of unreality for those who are. More broadly, by representing aspects of internal sensory experience, these light shows draw attention to the form of consciousness, providing multimedia expressions that resonate with the counter-culture ethos of consciousness expansion.

VJ Culture

> [M]any spliffs were smoked and much Pink Floyd listened to whilst using *Psychedelia*, and at computer shows we'd always play music whilst I would demonstrate the program to passers by.
>
> —Jeff Minter

The psychedelic light shows of the 1960s utilized what we might call a 'loose' form of synchronization with sound, since the possibilities for moving liquids precisely in time with music are somewhat limited. However, in the decades that followed, new technology began to emerge that offered more precise forms of control, in which visuals could be directly linked to the properties of audio signals. Following early sound-to-image synthesizers such as the Atari Video Music (1976), Jeff Minter developed several 'light synth' programs, including *Psychedelia* (1984), *Colourspace* (1986), *Trip-A-Tron* (1987), and the *Virtual Light Machine* (VLM, 1990–2003). These programs allowed the user to paint kaleidoscopic tunnels and symmetrical patterns of coloured dot particles, and in later iterations the amplitude and frequency spectrum of an incoming audio signal could be used to control properties of these animations. Jeff Minter's software was used to create live visuals for rave bands The Shamen, Primal Scream, and The Orb (Minter, 2005), and he even collaborated with composer Adrian Wagner on *Merak* (1988), an 'outer and inner space fantasy' that draws inspiration from the psychedelic space rock of Pink Floyd, and the 'star gate' sequence from Stanley Kubrick's *2001: A Space Odyssey* (1968).

Together with low-cost video compositing and 3D animations packages such as the NewTek Video Toaster, these tools were among those that shaped the design of rave culture in the late 1980s and early 1990s.[16] This gave rise to an emerging 'VJ culture', where videos were mixed alongside electronic dance music performances. For example, the *X-Mix* (Studio !K7, 1993–1998) series provided hour-long visual montages of looping computer graphics animations, which accompanied house and techno DJ mixes by artists such as Paul Van Dyk, Laurent Garnier, and Richie Hawtin. As also seen in The Prodigy's *One Love* (Howlett and Hyperbolic Systems, 1993), and The Future Sound of London's *Lifeforms* (1994), these videos represent the iconography of the rave culture through imagery that is suggestive of visual hallucinations, ecstasy tablets, tribal dancers in ancient temples, and alien worlds. In doing so, they reinforce the concepts of the music, while also providing visual stimulation to support the production of heightened states of arousal at raves. The use of audio-visual technologies to induce changes in consciousness is consistent with the 'technoshamanic' philosophies of Terence McKenna, who even participated in several of his own VJ performances in collaboration with video artist Rose X (e.g. *Alien Dreamtime*, 1993).[17]

As VJ culture and tools have developed, artists have been able to provide closely integrated visuals that respond to sound, presented using immersive projection technologies. For example, at the psy-trance festival Mo:Dem, The Extra-Dimensional Space Agency have provided large, highly detailed laser-cut sculptures, which are 'projection mapped'[18] using visuals by VJs (as for example in Figure 6.2). These sculptures incorporate circular portals, within which tunnels of light suggestive of visual hallucinations are projected. As shown in Figure 6.3, some of these projections even reference shamanic visionary experiences by incorporating Shipibo *ronin quene* designs.[19] Meanwhile, at Burning Man festival, artists have installed an immersive fulldome[20] environment, to project Android Jones' *Samskara* (with 360art, 2015–2016), which transports the viewer through disorientating[21] hallucinatory virtual environments that resemble the contents of a spiritual DMT trip

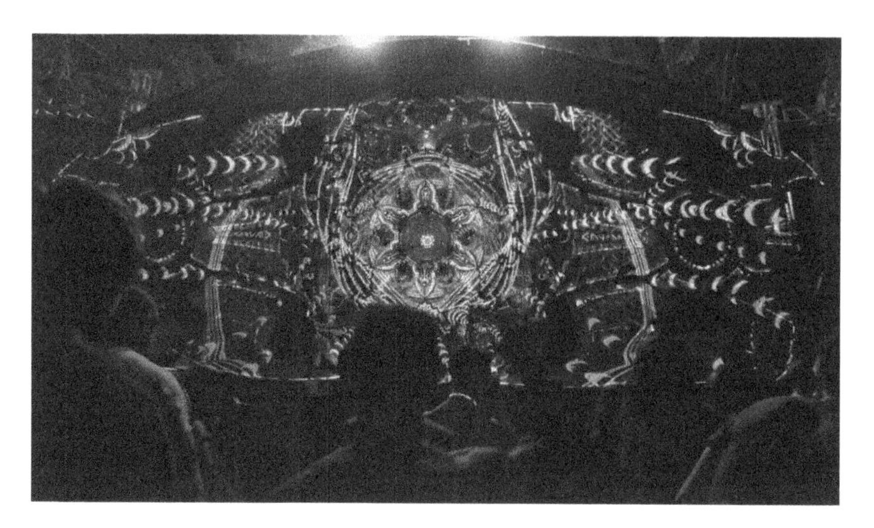

Figure 6.2. Projection mapped sculpture by the Extra-Dimensional Space Agency, with VJ mapping by TAS, Mo:Dem festival, Croatia, 2016. Copyright by TAS Visual Art.

Figure 6.3. Still image from VJ materials by TAS Visual Art (2015), showing Shipibo *ronin quene* designs. Copyright by TAS Visual Art.

(shown in Figure 6.4). This work was also screened at Fulldome UK 2016, alongside other outstanding pieces such as *Quadrivium* (Sol and Ralp, 2015) and *Remote Sense* (Knox and Britto, 2016), which similarly explore themes of unreality. Indeed, the latter work draws inspiration from entoptic phenomena and shamanic cave paintings, utilizing Lidar (laser scanned) data to construct a hallucinatory journey through ethereal architectural spaces that are rendered in pin-point clouds of light (Knox, 2017). Through technological approaches such as these, VJs are able to create a synthetic analogue of synaesthetic visual hallucinations, and in doing so they reinforce the 'technoshamanic' ethos of the culture.

Figure 6.4. Screening of *Samskara* by Android Jones and 360art (2015–2016), in a fulldome theatre at Burning Man festival, USA, 2016. Photo: Gilles Bonugli Kali—GBK photos.

Across these examples of visual music, psychedelic light shows, and VJ performances, we may observe the use of audio-visual technologies for representing experiences of synaesthesia and hallucination. Although these may be represented using various stylistic approaches, the use of computational sound-to-image processes and immersive technologies also reflects a trend towards improved levels of 'accuracy'. Yet while immersive technologies such as the fulldome 'transport' the audience into fictional diegetic spaces, psychedelic projections at festivals more commonly use a 'situational' approach that enhances sensory experience of the concert environment in the 'here and now'. For those works explored, the addition of visuals often reinforces the counter-culture themes of the music and vice versa, while their kinetic qualities may also support responses of low or high arousal.

* * *

This chapter has expanded our discussion of ASCs to consider audio-visual works such as avant-garde films, feature films, visual music, psychedelic projections, and VJ performances. Utilizing the 'representational component' of the conceptual model presented in the previous chapter allows us to distinguish different approaches in the design of these works. Audio-visual media may represent internal or external sensory inputs using various stylized approaches, yet as digital technologies have advanced, we have also witnessed a gradual progression towards more accurate modes of representation. At the same time, distinctions also emerge between those cinematic works that seek to transport the viewer into fictional diegetic spaces, and those VJ performances that overlay projections as a means to enhance sensory experience in the situation of the arena space.

Along similar lines, the 'affective component' can also be useful for distinguishing the type of emotional response that these audio-visual works promote. In many of the examples we have explored, music is used as a means to stimulate emotion. However, the design of visual media may also be used in ways that are more or less kinetic, supporting audience responses that are more meditative or trance-like in form. These properties may fluctuate within a work, yet the behaviours of audiences can also provide an indication of the affective response that a work elicits. For example, where we see seated audiences absorbed in contemplation of a visual music film, this may suggest a more meditative state than that experienced by energetic dancers beneath projection-mapped sculptures at psy-trance festivals, who appear to be in more trance-like states of high arousal.

Where representations of ASCs are included in audio-visual media, they may express a particular ethos. For example, we have explored works that utilize the cinematic medium in order to unlock dreams and the unconscious; develop counter-culture narratives; or tell cautionary tales of drug use. Meanwhile, within the trajectory of expanded cinema and synaesthetic projections we find works that reflect the consciousness expansion and technoshamanism of the musical cultures with which they are associated. In such cases, visuals reinforce the representational properties of the music, framing affective responses with meaning, thereby contributing towards cohesive forms of *gnosis*.

CHAPTER 7

Virtual Unreality

Can computers supplant psychedelics? As one of my fellow teachers at San Jose said to me, 'Computers are to the nineties what LSD was to the sixties'. With cool graphics and virtual reality, we can pursue the dream of the pure, nonphysical, software high.

—Rudy Rucker, *Mondo 2000*

Off a side-street in Manor House, North-East London, there is an industrial area, and down by the entrance to one of the warehouses there is a throng of people outside, some with thin blue plastic carrier bags containing cans of beer from the local off-license. From inside the darkness of the warehouse emerges the glow of blacklight, and the echoing thuds and hissing high-hats of some glitchy-techno. Going further in reveals a labyrinth of audio-visual installations using everything from neon strips and projectors, to web-cameras, gesture recognition devices, and biofeedback equipment.[1] In one area a guy mixes oils over an overhead projector producing classic liquid light psychedelia, while in the next a vast projection displays monochrome blocks that twitch and strobe at a dizzying pace to the pops and clicks of the music. In another room a girl sits patiently with a brainwave device on her head, while around the corner someone is waving their hands around some suspended circuit boards that emit a squealing cacophony of analogue noise. The event is VJ London's AV Depot (2016), and this is the hottest place to be right now to catch the latest wave of underground artworks involving synaesthetic combinations of light and sound.

In one area of the AV Depot swathes of dyed-fabrics are adorned with strange symbols, and are bathed in purple black light and the flickering of candles. Within a ritualistic circle, a man in a dark hooded robe presides over a virtual reality (VR) deck that spills out a torrent of wires in all directions. I lower into a cross-legged position on a cushion, placing the VR headset over my face, and for a moment all goes dark. Suddenly I am no longer in Manor House, but inside a galaxy of glowing purple words. Upon inspection some of the words are names like 'Carl Jung' or 'Terence McKenna', while others read 'Panspermia' or 'Psychedelics'. Using a controller I can move between these glimmering words, and draw connections between them, which seems to cause pulsing tubes of light to join them, forming shimmering constellations. At times I catch a glimpse of a holographic dancer, and notice spinning crystals glinting in the air, yet the meaning of it all remains enigmatic, and this compels me towards further exploration.

The video game I tried at AV Depot was a prototype of *Gnosis* (Fathomable, 2016), a game which places the player inside the 'memory palace' of a post-human consciousness of the distant future (as shown in Figure 7.1; Bogucki, 2016). The exploratory form of synaesthetic interactivity this provides, is just one example of audio-visual media pushing at the boundaries of experiences that can be provided using the latest VR hardware. In this chapter, we shall explore such media by looking first at the graphical and sound capabilities of video games, in order to see how these have advanced since the 1980s to offer the highly immersive 3D environments that are commonplace today. Following this, we begin a tour through the back-catalogue of existing video games that engage with altered states of consciounsness (ASCs) through the representation of dreams, hallucinations, or intoxicated states. Here these works will be separated into two broad trajectories. The first of these relates to action, driving, shooting, and adventure games that incorporate digital representations of drugs and psychosis; the second describes those more unusual games such as *Gnosis* that offer synaesthetic forms of interactivity, which expand our notions of what video games can be. Through the consideration of works from both of these categories, I will build upon the previous conceptual model in order to consider issues of interactivity for audio-visual media related to ASCs. Towards

Figure 7.1. Screenshot from the video game *Gnosis* (Fathomable, 2016), which allows the player to explore a 'memory palace' in virtual reality. Image: Robert Bogucki/Fathomable.

the end of this chapter this will then allow me to define the concept of 'ASC Simulations': interactive audio-visual systems that represent ASCs such as dreams or hallucinations with regards to the sensory components of the experience.

VIDEO GAMES

The origins of arcade games can be traced back to 'Bagatelle' in nineteenth-century France,[2] or the early coin-operated pinball tables of 1930s America. In the post-war period pinball games grew in popularity and evolved to include electromechanical parts, flippers, and lights. Yet it was the development of transistors and integrated circuit (IC) boards that would eventually give rise to the first electronic arcade games and microcomputers of the 1970s, launching a video games culture that continues to this day (Ceruzzi, 2012; Caulfield and Caulfield, 2014). In only a few decades we have seen the memory and processing speed of computers rapidly increase, providing ever more realistic and cinematic gaming experiences. In this section we take a brief tour through these technological advances, and consider how they may provide immersive experiences.

Technological Advances

The graphical capabilities of computer games have always been limited by the memory and processing capabilities of the hardware. Until the mid-1990s, most video games relied on combinations of text, backgrounds and 'sprites': two-dimensional visual objects that can be moved around on-screen. As memory capabilities increased through the 1980s and 1990s, these sprite-based graphics were able to utilize larger palettes of colours, and provide more detail through higher resolutions. Alongside this, a few early games such as *Battlezone* (Atari, 1980) provided 3D wireframe graphics, and later flat-shading, as seen in titles such as *Carrier Command* (Realtime Games, 1988). Yet it was not until the advent of Pentium PC gaming and fifth-generation video games consoles that 3D graphics would become dominant. Early titles such as *Doom* (id Software, 1993) offered a form of pseudo-3D[3]; however, with id Software's follow up *Quake* (1996), full 3D graphics became available, which could be further enhanced with accelerators such as the 3dfx Voodoo Graphics card. Such accelerator cards would eventually be fitted as standard in home computers and games consoles, allowing 3D games to use texture filtering (a process which allows the smoothing of textures), fog, transparencies, coloured lighting, and normal maps (or 'bump maps').[4] In the most recent video games, these effects have also been supplemented by bloom (or 'glow'), lens flare, depth-of-field, motion blur, and chromatic aberration, all of which simulate the artefacts of photographic lenses, allowing the visual style of games to become more photo-realistic.

The audio capabilities of video games have also undergone substantial advances, progressing from simple blips and bleeps to high-quality digital recordings. Most early systems used 'programmable sound generator' (PSG) chips such as the General Instruments AY-8910 series of the Sinclair ZX Spectrum, Sega Master System, and Atari ST;[5] or the MOS Technology 6581/8580 SID (Sound Interface Device) of the Commodore 64 (Collins, 2008). These chips provided the square, sawtooth, triangle, and noise waveforms that characterize the 'chip music' and sound effects of the era, and provided some limited digital sampling capabilities. While chip music dominated the early video games, improved memory capacities and the use of CD-ROM drives enabled a shift towards pre-recorded music and digital samples in the mid-1990s. This allowed Sony PlayStation games such as *WipEout* (Psygnosis, 1995) to utilize CD-quality music by electronic dance music artists such as The Prodigy, Leftfield, and the Chemical Brothers. Meanwhile, digital sampling enabled developers to utilize voice-actors on games such as *Command and Conquer* (Westwood Studios, 1995), and by the early 2000s 'triple A'[6] studios were contracting top Hollywood actors to provide this service.[7] Real-time effects processes were also gradually introduced, as on snowboarding games such as *SSX Tricky* (EA Canada, 2001), in which filters sculpt the sound of the board carving through the snow in real-time, and launching into the air applies a high-pass filter to the music, creating dramatic suspense (Sweet, 2014, pp.178–179). Real-time reverberation effects could also be used, which together with 3D audio techniques[8] provided an improved sense of aural spatiality in games. Lastly, tools for creating dynamic music allowed the design of musical soundtracks that seamlessly change based on events in the game. In the current state-of-the-art, then, video game sound designers may provide sophisticated forms of interactivity, utilizing tools comparable to those available in professional music production.

Presence and Immersion

Aside from graphics and sound, video games are distinguished from other audio-visual media such as films by their status as interactive, non-linear media. The player not only sees and hears virtual environments, but may explore and interact within them. Unpacking these forms of interactivity, Cajella (2011) proposes that games may offer kinaesthetic, spatial, shared, narrative, affective, and ludic forms of 'player involvement'. 'Kinaesthetic involvement' describes engagement of the player through control of a game character; 'spatial involvement' discusses the sense of a virtual environment that may be acquired through exploration; and the other types are related to social interaction, storyline, emotions, and the feelings of success or failure that are elicited as the player attempts to complete goals. According to Cajella, these six forms of involvement allow the player to build up a mental representation of a given virtual environment, and gain a sense of habitation within it.

This sense of habitation has been alternately described using the related terms 'presence'[9] and 'immersion'. 'Immersion' describes the capabilities of technology for submersing an individual into a virtual environment, while 'presence' describes the feeling of 'being there' that such experiences may produce (Slater and Wilbur, 1997).[10] Although many video games may be immersive, the latest VR headsets and fulldomes provide enhanced capabilities for this purpose, plunging the user into stereoscopic electronic worlds that completely engulf the senses. Being immersed in these electronic environments may lead to feelings of 'presence', as the user feels like they are 'really there'.

Through this phenomenon, video games may 'transport' the user from the physical arena space into synthetic virtual environments. However, it is also possible for video games to operate within the 'situation' of the arena space. This can be achieved through the use of 'augmented reality' (AR) or 'mixed reality' (MR) technologies. AR devices overlay synthetic visual or auditory information with the real, physical environment, providing a composite; MR technologies do the same, while providing improved integration and interaction between the two. For example, the Microsoft Hololens (2016) is a recent AR/MR device that consists of a wearable pair of glasses, which produces composites of the real physical environment, and synthetic graphics and sound.

Advances in graphics and sound technologies have enabled video games to provide increasing levels of realism. Yet just as other forms of electronic music and audio-visual media may represent unreal or hallucinatory experiences, so too can this be achieved in video games, and with increasing levels of detail and accuracy. In order to consider the design of these, we may utilize the conceptual model discussed previously, including the 'representational' and 'affective' components, while also considering the special concerns that interactivity generates.

DIGITAL DRUGS

She had just given me an O.D. of Valkyr. I could feel green fire eating my brains. They turned to steam . . . The shadows rushed me, bruised mug-shot faces hungry for revenge. They knew my weak spots and closed in for the kill. The floor turned into a vortex of green blood.

—Max Payne

Since the 1980s the average age of gamers has increased to thirty-five, and has grown to encompass a larger section of society.[11] This has come partly as a result of an ageing population of people who grew up playing video games in the 1980s, and can also be seen as a response to a market that has grown more diverse in an effort to sell games both to men and women, young and old. As part of this trend, the 1990s saw a significant increase in games aimed at a more mature audience, which incorporated sex, drugs, and violence. While such themes were not entirely absent before, the digitized violence of games such as *Mortal Kombat* (Midway Games, 1992) and *Night Trap* (Digital Pictures, 1992) attracted unprecedented levels of controversy, and appealed to rebellious teenagers in a similar manner as gangster rap or heavy metal. Meanwhile, a number of titles also began to incorporate drug use and hallucinations, either to provide deliberately shocking or exotic content, or simply as part of more 'grown-up' storylines involving elements of madness and psychological horror. In this section a selection of these games will be reviewed, in order to explore how they engage with ASCs through the interactive audio-visual medium.

Pixilated Sprites

Early representations of intoxicated states can be found in the two-dimensional sprite-based video games of the 1980s. For example, *Fantasy World Dizzy* (Oliver Twins, 1989) is an adventure game in which a cartoon egg-man (Dizzy) must save his egg-girlfriend (Daisy) who has been kidnapped by a troll. Along the way, one of the 'red-herring' items Dizzy encounters is a bottle of whisky, located temptingly near a moat that is occupied by an alligator. If Dizzy drinks the whisky, he becomes drunk and stumbles randomly from left to right, while the player must attempt to steer him away from the present dangers of the alligator and moat. These distortions to the interactive experience of physical control provide a simple yet effective means to represent the egg-man's inebriated state for a temporary time period, while also providing a ludic challenge.

Later on, in Remedy Entertainment's top-down racing game *Death Rally* (1996), hallucinogens perform a similar function. In some levels, small *Amanita muscaria* mushrooms appear on the road as collectable items. If the player picks them up, a visual rippling/wave effect is applied to the graphical display for a short period, making control temporarily more difficult. While the rippling effect signifies the perceptual distortions of the hallucinogen, an audio sample of a voice says 'woah man!', locating the brief episode within Cheech and Chong-style notions of 'stoner' culture (e.g. *Up In Smoke*, Adler, 1978). In terms of the game objectives, intoxication is once again used as a disruption to physical control; in this case, however, the effect is achieved by means of imposing a visual impairment.

Another notable example of intoxicated impairment also occurs in *Grand Theft Auto: Vice City* (Rockstar North, 2002). In the mission 'Boomshine Saigon', the protagonist Tommy Vercetti has to drive his friend Phil Cassidy to hospital, after Phil blows himself up with homemade moonshine and explosives. To complete the mission, the player must carefully drive Phil to the hospital within a time limit, while under the influence of the alcoholic fumes emitted from Cassidy's makeshift distillery. Here the intoxication of the player's avatar is represented through the use of drunken dialogue and a swaying camera effect, which fluctuates in intensity during the mission. On the PC version this is accompanied by oscillations in the brightness of the display, while on the PlayStation 2 version a 'visual trails' effect is used instead. The combination of spatial distortions caused by the swaying camera, and the visual impairments of the graphical effects make it harder for the player to control the vehicle, once again providing a ludic challenge.

Digital Stimulants

While Dizzy's whisky bottle impairs the player's abilities, many games incorporate 'power-up' items that bestow temporary advantages upon the player avatar, by increasing speed or other abilities. For instance, in *Sonic the Hedgehog* (Sonic Team, 1991) a glittery shield and speed boots can be collected, which respectively provide invincibility and faster running abilities. These items initiate a rush of excitement, as the player is required to think and act more quickly than usual in order to make the most of their temporary benefits. Yet collecting these items also precipitates a change in the musical soundtrack, triggering a celebratory anthem or increasing the tempo. This change reminds the player that the effects are time-limited, but also affords an increase in arousal and emotional valence through the quick tempo and melodic features of the music. In this way the items provide ludic involvement, while underscoring the sense of excitement through the affective properties of the music.

Where such power-up items occur in video games that are aimed at more mature players, they are sometimes presented as drugs. For example, in *Duke Nukem 3D* (3D Realms, 1996) a 'steroids' power-up temporarily boosts the Duke's running speed, accompanied by a rapid pulsing sound that indicates his elevated heartbeat and high arousal state. Elsewhere, in *Quake* (id Software, 1996), the 'quad damage' power-up initiates a temporary boost to the damage caused by the player's weapons. Collecting this item causes a rapidly flickering aura to form around the player, while the screen is tinted a blue-ish colour, and the face of the 'quake dude' avatar at the bottom of the screen twists into one of frenzied, ecstatic aggression. These graphical features suggest that the quad damage acts as an amphetamine for the game character, inducing a state of heightened arousal that recalls the use of *Amanita muscaria* mushrooms by Viking berserkers, to increase blood-lust and energy before going into battle.[12] Yet beyond this, the quad damage also affords a state of heightened arousal for the player, through ludic involvement underscored by a distorted noise that sounds with each gun-shot, adding to the player's sense of aggression through the affective properties of sound.

A similar collectable item is also found in the 'adrenaline pill' of *Grand Theft Auto III* (DMA Design, 2001) and *Grand Theft Auto: Vice City* (Rockstar North, 2002). While the stimulant items of *Quake* or *Duke Nukem 3D* increase excitement by ramping-up speed or damage capabilities, the adrenaline pill of *Grand Theft Auto III* actually slows down time, thereby reflecting an increase in cognitive ability, and giving the player more time to control the avatar's physical actions with improved precision. This effect is achieved in the third-person by slowing down the game, while sound represents the perceptual distortion by lowering the playback-speed of incidental dialogue in the game. Even though the item reflects a high-arousal state for the game character, here the player experience is the opposite, since it affords greater relaxation by reducing difficulty.

Waking Nightmares

Developed by Remedy Entertainment following *Death Rally* (1996), *Max Payne* (2001) is a third-person action game in a neo-noir style[13] that also features hallucination sequences as a means to enrich the narrative. The story follows Max Payne, a police detective seeking to avenge the murder of his family by criminals involved in the production of the designer drug 'Valkyr', a fictional hallucinogen that produces dangerous states of psychosis. At several points in the game,[14] Max is drugged with Valkyr and enters a nightmarish hallucinatory dream world. In each of these sequences, the player must navigate through a maze of corridors, while Max experiences auditory verbal hallucinations, and the blood curdling screams of his murdered family. Here reverberation is used to reflect the unreality of these voices, which emerge as if they are echoes from Max's past. The hallucinatory mazes are metaphors for Max's troubled psyche, containing rooms and objects that reflect fragments of his memories, which Max must navigate in order to advance the narrative. Besides the ludic challenge of completing the maze, these sections also require the player to balance the avatar on trails of blood, to prevent him from literally falling into an abyss of darkness. All the while we hear the beating of his own heart, and thus these sequences symbolize the 'internal' experience of Max's hallucinations, from which he must eventually emerge into 'external' reality as he regains consciousness.

The use of hallucinatory psychoses to develop storylines by interrogating the internal spaces of a character's psyche, is also found in several other video games. For example, *Eternal Darkness: Sanity's Requiem* (Silicon Knights, 2002) is a third-person adventure game that incorporates a 'sanity meter' patented by Nintendo (Sterchi, Ridgeway and Dyack, 2005), which reflects the level of 'sanity' held by the game character. As this bar decreases, various effects are introduced such as skewed camera angles, mysterious occurrences such as blood dripping from the ceiling, and auditory hallucinations of whispering voices. More recently *Batman: Arkham Asylum* (Rocksteady Studios, 2009) uses scripted animations and voices that are processed with reverse, echo, and reverb effects, to suggest Batman's intoxicated state under the influence of the Scarecrow's hallucinogens. As with *Max Payne*, these 'internal' scenes provide a means through which to develop the plot by exploring Batman's memories, as he recovers childhood recollections of his parents. Along similar lines, in *Alice: Madness Returns* (Spicy Horse, 2011; adapted from Carroll,

1865–1871), Alice begins in the 'external' reality of a mental institution, before this world disintegrates, causing her to tumble down into the 'internal' unreality of Wonderland, which reflects her troubled psyche.

Psychedelic Flux

Video games that incorporate ASC sequences also do so utilizing scripted changes to visual effects and sounds. For example, exploring this concept in 'Quake Delirium' (discussed in Weinel, 2011), a prototype video game modification for *Quake* (id Software, 1996), I utilized several time-varying visual effects, which fluctuate during the game as a means to represent the perceptual distortions of ASCs. Here the changing visual parameters were also mapped to filters and other aspects of sound, as a means to generate a synaesthetic aural accompaniment. As developers began to provide more elaborate sequences that represent hallucinations, this type of approach would also be used in a variety of titles, most notably *Far Cry 3* (Ubisoft Montreal, 2012). In the 'Mushrooms in the Deep' mission of *Far Cry 3*, extensive 'key-framing'[15] of visual effects is used, so that the camera reflects shifts in visual perception caused by the psychedelic mushroom trip. Scripted animations are also provided in this sequence to show objects mysteriously levitating, while swirling layers of sound suggestive of auditory hallucinations provide a sonic accompaniment.

Scripted ASC sequences were also used in *Grand Theft Auto V* (Rockstar North, 2013), to provide a number of drug episodes. For instance, during the 'Grass Roots' mission, the character Michael De Santa smokes a potent marijuana joint, causing the onset of violet fog, chromatic aberration, and tunnel vision effects, while a negative pitch transformation is applied to the dialogue. Elsewhere, an in-game 'easter egg'[16] allows Michael to smoke a bong in his son's room, following which an increase in colour contrast and a glow effect temporarily reflects his altered state, while we hear rambling stoned dialogue. However, the most elaborate drug sequence occurs in the 'Did Somebody Say Yoga?' mission, during which Michael is drugged with an anaesthetic. At the *onset* of the effects of the drug, we see a glowing effect; changes to the camera field of vision; and flickering coloured tints that indicate intoxication. On the audio track, dialogue is processed with a pitch transformation and reverberation, suggesting the dissociative effects of the drug as cognitive abilities become slow and 'distanced' from reality. Following this, Michael enters a *plateau* phase of figurative hallucination during which he is surrounded by screaming monkeys, and is abducted by aliens that recall the 'entities' of Strassman's (2001) DMT (*N,N*-dimethyltryptamine) studies. During this phase we hear the beating of Michael's heart, before the alien ship drops him from the sky, precipitating a free-fall descent controlled by the player, above a glowing, distorted view of the city with enhanced colour contrast.[17] During this phase we hear dialogue that reflects Michael's memories, which are signified as inner speech through the use of an echo effect. After he reaches the ground, the scene cuts to show him lying on his back, whereupon he stands up, and the glowing and blurring effects gradually subside as the trip *terminates*.

Scripted sequences from *Far Cry 3* (Ubisoft Montreal, 2012) and *Grand Theft Auto V* (Rockstar North, 2013) provide detailed representations of hallucination that have greater levels of 'accuracy' than previous games, though we may note that the latter also includes obviously 'stylized' elements of parody. This comic approach is epitomized in the 2014 'enhanced edition' of *Grand Theft Auto V*, during which the player may take peyote in a series of hidden missions. Rather than providing any serious engagement with peyote as a religious sacrament, these missions offers a somewhat juvenile parody of *The Teachings of Don Juan: A Yaqui Way of Knowledge* (Castaneda, 1968), as the player character transforms into pigeons and other animals and makes inane jokes about defecation. In this case stereotypical 'tribal' music consisting of clapping, bells, and flutes plays in the background to provide an exotic feeling.

The incorporation of ASCs and drug sequences in video games typically reflects material aimed at more 'mature' audiences of teenagers and young adults. Increasingly these sequences have been constructed using scripted visual effects and sounds, which reflect a trend towards improved levels of 'accuracy' through means of technology. Graphics provide representations of hallucinatory virtual environments, while sound is often used to provide auditory hallucinations or affective properties via music. When these are experienced interactively, they may distort the kinaesthetic and spatial experience of the player, and contribute towards the ludic involvement that the game provides, by impairing or enhancing the abilities of an avatar. Meanwhile, they may also develop narratives, by giving insights into the internal psychology of characters. In general these games reflect a predominantly negative attitude towards ASCs, since they are either used to provide juvenile 'stoner' humour or develop explorations of gothic horror.

INTERACTIVE SYNAESTHESIA

'Get ready ... get ready!': bit-crushed sirens ring out and the screen strobes red and blue, as the red eye of a llama stares out through a pyramid with the word 'HARDCORE' emblazoned above. As Jeff Minter's *Hardcore* (1992) begins, a techno bass drum pounds and the re-triggered words 'ec-ec-ec-ecstasy' sound as the zone title is written in exploding cans of Coke, before the screen erupts with torrents of laser cannon fire. Along with other Atari ST titles such as *Xenon II Megablast* (Bitmap Brothers, 1989), which sampled Bomb the Bass ('Megablast [Hip Hop on Precinct 13]', 1988), *Hardcore* was an early computer game to incorporate rave music on its soundtrack. Throughout the 1990s the links between electronic dance music would grow, as CD-ROM games were able to utilize full digital music tracks by popular dance artists. Eager to market the first PlayStation console to young adults (Poole, 2004, p.7), Sony sought to promote the console as a cool technology to be used by clubbers, and even hosted a lounge at the Ministry of Sound nightclub in London (Kushner, 2012, p.28).[18] Born out of this marketing strategy, a number of music games emerged that expanded the idea of what a video game could be, providing interactive synaesthetic audio-visual experiences that were characterized as more dreamlike, meditative, or psychedelic. In this section we consider key works from this trajectory, which recall the VJ performances of the previous chapter, and the synaesthetic hallucinations that are often experienced during ASCs.

Synaesthetic Adrenaline

> One sensation I remember influencing me was being in a car with my mates, going to one of the Blackburn raves somewhere over the hills of the Pennines, and hurtling down the motorway at night . . . We were riding up and down the hills, seeing the angles of the embankments, which were very much like the *WipEout* tracks, with those little dotted white lines and the cats eyes rushing past us, with the music cranked up . . . It's all very visceral, and I think in some ways I subconsciously tried to bring those sensations into the track design and to the speed of the ships.
>
> —Nick Burcombe

Four-to-the-floor bass drums thump and jagged TB-303s pulse as a shard-like racing vehicle tears through the tunnels and ramps of a futuristic racing circuit. This is *WipEout* (Psygnosis, 1995), a high-speed 3D racing game for the PlayStation, with a techno soundtrack that includes music by popular producers of the day such as Leftfield, the Chemical Brothers, and Orbital.[19] *WipEout* prioritizes high-adrenaline gameplay, which seeks to excite players by plunging them forwards through the 3D racecourse at high velocity, while challenging them to maintain control of their craft. The quick tempos and rhythmic attack of the rave soundtrack support this, heightening the experience for the player through the affective properties of the music. At the same time, the bleeps and pulses of the synthesized instruments on pieces such as CoLD SToRAGE's 'Cairodrome' assist with eliciting the futuristic representation of the game. In this way *WipEout* finds a synergy with rave culture, which Burcombe suggests was actually inspired by the exhilaration of hurtling down motorways on the way to raves. By imitating this excitement, the game provided an audio-visual electronic high, which could even be used to boost energy levels before a party or sustain them for a while longer afterwards. Of course, these associations with rave culture were also consistent with Sony's marketing strategy for the PlayStation, and were seemingly emphasized through other aspects of the game, such as the capitalized 'E' of the title—a subtle allusion to ecstasy culture.[20] At the time the game was even advertised with a highly controversial poster, in which two gamers (one of whom was Sara Cox, who later became famous as a BBC Radio 1 DJ) were shown having nosebleeds after having overdosed on the 'dangerous game'.[21]

Around this time, thumping techno beats would also see increasing use as a complement to high-energy action in other titles such as *Panzer Dragoon* (Team Andromeda, 1995), an 'on-rails shooter'[22] set in a fantasy landscape. Several members of the development team behind *Panzer Dragoon* (and sequel, *Panzer Dragoon II Zwei*, 1996) would go on to make *Rez* (United Game Artists, 2001), which pushed yet further into the territories of electronic dance music and futuristic aesthetics. The title of the game was inspired by a track of the same title by dance band Underworld (1993), and a beta version of the game included this song and the group's hit *Born Slippy* (1995) on the soundtrack. Although these tracks were not used on the final game due to licensing restrictions, *Rez* nonetheless included a soundtrack with electronic dance music by artists such as Ken Ishii, Adam Freeland, and others. The game utilizes techno music to heighten the sense of energy, while the futuristic soundtrack matches the visual style of the graphics, which use wireframes and flat shading in a style that recalls the movie *Tron* (Lisberger, 1982). Here music is not only used as background audio, but is also integrated into the interactive experience, since shots fired by the player trigger percussive sounds, and are quantized with the music to form rhythms. In this way the game provides a synaesthetic experience in which the kinaesthetic, visual, and aural sensations merge together.[23] In order to enhance the multi-modal experience of the game, *Rez* was even released as a limited edition version with a 'trance vibrator', a specially designed vibration pack that stimulates the player in time with the music. *Rez* was revamped as *Rez HD* (United Game Artists, 2008), and followed by a similar sequel *Child of Eden* (Q Entertainment, 2011). In 2016 a VR version of the game was released as *Rez Infinite* (Enhance Games and Monstars, 2016), which was demonstrated with a haptic 'synaesthesia suit'.

Dream Emulation

Deep bass throbs below drum machine ticks, re-triggered samples processed with a pitch transformation, and an overdriven lead synthesizer. The words 'Linking Sapient Dream' rendered in multi-coloured lettering shake and jitter over a time-lapsed view of the clouds, before the mask of an oddly shaped being comes into view and shatters. Strange high-contrast faces and the letters 'L-S-D' scroll back-and-forth vertically over a city skyline, before the display cuts rapidly between spirals of spheres; an expressway; industrial sprawl; and a Shinto shrine. All the while coloured circles, stars, hearts, and inky characters in traditional Japanese attire explode across the screen.

This is the title sequence for *LSD: Dream Emulator* (Asmik Ace Entertainment, 1998), a rare Japanese title for the PlayStation that is based on a dream journal by one of the game artists, Hiroko Nishikawa (1998). In the game the player undergoes a 'dream' for each incremental day, during which he or she may explore a number of unreal 3D environments. These include indoor and outdoor spaces; city-scapes; natural environments; luminescent neon castles; corridors suspended in the sky; and fleshy womb-like tunnels. Scattered throughout are artefacts such as bird-cages and TVs; the historical monuments of Big Ben and the Moai of Easter Island; graffiti; and trees. As the player navigates these environments, he or she also encounters animated characters such as geisha, ghosts, flying elephants, children playing, and a sinister 'grey man'. Walking up to any of these causes the player to 'link' and be transported to another dream-space. In each new area, the starting location, colours, textures, and accompanying music may change. The latter of these processes occurs by altering the instrumental voices used to perform the sequences, resulting in a variety of quirky techno, ambient, and drill 'n' bass.[24] Due to the generative features of the environments, the game is capable of producing a large number of possible permutations, so that each 'dream' is unique. Crucially, the actions of the player within each space are involved in defining how the dream unfolds through different locations and variations; however, the manner in which this occurs is largely enigmatic. At the end of each dream it is located on a cryptic chart in the shape of a face, with the *x* axis labelled 'static/dynamic', and the *y* axis labelled 'upper/downer'.[25] Through this system, dreams are retrospectively ranked according to their positive or negative valence, and relaxed or energetic qualities, in a manner that recalls Russell's (1980) 'circumplex model of affect'.

LSD: Dream Emulator (Asmik Ace Entertainment, 1998) can be understood as representing the bizarre experiences that people often report from their dreams, in which positive or negative emotions may carry the individual through various scenes and non-sequitur events. The generative levels allow the familiar to be revisited but somehow altered each time, in a manner that reflects the way in which actual dreams often involve scenes or locations that are somehow distorted from their experience in normal waking consciousness. The 'linking' process is synaesthetic, since it forms associations between events, objects, and visual and aural elements of the game. For instance, seeing a woman whose head detaches from her body in one area may suggest a negative or violent emotion, which precipitates a blood red sky in the next sequence of the dream. These associations are frequently enigmatic, enticing the player to explore synaesthetic connections by freely probing the contents of the levels to see what metaphorical or symbolic links they may discover. In this way the game has no clearly defined goals, but encourages an impulsive mode of play in which the player may explore based on whatever he or she feels aesthetically drawn towards.

The drug allusions in the title of the game and the electronic soundtrack are clearly sculpted to appeal to rave audiences, as are the VJ-style interlude videos, with their flickering kaleidoscopes of neon imagery, dot funnels, and cryptic symbols. Indeed, the form of *LSD: Dream Emulator* (Asmik Ace Entertainment, 1998) may also afford the use as a casual audio-visual experience for 'chill-out' zones or post-clubbing parties. When used in such contexts, the synaesthetic qualities of the music and graphics, the dream theme, and the relatively stress-free experience that arises in the absence of clearly defined goals, may be desirable features.

Audio-Visual Meditations

Over time the provision of video games that offer 'experiences' rather than clearly directed challenges has steadily grown, expanding the idea of what games can be. Within this area we also find games related to the concept of meditation, such as *Deepak Chopra's Leela* (Curious Pictures, 2011), which was designed with the assistance of new-age guru Deepak Chopra, and intended to elicit a form of ludic meditation. The main part of the game consists of seven sub-games that correspond with 'chakra points'[26] on the body. Each sub-game asks the player to engage in a challenge that is metaphorically related to the meaning of the corresponding chakra point. The first of these relates to the 'origin' chakra at the base of the spine, which is associated with stability and the earth; thus the game requires the player to assist with the planting of seeds that take root and grow into trees and other plants. For each of the other sub-games the thematic metaphor is varied according to the meaning of the corresponding chakra; for example, the 'life' chakra sees the player fertilizing seeds, while the 'fire' chakra has the player launching fireballs to activate gemstones. Each game involves gradual tilts of the body, and advises the player to undertake actions in time with breathing, thereby providing kinaesthetic forms of involvement that draw some comparisons with yoga techniques.

Music plays an integral role throughout *Leela* as a means to establish a relaxing mood and give an impression of Eastern spirituality. Each game utilizes new-age music, consisting of droning, and harmonic melodies that have long attack and decay times. As the player completes the activities within each sub-game, the intensity of the music increases through additional layers of harmonic material and gentle rhythms. Specific events trigger pitched notes to form melodies that blend with the soundtrack. Through low-arousal properties, the music affords a calm affective response for the player, while he or she completes the tasks, thus promoting a focused state of relaxation similar to yoga or meditation. Of course, the sub-games are probably less effective as a means for drawing attention to breathing or body movement than these traditional techniques, and for some players the possibility of failure could provoke feelings of frustration or disappointment. However, the game does seek to provide a less stressful ludic experience by using dissonant sounds to indicate incorrect actions in a relatively subtle way.

Meditation games have also recently been created for VR technologies. For example, *Guided Meditation VR* (Cubicle Ninjas, 2016) situates the player within virtual environments such as a tropical island, desert canyon, zen garden, and forest. Each location uses sound to elicit a guided meditation. For instance, the canyon level is introduced with a background of gentle acoustic guitar melodies, and the diegetic sounds of wind, running water, and galloping horses. As the meditation dialogue begins on a cliff-top, the player is instructed to attend to his or her breathing, and focus on different areas of the body, before moving their attention outwards to the surrounding virtual landscape. Both synthetic sounds and visuals are involved in the meditation, as the player is instructed to focus on aspects of the surrounding cacti and the wind that rushes past. In this way *Guided Meditation VR* supplements the aural experience of a typical guided meditation audio-CD with a virtual environment, effectively staging a meditation class in VR. Just as a guided meditation CD seeks to 'transport' the individual to a virtual location through sound, *Guided Meditation VR* suppresses the external environment through the audio-visual medium. The use of synthetic virtual environments as a basis for meditation is also used in several other titles such as *Zen Zone* (Unello Design, 2015), which provides attention and breathing meditations in VR; and *Deep VR* (Harris and Smit, 2016), in which pranayama (yogic) breathing controls the movement of the player within an aquatic environment.

Interactive Psychedelia

Within the area of games that avoid any conventional forms of ludic interaction, we also find some titles that are related to psychedelic states. One of these is my own *Psych Dome* (Weinel, 2013) project, a prototype 'ASC Simulation', which provides a real-time audio-visualization based on Klüver's (1971) form constants.[27] Originally presented in a fulldome, it was designed for an individual participant wearing a Neurosky Mindwave, a consumer-grade electroencephalograph (EEG) brain-computer interface (BCI). The player puts on the EEG headset, which provides a control signal that affects properties of the sound and graphics, such as the colours of the visualization and the frequencies of the sound generating processes. In doing so the system provides a form of 'passive'[28] connection between the individual and a synthetic representation of visual hallucinations.

Other artists have also explored the use of novel forms of interactivity and immersive technologies in order to create psychedelic forms of audio-visual media. For example, Robin Arnott's *SoundSelf* (2016) uses the human voice to control parameters of a visualization that also resembles visual hallucinations (shown in Figure 7.2).[29] Described as being 'inspired by a group-ohm on LSD', the game applies sound processing to the audio input from a microphone, allowing the player's voice to create long droning sounds that take on qualities of the numinous. Sound also provides a control signal for the generation of the visuals, thereby simulating the sound-to-image hallucinations that are commonly experienced when using psychedelic drugs. As with Arnott's previous fear-based game *Deep Sea* (2011), which utilized a mask to provide sensory deprivation in order to emphasize sound, *SoundSelf* encourages the player to suppress the sensory input from the 'arena space' by turning off the lights and wearing headphones. In recent editions of the game, a VR headset provides a means through which to further this effect by

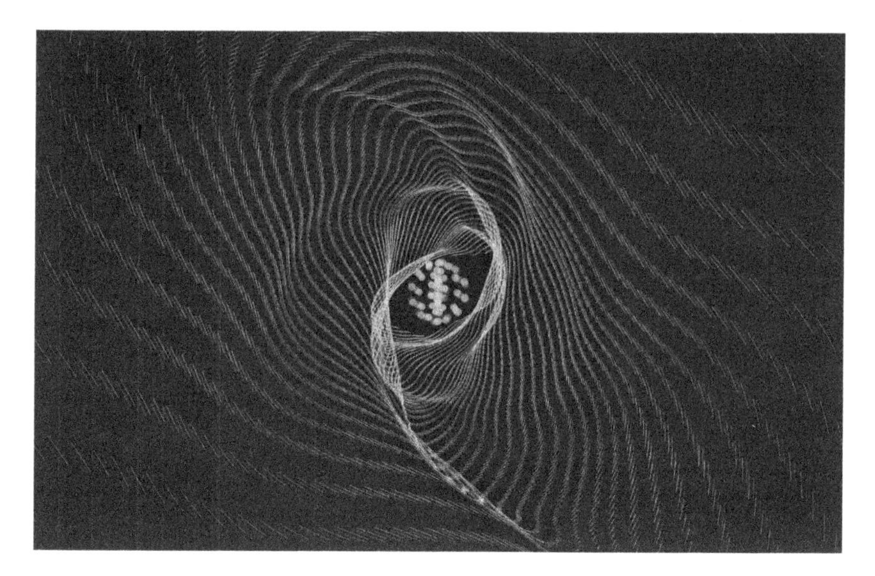

Figure 7.2. Screenshot from the video game *SoundSelf* (2016), which its creator Robin Arnott describes as 'a technodelic VR experience'. Image: Robin Arnott.

blocking out external visual stimuli, in order to promote immersion into a 'transported', hallucinatory environment.

Since the 1990s, games have developed not only to offer increasingly realistic and cinematic experiences but also to provide a wider breadth of experiences. The synaesthetic examples explored in this section can be seen as part of this trend, and show a movement away from traditional models, towards forms of dreamlike, meditative, or psychedelic gaming. Many of these games achieve this by de-emphasizing the win/lose ludic paradigm of gameplay, to instead offer synaesthetic explorations of sensations and emotions. New hardware also has a role to play in this, as VR equipment can be seen as a means to manipulate sensory inputs, while biofeedback and neurofeedback devices provide a means through which to directly incorporate the cognitive and physiological responses of the player. While mainstream titles typically depict ASCs in a negative light, the games in this section promote an entirely different viewpoint in which interactive technologies are treated as tools for exploring and shaping conscious experience.

ASC SIMULATIONS

Through the course of this chapter we have seen how interactive video games can represent ASCs in ways that are more accurate than ever before. This points towards the concept of 'ASC Simulations': interactive audio-visual systems that represent

ASCs with regards to the sensory components of the experience. These simulations may recreate the visual and auditory components of ASCs that are experienced subjectively, using corresponding graphics and sound. In what follows I define the concept of ASC Simulations, which advances that of first-person point-of-view (POV) by considering in more detail how sensory experience changes subjectively during a variety of conscious states, and indicates how designs may be created in accordance with this.

ASC Simulations

Figure 7.3 illustrates the concept of 'ASC Simulations'. The simulation is based on the sensory experience of a conscious individual, or 'host', who may be real or fictitious. Here the host is indicated as the larger head in Figure 7.3. Sound and graphics can be designed which are based on the sensory experience of the host, and these are presented using loudspeakers and a projector screen. In the conceptual illustration, the audience of this audio-visual system is metaphorically depicted as a homunculus inside the host, but of course, in practice, the system could be located in a normal living room, and used by a regular sized person. Drawing upon Baars's (1997) metaphor, then, ASC Simulations can be provided which literally situate an audience within a 'theatre of consciousness'.[30]

Figure 7.4 illustrates the ASC Simulation concept within a system. The left-hand section indicates the material properties of the simulation, which may include representational and affective audio-visual properties. These can be described using the 'representational component' discussed previously, and may therefore include 'external' or 'internal' sensory inputs; be presented using various 'stylized' or 'accurate' modes of representation; and use 'situational' or 'transported' approaches within the arena space. Similarly, the system may also provide 'affective properties' which are based on the emotions of the host. These may be provided through music or other means, and may be defined using the arousal and valence dimensions of the 'affective component'.

The central section of Figure 7.4 shows the 'user' of the ASC Simulation. If the user attends the ASC Simulation, the 'representational properties' may allow him or her to perceive analogues of what the host sees and hears subjectively, while the 'affective properties' may be used to communicate an emotional state. This may produce forms of *gnosis*, which are related to the ethos of the simulation.

As indicated in the right-hand section of Figure 7.4, 'feedback systems' can also be used to provide interactive features, routing signals back into the ASC Simulation. For example, haptic or gestural controllers may provide the user with spatial control over an avatar of the host who is undergoing an ASC. These may provide forms of involvement that enhance the user's sense of presence within the simulation. Biofeedback devices may also be used to link the user's physiology or

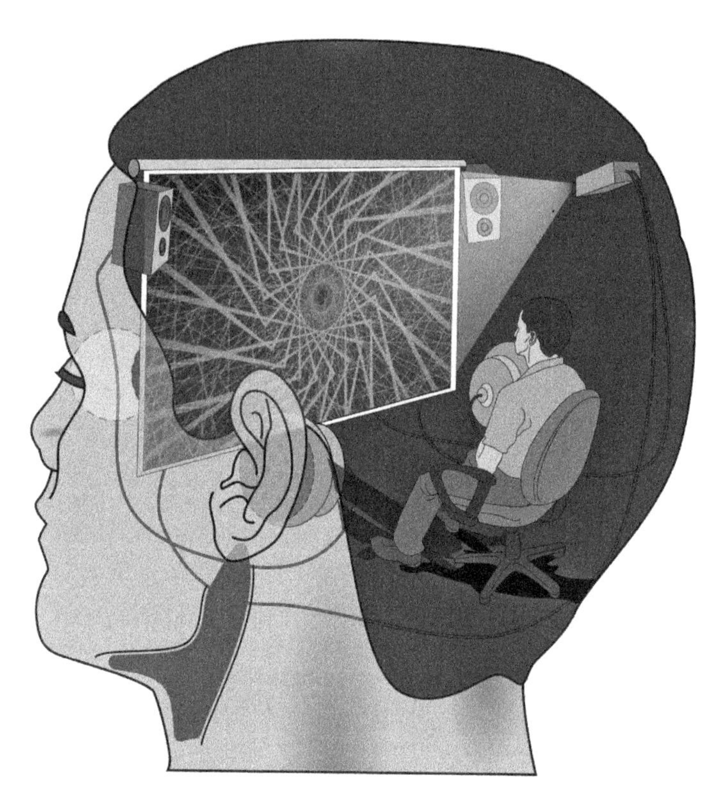

Figure 7.3. Conceptual illustration of an 'ASC Simulation'. Adapted from J. Garcia's 'Cartesian Theatre', 2006, Creative Commons: CC BY-SA 3.0.

neural activity to features of the simulation, thereby forming correspondences with aspects of the user's conscious state.

Varieties of ASC Simulation

The concept of ASC Simulations is not a singular design, but may utilize a variety of configurations as defined by the axes of the representational and affective components. For instance, with regards to the input axis, some simulations may present both synthetic 'external' and 'internal' material, while others may present internal material only, and relatively more 'accurate' or 'stylized' approaches are possible. The use of arena space also presents a particularly interesting range of possibilities, which have important implications for the technologies that are used to create ASC Simulations. In particular, the opposite poles of the arena space axis imply two distinct varieties of ASC Simulation, which correspond with the concepts of 'virtual reality' (VR) and 'augmented reality' (AR) in computing.

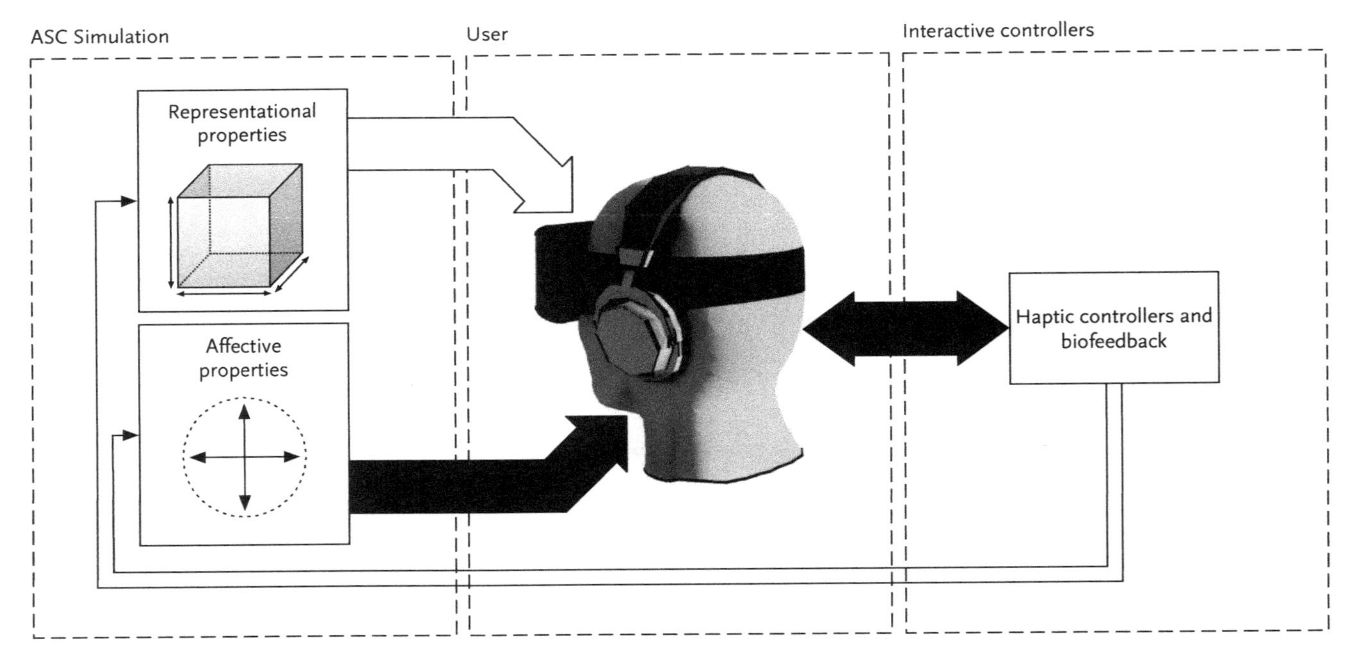

Figure 7.4. Diagram showing an ASC Simulation within a system, which is operated by a user via interactive controllers.

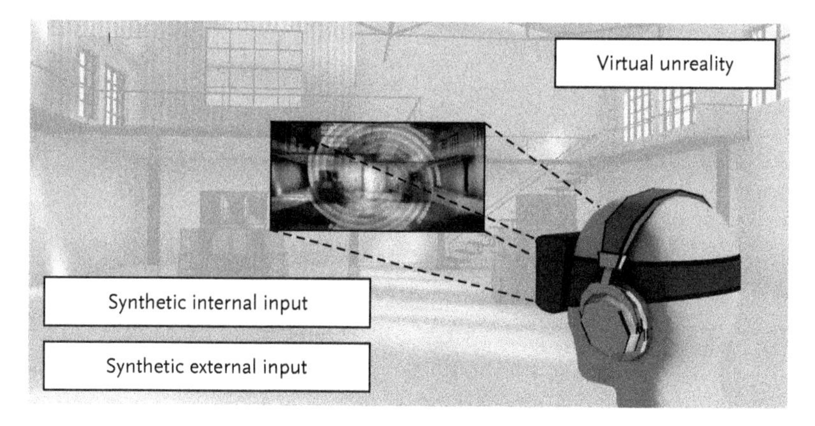

Figure 7.5. Illustration of 'virtual unreality', a specific type of ASC Simulation, in which the user is 'transported' into a synthetic hallucination.

'Virtual unreality' constructs a simulation of ASCs using a 'transported' approach in the arena space. As illustrated in Figure 7.5, a VR headset and headphones can be used to provide the synthetic external and internal sensory inputs of an ASC Simulation. Here the VR headset suppresses visual awareness of the natural physical environment, by blocking out light other than that which comes from the display, while the noise-isolating features of the headphones perform an equivalent function for sound. By suppressing the natural inputs of the arena space and replacing them with synthetic ones, the simulation immerses the individual in virtual unreality.

'Augmented unreality' constructs a simulation of ASCs using a 'situational' approach in the arena space. Figure 7.6 illustrates this using an AR/MR device such as the Microsoft Hololens, which provides a composite of the synthetic internal input provided by the device, and the natural external input from the physical environment. This allows the device to alter the real surroundings of the user, by enhancing their sense of unreality through synthetic imagery such as visual patterns of hallucination based on Klüver's (1971) form constants.

The two forms of ASC Simulation proposed are illustrative examples only, and need not necessarily be constructed with VR and AR/MR equipment. Forms of virtual unreality could also be constructed using other 'transporting' immersive environments such as fulldomes; augmented unreality, in contrast, could be created with projection mapping and loudspeaker technologies. We may also note that the solitary and social dimensions of the respective technologies will feed back into the affective response of the user, supporting experiences that are more meditative or trance-like respectively.

This section has introduced the concept of 'ASC Simulations': interactive audio-visual systems that represent ASCs with regards to the sensory components of

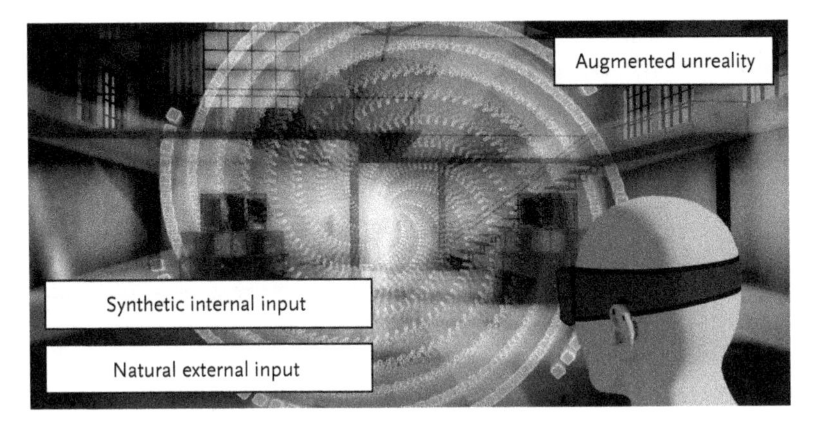

Figure 7.6. Illustration of 'augmented unreality', a specific type of ASC Simulation, in which the user experiences synthetic hallucinations as composites within the real-world 'situation'.

the experience. This concept is not a singular design, but encompasses a variety of fluid possibilities that relay the subjective experience of a host to the user through means of interactive audio-visual technologies, which place him or her in a 'theatre of consciousness'. Among the many possibilities that this concept encompasses, 'virtual unreality' and 'augmented unreality' are two distinct configurations.

* * *

In this chapter we have taken a tour through a variety of interactive video games from the past few decades that are related to ASCs. The development of sound and graphics has enabled video games to become more realistic; however, these advances have also yielded ever-more accurate approaches for the representation of ASCs. Where they are used in games, we find that these representations of ASCs may distort the spatial and kinaesthetic experiences of the player, and may be used as a means to introduce ludic novelty or develop interesting storylines. Most mainstream games that use ASCs do so in ways that are intentionally controversial, comedic, or horrifying, and reflect predominantly negative attitudes towards ASCs within Western culture. However, within the trajectory of games that explore synaesthetic forms, we also find a variety of alternative approaches, where ASCs are seen in a more positive light, and games provide a means to elicit dreamlike, meditative, or psychedelic forms.

Through consideration of these existing works, this chapter has defined the concept of 'ASC Simulations': interactive audio-visual systems that represent ASCs with regards to the sensory components of the experience. As advances in immersive technologies continue, we can expect that these ASC Simulations will provide ever-more accurate and convincing experiences, perhaps even become indistinguishable from reality within the near future. Yet as our discussion has revealed, the design of these simulations may also reflect different sets of values, and thus the reasons why we might create analogues of the 'theatre of consciousness' prompts a variety of ethical concerns. In order to consider these, the final chapter takes a step back to explore connections with the shamanism of old, in order to consider what role the new technoshamans of virtual unreality might have in the not-so-distant future.

CHAPTER 8

Abstractions

The emphasis in house music and rave culture on physiologically compatible rhythms, and this sort of thing, is really the re-discovery of the art of natural magic with sound. That sound, properly understood, especially percussive sound, can actually change neurological states, and large groups of people getting together in the presence of this kind of music are creating a telepathic community, a bonding, that hopefully will be strong enough to carry the vision out into the mainstream of society.

—Terence McKenna, *Re:Evolution*

Upstairs at a building on Old Street (Shoreditch, London) there is a buzz happening as 'alt[ered] state[s] pioneers, tech dreamers, creators, and hackers [transcend] the limitations of perception and reality' at #Hackstock—Immersive Art Without Boundaries (Sci-Fi-London, 2016). Around the room various immersive technologies and biofeedback gadgets are in operation. Over on one side of the room some Samsung Gear VR headsets are actually being handed out from a table. 'We're running out of VR kit', says one of the team responsible for dishing out the gear. 'Get the cardboard ones'. The users with headsets on already are scattered around as if caught in a trance, some adopting distanced stances and expressions or reclining in chairs as they take their first hit of the immersive technology. The headsets are running a selection of 360-degree videos: short demonstrations that throw the user into scenarios involving computer animated space-craft, zombies, or arty live-action films. The atmosphere in the room is electric, and captures the latest upsurge of cyberculture, a scene that has its roots in the techno-utopianism of Terence McKenna and Douglas Rushkoff's *Cyberia* (1994); among the pages of *Mondo 2000* (Rucker, R.U. Sirius and Queen Mu, 1992) and Timothy Leary's *Chaos & Cyber Culture* (1994); and in London, nightclubs like Megatripolis.[1] In the centre of the room a man with a headset and a microphone sits in the middle of a circular table and leads an open discussion with tech experts, start-up entrepreneurs, psychedelic gurus, and curious passers-by. As the microphone is handed back and forth, the discussion evolves through a myriad of topics from raves, psychedelics, and 1960s counter-culture; to 3D printing, holograms, haptic feedback devices, biofeedback, gestural controllers, wearable technologies, and VR headsets.[2] Participants come and go, yet somehow the debate always comes back to issues of ethics and ethos, as the contributors debate the potential uses, benefits, pitfalls, and implications of these technologies for society.

In this final chapter, we consider some of these issues of ethics and ethos with regards to altered states of consciousness (ASCs) in electronic music and audio-visual media, and the concept of 'ASC Simulations'. First, I recapitulate the territory that has been covered, as we recall the journey we have taken from the ayahuasca ceremonies of the Peruvian Amazon to psychedelic rock concerts; from sound system raves to the Athenian electroacoustic concerts; and from avant-garde trance films to meditations on the shores of virtual reality. Through this, we shall see how there are some similarities in the underlying principles of the art and music across these various areas in culture, and that the concept of ASC Simulations finds its basis in traditional shamanic arts. Yet while there is nothing new under the sun, clearly the technologies for creating representations of ASCs have changed, as we have progressed from cave paintings to complex audio-visual hallucinations rendered in 3D computer graphics. Technologies have allowed these simulations to become more accurate, to the point where they may even become indistinguishable from reality within the near future. This raises important questions about how and why they should be used, and for what purposes. While these are questions that must necessarily remain open, towards the end of this chapter I look forwards to consider these possibilities and give some speculative suggestions. Consequently, as *Inner Sound* draws to a close I hope to open new debates and lines of enquiry.

FROM SHAMANISM TO TECHNOSHAMANISM

The journey of *Inner Sound* began with a discussion of William James's (1890) concept of the 'stream of consciousness', which proposed that consciousness is composed of a continuous flow of sensory experiences, thoughts, and emotions. Developing these ideas, we then explored Baars's (1988; 1997) Global Workspace (GW) theory, and saw how various cognitive systems such as attention, memory, and emotion come together to form a 'theatre of consciousness'. With regards to various ASCs such as dreams, hallucinations, and trances, we saw how these may shape consciousness in various ways, such as by turning our attention inwards towards internal sensory inputs, or by producing heightened states of arousal. In addition, the concepts of 'representational' and 'affective' properties of sound were also introduced, allowing us to begin to consider how sound might be used to represent or induce ASCs.

Throughout the book, we then proceeded to explore how artists and musicians have used these properties in order to represent or induce ASCs. Beginning with shamanic traditions, in Chapter 2 we saw how San, Native American, Huichol, Tukano, and Shipibo people have represented internal visionary experiences through visual art. We also saw how music from Haitian Vodou, Tukano, Mazatec, Kiowa, and Mayan traditions invokes a sense of the numinous, through sonic representations of spirits. These practices not only represent visionary experiences in a passive or detached manner, but also establish their efficacy, and may shape the experience of ASCs, or induce states of trance, such as through the use of rhythmic percussion. Many of these examples reflect practices that have been established through traditions that are thousands of years old, and thus we find that the representation of ASCs is ancient, and may even be one of the original functions of art and music.

Progressing into the world of rock 'n' roll music, we found that driving percussion, blues melodies, and distortion effects provide highly energetic properties. These forms are not so far removed from those of Vodou trances, and one might readily draw comparisons between the sexualized dances of Ghede and the rock 'n' roll sermons of Little Richard. Yet where Vodou drumming patterns were associated with different spirits, rock 'n' roll music framed these energetic properties with secular meanings related to the concerns of youth culture. As I demonstrated in Chapter 3, these meanings were elicited not only through lyrics but also through sound with the aid of analogue electronics. Thus, we saw how reverb was used to conjure illusory impressions of coastal bliss; sampled engine noises communicated the speed and excitement of teenage hot-rod culture; warped effects and time-distortions reflected psychedelic counter-culture; and electronic sounds suggested science fiction voyages into outer or inner space, in space rock and space jazz. Notably in the case of psychedelic rock, audio technologies were even used to represent 'internal' experiences of hallucination, drawing direct comparison with ancient shamanic traditions.

While many productions in psychedelic rock accomplished more 'out there' sounds in the studio than could be achieved on stage, the sound system cultures we examined in Chapter 4 overcame this problem by using loudspeakers and turntables as the primary tools of dissemination. Through the sound system, dub-reggae brought the sonic capabilities of the studio to the forefront in situations of communal dance, harnessing their full potential to elicit various forms of conceptual meaning that constructed empowering visions of African utopia. As we saw in this chapter, these approaches would later be developed in various forms of electronic dance music, including the acid house, Detroit techno, UK rave, and global psytrance scenes. For each of these, sampled materials and sound design techniques allowed the music to provide various conceptual meanings, ranging from hedonistic sexuality to Afrofuturism and technoshamanism. These allowed the relentless energy of electronic drum machines and sampled breakbeats to become framed by conceptual meaning, leading to experiential forms of knowledge or *gnosis*. This *gnosis* encompassed the ethos of the music, and was closely related to what St. John (2009) and Henriques (2011) have referred to as 'the vibe'. Although not all of these musical forms represent drug experiences, in some areas such as psy-trance, experiences of hallucination are sometimes seen in quasi-religious terms, and here we find the form of the music incorporates features that reflect hallucinations in accordance.

Moving on to consider electroacoustic music in Chapter 5, we were able to reflect on an alternative approach, where multi-speaker diffusion systems were being used to construct unreal journeys. In such cases, sound is used to construct imaginary soundscapes through dreamlike, hallucinatory, or shamanic worlds. Foregoing the dancefloor sensibilities and energetic priorities of electronic dance music, these electroacoustic works offer a more meditative and introspective listening experience. As the listener focuses his or her attention in dimly lit concert halls, the associative properties of sound allow the listener to undergo voyages into rich dreamlike and hallucinatory sound worlds rendered in exquisite spatial detail. In accordance with the ethos of soundscape composition, these 'imaginary soundscapes' prompt us to reflect on internal experiences of sound. By considering these approaches and those areas visited previously, I proposed a conceptual model that articulated a range of possible approaches for creating work related to ASCs, according to several 'representational' and 'affective' dimensions. This model not only showed how music may represent ASCs, but also suggested that affective properties may afford states of high or low arousal for the listener, and may therefore provide a form of ASC.

Expanding our discussion into the realm of audio-visual media in Chapter 6, we used the conceptual model as a tool to consider avant-garde films, feature films, and works of expanded cinema that are related to ASCs. While pioneering surrealist and trance films initially used visual techniques such as montage to represent dreams or hallucinations, gradually sound was introduced in order to provide subjective, diegetic representations of auditory hallucinations. By the 1990s feature films were able to utilize sophisticated computer graphics and digital audio techniques in order to render hallucination sequences with improved levels of accuracy, so that they began to resemble what one might actually see or hear during an ASC. These narrative films explored various themes ranging from dreams and the unconscious, to counter-culture narratives and cautionary tales of drug-use. Meanwhile, within the alternative trajectory of expanded cinema, visual music films, psychedelic lightshows, and VJ performances provided progressive levels of integration between sound and image using sound-to-image computer techniques. Here these works often reinforced the psychedelic themes of the counter-culture by representing visual patterns of hallucination such as the 'form constants' (Klüver, 1971). Through the design of these works, we also saw further examples that afford meditative or trance-like responses, and may 'transport' their audience into synthetic worlds, or form audio-visual composites within the 'situation' of the arena space.

These trends were also mirrored in the video games culture that was explored in Chapter 7. While improvements in sound and graphics enabled games to provide higher levels of realism, these technologies were also used to depict ASCs with improved levels of detail and accuracy. In this chapter we explored issues of interactivity, and saw how video games may involve the player through various kinaesthetic, ludic, and narrative mechanisms, providing immersive representations of ASCs. Here ASCs are often used to reflect psychotic states, as a means to enrich storylines involving psychological horror, or may be provided simply for comic amusement or exoticism. Mirroring the trajectory that extended from expanded cinema in the previous chapter, we also observed various examples of video games that move beyond traditional ludic notions of play, in order to provide synaesthetic experiences that reflect dreamlike, meditative, or hallucinatory states. Where these are associated with rave culture, they express similar values through their design, and in some cases may be used in pre- or post-clubbing situations. Many of the examples explored in this chapter point towards the concept of 'ASC Simulations': interactive systems that represent the sensory experience of ASCs within the 'theatre of consciousness'. Here I defined this concept not as a singular approach, but as a range of possibilities, of which 'virtual unreality' and 'augmented unreality' are two significant configurations. As the trend towards ever-more convincing illusory sounds and graphics continues with the aid of new immersive technologies and biofeedback, we can expect the gap between the user and these ASC Simulations to grow smaller, to the point where they may even become indistinguishable from reality in the near future.

While the technologies may have changed, one of the fascinating features to emerge from this journey is that many of the underlying principles of ASC Simulations are not so different from those found in shamanic art and music. For example, the dimensional axes of the conceptual model can readily be applied to many of the shamanic examples explored in Chapter 2. In shamanic art, we find representations of 'internal' and 'external' inputs, presented using a variety of modes of representation. Indeed, we may recall that the Shipibo *ronin quene* designs were even conceived based on shamanic songs, and find direct correspondence with the sound-to-image techniques of modern VJ performances. We also find the use of rhythmic properties to manipulate arousal levels, sometimes as a complement to the use of intoxicating substances; thus the percussive stomping and pan-pipes of Tukano chicha gatherings are not so different from the electronic throb of Scandinavian forest trance parties. This comparison became evident to me when I recently attended an underground forest trance party along the coast of the Northern Jutland of Denmark. As revellers exchanged their chillums and danced beneath the full moon, the scene immediately recalled the passing of ceremonial leaf-bound cigars at the party described in Donald Tayler's (1972) account of a Makuna-Tukano party. While such parties could be viewed as making 'situational' use of the arena space, in the darkened caves of Upper Palaeolithic rituals one imagines that the experience may have been one of 'transportation'. Here the use of darkness to shut out external sensory inputs may have provided a means through which to manipulate the senses, in order to heighten immersion into visionary experiences of the underworld. This may have provided an early form of virtual unreality, which today we achieve through darkened warehouses, expansive full-domes, and VR headsets, all of which shut out natural external inputs in order to induce synthetic illusory experiences of ASC.

SONIC MYTHOLOGIES

Throughout *Inner Sound* I have utilized the concepts of 'representational' and 'affective' properties to describe the material forms of electronic music and audio-visual media. These concepts are not new, since they find their basis in the 'mimesis' and 'catharsis' of Aristotle, and have probably been known long before this through their functional use in music. In this book I have argued that these properties are not separate, but related, and that representational properties allow affective responses to music to become framed by conceptual meaning. This combination leads to experiential forms of knowledge or *gnosis*. *Gnosis* can be understood as multi-modal, engaging cognitive, physiological, and behavioural systems.

Gnosis may encompass a particular ethos, or mythological vision. For example, in Chapter 2 we saw how shamanic visual arts often depict visionary experiences, while musical practices symbolically represent spirits. These representations are related to the animist mythologies of the respective cultures, which promote existence in harmonic balance with nature. They therefore produce experiences of *gnosis* that are aligned with these beliefs. This is perhaps best illustrated through the Haitian Vodou trances, where we find that percussive rhythms produce experiences of heightened arousal, while also representing spirits, thereby producing powerful forms of *gnosis* that reinforce the animist belief system.

Such processes are instructive when we consider the function of modern forms of electronic music and audio-visual media in society. In each case the representational properties elicit a different ethos that is appealing for their audience. For instance, in Chapter 3 we saw how rock 'n' roll, surf rock, and hot-rod music expressed an ethos of exuberant teenage freedom through speed, cars, and sex. With each permutation of rock 'n' roll music, adjustments were made to this conceptual vision. Psychedelic rock introduced a 'man-meets-cosmos' discourse, which called for audiences to revaluate their ways of living and spirituality, while space-rock added a further adaptation to this to construct visions that interrogated where space race technologies might lead humanity in the future. Each of these themes expresses a different kind of mythology that is appealing for their audience, which frames energetic experiences of dance and produces a different kind of *gnosis*.

Crucially, as I have emphasized throughout *Inner Sound*, these representational properties are provided not only through lyrics but also through sound design. This becomes especially significant as we consider the various permutations of sound system culture explored in Chapter 4, which de-emphasize lyrics and bring studio production and sampling techniques to the forefront in situations of communal dance. For example, in dub-reggae the use of echo and reverb are essential as means to elicit visions of African utopia. Here in the absence of lyrics, the music continues to deliver a message of righteous exultation in the face of oppression, which is empowering for its audiences. Along similar lines, Detroit techno uses high-tech electronic sounds to express an ethos of technological empowerment in the face of *Future Shock* (Toffler, 1970). In each case, the sonic representations elicit a different ethos, leading to forms of *gnosis* that the audience may find appealing. Many post-millennial forms of sound-system music such as dubstep[3] (e.g. Kode9 and The Spaceape, *Memories of The Future*, 2006) extend and adapt Afrofuturist mythologies such as these, creating further permutations that we could almost trace genealogically.

Among those areas of music and culture explored in *Inner Sound*, we found several that explicitly reference psychedelic states, through sounds and visual projections that are suggestive of perceptual distortions and hallucinations. Where we find such materials, it is usually because the music expresses a view of ASCs that is integral to the ethos of the culture. For instance, in 1960s counter-culture we saw how psychedelic experiences were considered as a means to break previous traditional thought structures, following the 'turn on, tune in, drop out' message of Timothy Leary. Later, in the technoshamanic rave and psytrance culture that descends from this, via the hippy parties of Goa, the psychedelic experience is seen in similarly positive terms. Following the philosophies of key figures such as Terence McKenna, here psychedelic experiences and electronic dance music are seen as complementary spiritual technologies that reconnect members of the 'global village' (McLuhan and Fiore, 1968) with the 'Gaian mind'. According to this viewpoint, such experiences provide a means to advance consciousness and gain greater awareness of issues such as global ecological crises.

What our discussion here reveals, is that music can elicit mythological visions through sound, which provide forms of *gnosis* that align the ethos of the audience. These may be religious, quasi-religious, or secular. As I have noted, experiences of *gnosis* may encompass heightened emotional states that move consciousness away from a 'normal' baseline (following Fischer's 'cartography of ecstatic and meditative states', 1971), and thus they can be thought of as a unique form of ASC, which may or may not be enhanced through the use of intoxicating substances. Such experiences could be considered 'shamanic', in that they involve the production of ASCs as a means to facilitate a form of symbolic manipulation, which aligns the ethos and intentions of the cultural group, remaking their understanding of the world. However, it is by no means essential for the music and cultural artefacts to incorporate representations of ASCs or psychedelic drugs to produce powerful experiences of *gnosis*; where these representations do occur, it is simply because the ethos of the culture places some special significance upon them.

APPLICATIONS OF ASC SIMULATIONS

These considerations are also applicable to the concept of ASC Simulations, since the way in which ASCs are portrayed may express a particular ethos. ASC Simulations also generate special ethical concerns, since as they continue to grow in sophistication and accuracy, they may provide powerful new forms of experience. In replicating the experience of ASCs, they have the potential to induce a range of effects from the pleasurable to the truly horrific, and therefore we should consider carefully how they might be used in positive ways. With this in mind, in this section we will now look forwards to consider the technologies of the future, as I outline several possible practical applications of ASC Simulations.

One of the most obvious areas where we may expect to see ASC Simulations is to provide states of dreaming, psychosis, or psychological horror within video games. Indeed, this seems to be the most common area within which we find them already, and the popularity of genres such as the psychological horror game suggests that we will see many more of these titles in the future, which will include increasingly accurate depictions of hallucinations. Typically, these sequences provide a means through which to enhance the narrative of the game, and may also provide ludic elements that enrich the experience. In VR these games may provide genuinely terrifying moments, and their designers will need to balance these appropriately to provide experiences that audiences ultimately find enjoyable. Equally, when dealing with schizophrenia and states of psychosis, we might hope to see such conditions portrayed with respect, in order to avoid perpetuating negative stereotypes that could ultimately be harmful to those who experience these conditions. If such materials are treated appropriately, there is no reason why ASC Simulations in this context could not provide a route towards generating interesting gothic storylines, perhaps looking back towards authors such as Samuel Taylor Coleridge (e.g. 'The Rime of the Ancient Mariner', 1798), Edgar Allan Poe, or H.P. Lovecraft for inspiration.

Another area where we are likely to see more ASC Simulations is within synaesthetic video games and immersive audio-visual artworks. These simulations will provide psychedelic experiences of sound-to-image synaesthesia that imitate the function of listening to music under the influence of drugs such as LSD. Within the design of these simulations, there is some scope to adapt the representations in order to reflect different kinds of mythological visions. These may reflect the themes that are already present within musical culture; hence following the example of fulldome works such as *Samskara* (Android Jones and 360art, 2015–2016), we may see more works that provide immersive psychedelic experiences that explore spiritual or ecological themes. Conversely, following games such as *Gnosis* (Fathomable, 2016), we may also find works that deliver darker voyages closer to the virtual reality hallucinations of William Gibson's novels (e.g. *Neuromancer*, 1984) that interrogate ideas of machine consciousness, post-humanism, and the ASCs of artificial intelligences.

With the recent resurgence of VR, there has been an explosion of immersive games that offer experiences of meditation or relaxation. Following this trend, we may see more ASC Simulations that provide different forms of meditation in the future. As explored in *Deep VR* (Harris and Smit, 2016), these may benefit from biofeedback technologies, which allow the system to recognize the breathing patterns and attention of the user, providing improved capabilities for training the user and inducing deeper states of meditation. Of course, more research will be needed to develop these systems and prove their efficacy, but in principal these simulations have therapeutic applications as a means to facilitate pain-management, or reduce stress and anxiety.

Along similar lines, ASC Simulations may also be used for therapeutic purposes to assist people who suffer from psychoses or schizophrenia. For instance, there is already work being done in which virtual avatars are used to simulate experiences of auditory hallucination in schizophrenia (Craig et al., 2015). By creating synthetic hallucinations, this research aims to provide better assistance for schizophrenics to help them manage such experiences. It is interesting to consider these therapies in terms of Hobson's (2009) argument that dreaming provides a form of 'virtual reality pattern generator', which allows unborn children to develop their conscious mechanisms before leaving the womb. If we follow the view that dreams provide 'dry runs' of experiences that we may encounter in the real world in order to prepare us for them, then conversely ASC Simulations might also allow us to generate synthetic dreams that fulfil a similar purpose.

Besides treating such conditions, ASC Simulations could also be useful as communicative tools that foster improved awareness of these states within society. Along similar lines, we have already begun to see the use of movies such as the *Autism TMI Virtual Reality Experience* (Happy Finish, 2016), as a means to increase awareness of subjective experiences of autism. In such cases VR allows another person to gain an impression of the subjective experience of another, perhaps leading to an improved sense of empathy.[4] In a similar mould, ASC Simulations could provide a means through which to increase awareness of conditions such as schizophrenia.

This last application is perhaps one of the most interesting, since it implies the use of ASC Simulations as a new form of communication, which allows us to perceive the subjective experiences of others. Such systems could allow us not only to experience what it is like to be in the same situation as another person, but to actually perceive what their subjective experience is like. In an increasingly digital society where communication occurs over computer networks, such tools could provide a means through which to foster more meaningful interactions. This imperative could be considered in terms of McLuhan's (1964) view of communication technologies as extensions of the human nervous system, or as an expansion of Picard's (1997) discussion of computer systems that respond to or exhibit human emotions.[5] Yet beyond this, they could also provide us with unprecedented insights into the human mind. Imagine if you will, what we might learn if we could record our dreams, and share them with each other. The implications are perhaps as terrifying as they are fantastic, as has been explored in numerous works of science fiction that contemplate such technologies.[6] Yet what has existed before only in fantasy could soon become reality.

DECOMPRESSION

Through the course of *Inner Sound* I have sought to illuminate practices in twentieth-century electronic music and audio-visual media, which have considerable history as we look backwards towards the art and music produced in the past of our species. Many of the areas of culture explored herein have too often been overlooked or ignored in academic research, with notable exceptions found among the work of those authors who I have referred to. Even so, there has been a recent trend towards considering the internal experience of sound and music, as well as a renewed interest in research exploring altered states of consciousness, and I hope that *Inner Sound* will provide a valuable contribution to this field.

In particular, *Inner Sound* has drawn connections between a range of electronic music and audio-visual media, and provided a new conceptual model that allows us to consider how the material design of these works may represent or induce ASCs. This conceptual model may be useful to artists, composers, and programmers for the creation of new work, while also providing analysts with a tool for examining other existing works. Throughout the book I have also endeavoured to explore how these cultural artefacts may communicate a particular ethos, which is important as we seek to understand the place and function of these works within culture and society. Such issues are especially significant when we consider the concept of ASC Simulations that I have defined here, as in the future these may provide powerful experiences, and we should consider carefully how and why they might be used.

Finally, while *Inner Sound* may have provided some answers, I also hope that it will have provoked yet more questions that others will seek to explore through both creative work and theoretical discourses. For instance, although my main focus here has been on works that are explicitly related to ASCs, aspects of my discussion could be applied much more broadly to other forms of music. In the future then, we might hope to see further work that illuminates the connections between sound design and ethos, for other music genres and artefacts that I have not explored here. Further scientific research must also be undertaken to explore how the materials properties of these works lead to corresponding responses, and yield experiential forms of knowledge that I have referred to here as *gnosis*. Meanwhile, within the area of ASC Simulations, technical advances in sound, graphics, interactivity, and biofeedback are needed, which may ultimately allow us to abstract from the theatre of consciousness and bring its contents into the digital domain.[7] In doing so we may begin to unlock the secrets of human consciousness, and even transcend their boundaries through *inner sound*.

NOTES

INTRODUCTION

1. Franciscan friar Bernardino de Sahagún (1499–1590a, p.173; 1499–1590b, p.129) described the Aztec use of peyote in the sixteenth century. For a further discussion of this and other early accounts of peyote use among the Aztecs, see Schaefer (1996, p.141).
2. 'Phosphenes' are visual experiences of light that are caused by physical stimulation, such as may occur when applying pressure to the eyeball, or due to a change in blood pressure. These can be differentiated from form constants, which are generated within the brain.
3. The theory has sparked an extensive debate spanning several decades. For further discussion see Lewis-Williams (2007), Dowson (2007), and Luke (2010).
4. For example, Nishimoto et al. (2011) have used blood oxygen level-dependent (BOLD) signals measured via functional magnetic resonance imaging (fMRI: a neuroimaging technique), in order to measure brain activity evoked by movies. By registering patterns of activity evoked by the movies, the researchers were able to devise a decoding system that predicts the visual stimuli a person is seeing based on their brain activity.
5. This is the estimate provided in Schultes, Hofmann, and Rätsch (1996, p.182). For further information on pituri, see also Ratsch, Steadman, and Bogossian (2010).
6. For example, Sherratt (1991) discusses the evidence for ritual opium and cannabis use in Neolithic Europe. In particular, he suggests that pottery artefacts such as bowl-like containers that carry traces of burning may have been used for the purposes of ritual intoxication.
7. The contents of soma have been the subject of much debate. For example, Wasson (1968) proposed that soma was the *Amanita muscaria* mushroom; Flattery and Schwartz (1989) proposed it was *Paganum harmala* (Syrian rue); McKenna (1992, p.120) argued for *Psilocybe cubensis* mushrooms; and Sherratt (1991, pp.29–30) indicated an infusion of various plant products.
8. For further information on these 'mushroom stones' and their suggested connection with mushroom rituals, see Wasson and Wasson (1957, pp.274–286), Borhegyi (1961), and Lowy (1971).
9. For an overview of the hexing herbs used in witchcraft, see Schultes, Hofmann, and Rätsch (1996, pp.86–91).
10. The term 'entheogen' refers to the spiritual or religious use of psychoactive plants.
11. In their history of opium, Goldberg and Latimer (2014) discuss changing attitudes towards the use of opium as a medicine and recreational substance. Significant factors they identify include trade and political interests, and the increased potency and addictive properties of morphine and heroin.

12. For further discussion, see also Ott's (1976, pp.83–102) comments on hallucinogens; and Sherratt's (1995) views on how alcohol and other intoxicating substances have fallen in and out of favour in different regions and cultural traditions throughout history.
13. Other possible examples include: the Megalithic markings seen at the Er Lannic and Gavrini's sites, which Patton (1990) has argued are similarly based on entoptic phenomena; the mushroom-like figures found on bronze razors in Scandinavia (Kaplan, 1975); and the mushroom-figures found in the rock art of the Tassili n'Ajjar plateau in Africa, as documented in Lajoux (1963) and discussed with regards to their ASC interpretation in McKenna (1992, pp.70–73).
14. In this context, 'cyberculture' describes the culture of networked computers and associated technologies such as human-computer interfaces.
15. Though the original artefacts are often preferable, many of the musical examples discussed can be found using digital music services such as iTunes, Spotify, or Bandcamp. For some of the harder-to-find field recordings of shamanic music discussed in Chapter 2, the Smithsonian Folkways website (http://www.folkways.si.edu/) and the British Library Sound Archive (http://sounds.bl.uk/) are also invaluable resources. Many of the electroacoustic compositions discussed in Chapter 5 can be heard using Electrothèque (http://electrotheque.com/). Video examples can be viewed using Netflix, Amazon Video, YouTube, or Vimeo. Video games can be accessed using Steam or the PlayStation Network.
16. The 'Gaia hypothesis' as discussed by Lovelock (1979) suggests that the earth functions as a global self-regulating system in order to sustain life.

CHAPTER 1

1. This conceptual model was also later expanded to include a temporary store of multimodal information: 'the episodic buffer'; see Baddeley (2000).
2. The order in which these processes occur has been a source of debate; for a comparison of theories see Rosenzweig et al. (1999, p.412).
3. For a further discussion of the various means through which ASCs can be produced, see also Huxley (1954–1956) and Blackmore (2003, pp.308–309).
4. Strassman's (2001) studies focused on the synthetic form of DMT, which onsets rapidly and lasts for around 15 minutes. During peaks of intensity, synthetic DMT can cause 'total hallucinations', during which the participant perceives vivid hallucinations, and may be completely unaware of their external environment.
5. Neher (1961; 1962) carried out experiments to explore his hypothesis that trance states are produced through 'audio driving' effects of rhythms, which cause brainwaves to synchronize with the tempo of the music. For a further discussion see Chapter 2, p.50.
6. For example, Carl Jung considered that dreams were an important expression of the unconscious. According to his view, if the unconscious was not properly managed, it could impact negatively on society, and hence methods of psychoanalysis were necessary as a means to address this by giving individuals an improved connection with dreams and the unconscious (see Jung, 1978).
7. Not everyone follows these definitions of ecstasy and trance. For example, Penman and Becker (2009) prefer to use 'ecstasy' and 'trance' interchangeably, adapting Rouget's (1985) model so that experiences of still, silent introspection are classed as 'meditation'.
8. The capability of sound for referencing non-musical properties is related to Emmerson's (1986) 'mimetic discourse', which will also be explored in more detail in Chapter 5 p.98.
9. Smalley's (1986) concept of 'spectromorphology' considers sounds in terms of their constituent frequency spectrum and how this is shaped in time.

10. This method of representation may be more accurately described as a presentation of comparable stimuli to that which was experienced in the original scenario. The image will provide a similar stimulus to that provided by the original object. However, since it communicates significant aspects of first-person perspective, it will be sufficient for the purpose of 'representation' discussed here.
11. Binaural recording is a sound recording technique, where two microphones are used to record the sounds that would be heard through a pair of ears in a given situation. The resulting 'binaural recordings' are listened to using headphones, and provide a realistic spatial impression for the listener.

CHAPTER 2

1. Criticisms of Eliade's (1964) study typically discuss the limitations that arise due to overgeneralization; its exclusive basis in literary resources (rather than fieldwork); and failure to recognize the fluid boundaries between magic and religion (e.g. Harvey, 2003, pp.7–8). For our purposes here it is also notable that Eliade de-emphasizes the role of hallucinogenic plants in shamanism, in conflict with subsequent surveys such as Furst (1976) that show their pervasive use, especially in the Americas.
2. For further discussion of cultural continuity and change in San culture, see Barnard (2007, pp.4–5).
3. Examples of San rock art are distributed across a variety of sites in South Africa. Digital photographs are available via The African Rock Art Digital Archive (http://www.sarada.co.za/).
4. Soloman (2013) has argued that Lewis-Williams's theories are undermined by a lack of distinction between San (/Xam) and Kalahari San traditions.
5. A study by McLeary, Sypherd, and Walkington (1960) suggested that besides its shamanic function, peyote may provide antibiotic activity through its chemical makeup.
6. For reproductions and discussion of Huichol art and textiles, see Berrin (1978).
7. For further discussion of ASCs and psychedelic themes in visual art and fine art, see Grunenberg (2005), Rubin (2010), and Johnson (2011).
8. For a review of musical practices across different traditions, see Dobkin de Rios and Katz (1975, pp.74–75).
9. For example, Moser has discussed the transformative effects of the international cocaine trade on Tukano culture (sleeve notes of *Music of the Tukano and Cuna Peoples of Colombia*, 1987), while María Sabina claimed that her shamanism lost its efficacy as a direct consequence of contact with outsiders (Estrada, 1981).
10. Deren's recordings were first released on the out-of-print 10″ vinyl *Voices of Haiti* (1953), and documented in her (1953) book. Various other recordings of Haitian Vodou music and drumming are also available, such as the currently in-print Folkways *Music of Haiti Vols 1–3* (Various Artists, 1950, 1951, 1952) series.
11. Wilcken's (1992, pp.52–53) discussion of the *kase* is supported by the example 'Yanvalou' on the accompanying CD with Frisner Augustin, *The Drums of Vodou* (1994).
12. Brian Moser and Donald Tayler's recordings were also re-mastered for the single LP *Music of the Tukano and Cuna Peoples of Colombia* (1987), and digital versions of the original source tapes are available in the British Library Sound Archive (1960–1961). For further details of the expedition and the sound recordings, see Tayler's extensive accompanying notes for *The Music of Some Indian Tribes of Colombia* (1972); Moser and Tayler's book *The Cocaine Eaters* (1965); and their interview with Landau (2010).
13. The audio referencing system used here is preserved from the original recordings and notes (Tayler, 1972). MC2.A.4d indicates the second record, side A, fourth band, fourth item within the band.

14. *Salvia divinorum* is a psychoactive plant, which in a ritual context is usually chewed or ground, mixed with water, and strained, see Schultes (1972, pp.22–24).
15. It is also of note that the ritual captured on *María Sabina and her Mazatec Mushroom Velada* (1974) is reported to involve successful contact with the mushroom spirits. In Sabina's account this is not the case for the one featured on the María Sabina Folkways LP (liner notes of *Mushroom Ceremony of the Mazatec Indians of Mexico*, 1957).
16. The referencing system here indicates excerpts on cassette tapes. C1.A.2 indicates the first cassette, side A, second band.
17. As with Native American peyote shamanism, the Mazatec are known to incorporate symbols of Christianity; see La Barre (2011, pp.292–294).
18. For a discussion of the Tambaran cult among the Ilahita Arapesh of Papua New Guinea, see Tuzin (1980).
19. A 'bullroarer' is a musical instrument consisting of an aerofoil attached to a cord. When swung in a circular motion, it producers a characteristic vibrato sound.
20. Neher's (1961; 1962) studies were based upon similar work in 'photic driving': a known effect in which repeating flashes of light cause changes to brain waves (as measured using electroencephalography), and can induce increased visual imagery and changes in mood (for example, see Gizycki et al., 1998). As Fachner (2011) comments, rhythmic entrainment has been shown in the laboratory; however, the precise effect described by Neher in which brain waves become sychronized with musical bpms (beats per minute) would require further scientific evidence.
21. Peak experiences are 'intense positive affective states in response to music' (Whaley, Sloboda, and Gabrielsson, 2008). The authors describe these states as having 'powerful, valued [and] lasting effects', including the potential for 'transcendent, transformational [or], even spiritual' states. They suggest that this capability may be among the reasons why music is used in ritual contexts, including the meditative or ecstatic states discussed by Becker (2001).

CHAPTER 3

1. 'Shepard tones' are superimposed rising tones that create the illusion of a perpetually rising tone.
2. For a historical account of the sound recording from Edison to digital multi-tracking, see Milner (2009).
3. A technical discussion of analogue and digital audio technologies is available in Rumsey and McCormick (2009).
4. For a further critical discussion of 'acousmatic listening' and the associated Pythagorean myth, see Kane (2014b).
5. Milner (2009, pp.129–182) discusses trends in popular music regarding the use of artificial reverberation to provide 'presence' or authenticity. The role of architectural acoustics in dampening sound is also explored in Thompson (2002).
6. For a discussion of the acoustic properties and architecture of sites of spiritual significance, see also Eneix (2016).
7. In audio engineering, 'clipping' is the term used to describe signals that are over-amplified to the point where the peaks of the waveform exceed the dynamic range of the equipment, causing the peak to become distorted (for more details, see Rumsey and McCormick, 2009, p.141).
8. There are some direct connections between surf groups and psychedelic groups. For example, Frank Zappa created surf rock in the early 1960s before creating psychedelic records with The Mothers of Invention, such as *Freak Out!* (1966). Similarly, Merrell Fankhauser was in surf group The Impacts, and later recorded psychedelic music as Fapardokly (1966).

9. Electronic tremolo produces a vibrato effect by varying signal amplitude over time.
10. To create 'oil can echo reverb', an oil-filled can is rotated by an electric motor (Thompson, 1997, p.67; see also Teagle and Sprung, 1995, p.170).
11. For a further discussion of the way music can construct fantasies and ideas of personhood that are appealing for adolescent listeners see Frith (1987) and Shepherd and Giles-David (1991).
12. The Byrds' *Eight Miles High* (1966) was banned from radio shortly after it was released, due to the perceived drug references. The band denied these, claiming the song was about an aeroplane trip to London, though years later commented that it could also be interpreted as a drug song (Rogan, 2001, pp.152–164).
13. A 'rotary effect' is a type of audio effects process created using a rotating speaker or baffle, or electronic simulation of this.
14. Tommy Hall discusses the 'electric jug' instrument and the inspiration of LSD in Trybyszewski's (2004) interview.
15. Although effects processes may be less widely used in psychedelic folk, Leech (2010) notes their use on some records, such as Linda Perhacs's *Parallelograms* (1970). As Turner (2008) discusses, the use of technology can also be seen as a means to empower naturalistic communities such as hippy farming projects, and is therefore not necessarily antithetical to the ecological imperatives present in the psychedelic movement.
16. A studio version of 'Sonic Attack' was also later featured on Hawkwind's *Sonic Attack* (1981).
17. The impact of the Cold War threat of nuclear attack on popular culture is discussed by Sontag (1965), Nuttall (1968), and can be heard in other examples of pop music from the era, such as Black Sabbath's 'Electric Funeral' (on *Paranoid*, 1970).
18. For a discussion of Sun Ra's music in relation to racial issues in the USA, see Szwed (2000).
19. The term 'Afrofuturism' was first coined in Dery (1994). For a further discussion of Afrofuturism across a range of media, see the edited volume *The Black Imagination: Science Fiction, Futurism, and the Speculative* (Jackson and Moody-Freeman, 2011).

CHAPTER 4

1. Henriques (2011, p.23) argues that the sound system performance is not a mere recreation of a musical performance, but a 're-presentation'; this term emphasizes the newness and primacy of the music when realized on a well-tuned sound system.
2. St. John's (2009, pp.146–155) discussion of 'the vibe' draws upon Victor Turner's (1982, p.48) concept of spontaneous communitas, which occur in liminal situations and provide a 'flash of mutual understanding on the existential level, and a "gut" understanding of synchronicity'. In more recent work St. John (2012, pp.327–328) has discussed this concept further, arguing that psy-trance is a 'culture of liminality'.
3. For further discussion of the transcendental capabilities afforded by representational properties in music see also Kane (2014c) and Weheliye (2005).
4. Pan-Africanism is the movement discussed by Marcus Garvey and others that encourages unity between people of African descent across the world. Rastafarianism is a related system of beliefs that venerates Haile Selassie I.
5. These mimetic properties are also discussed by Veal (2007, pp.83–84), who draws comparisons with psychedelic rock music. Veal refers to the 'psychedelic coding' of dub music, whereby the music externalizes typical aspects of THC intoxication such as changes to the perception of movement, spatiality, and time.
6. As Katz (2006) discusses, Perry's personas include the Upsetter, the Super Ape, Pipecock Jackson, and others. These reflect visions of Africa, creation, apocalypse, the forces of

nature, and Perry's interest in film and TV such as Clint Eastwood's Western characters (e.g. as The Upsetters, *Clint Eastwood*, 1970); the movie *The French Connection* (Friedkin, 1971) (*French Connection*, 1972); and martial arts films such as Bruce Lee's *Enter the Dragon* (Clouse, 1973) (*Kung Fu Meets the Dragon*, 1975).

7. Nyahbinghi is a form of traditional drumming associated with Rastfarianism.
8. For example, Katz (2006, p.77), Veal (2007, p.142), and Davis (2010) are among those who have discussed the influence of magic, animism, and spiritual belief in Perry's music.
9. Pocomania is a Jamaican folk religion involving spirit possession. Perry also grew up around traditions of Ettu, Pentecostal, and Revival Zion churches in which spirit possession occurred (Katz, 2006, pp.67–68).
10. At this time this motif is prevalent on Scientist's records, in which he triumphs with Prince Jammy 'a long time ago in a galaxy far, far away' (*Scientist and Prince Jammy Strike Back!*, 1982); over supernatural forces (*Scientist Rids the World of the Curse of The Evil Vampires*, 1981); video game characters (*Scientist Encounters Pacman*, 1982); and even defeats the world's football teams through dub (*Scientist Wins the World Cup*, 1982). Indeed Prince Jammy and Scientist were protégés of King Tubby who worked together and went head-to-head on *Scientist vs. Prince Jammy: Big Showdown* (1980), and *Prince Jammy Destroys the Invaders*... can be seen as an answer to *Scientist Meets the Space Invaders* (1981).
11. Veal's (2007) argument is ambiguous not least because he does not clearly define what is meant by 'pseudo-possession', and seems to conflate ecstasy/ecstatic contemplation with trance/spirit possession (e.g. use of the phrase 'ecstasy of possession', p.201). Although the term 'ecstasy' is commonly used as a synonym for trance, in Rouget's (1985) definition 'ecstasy' and 'trance' are opposite terms that reflect the poles of low and high arousal on Fischer's (1971) continuum (see Chapter 1 pp.24–25; Penman and Becker, 2009).
12. Marijuana is used in Rastafarian culture as a ritual sacrament and is more widely associated with reggae culture. However, in considering the influence of the drug in dub-reggae, it should be acknowledged that some figures such as King Tubby were opposed to its use in the studio, while others including Scientist (King Tubby's protégé) and Lee 'Scratch' Perry have commented on the way marijuana changed their perception of sound (Veal, 2007, p.82; Katz, 2006).
13. 'Jack' refers to the dominant dance style of 'jacking' that was popular in the Chicago house scene, which involves jerky body movements (Reynolds, 2008, pp.20–21).
14. The gospel association permeates a great deal of blues music in general, and was explored in Reginald D. Hunter's (2015) *Songs of the South* TV documentary exploring the music of the Southern states of America. Rock 'n' roll singer Little Richard is a notable example whose performances resemble religious sermons. For an example, see his live versions of 'Get Down with It' and 'Whole Lotta Shakin' Goin' On' on *Little Richard's Greatest Hits* (1971), during which Richard invites his audience to 'testify', and describes his music as 'the healing music'. Little Richard also recorded gospel and worked as a preacher at points during his career.
15. 'Acid house' is a variation of Chicago house that utilizes the sounds of the Roland TB-303 Bass Line Synthesizer.
16. Detroit techno can be seen as part of the Afrofuturist canon, and as an empowering response to Detroit as a technological city that suffered economic problems following the decline of the auto industry (Bredow, 2006).
17. As discussed by Katz (2010, pp.126–127), in early hip-hop culture these breakbeat sections were looped by fading between two copies of the same record on different turntables. In the 1980s the digital sampler enabled the convenient looping of breakbeats: a technique that was used extensively in hip-hop and electronic dance music genres such as drum & bass. Popular examples include the 'amen' breakbeat, which was taken from The

Winstons' 'Amen Brother', a B-side on the 7″ single *Color Him Father* (1969); the 'funky drummer', from James Brown's (1970) song of the same title; and the 'think break' from Lyn Collins's 'Think (About It)' (1972). The 'amen' break was one of the most widely sampled breakbeats, as discussed in Nate Harrison's video documentary *Can I Get an Amen?* (2004).

18. For a further discussion of reggae and dancehall influences in UK rave music see also Collin (1998; p.72) and Veal (2007, pp.220–260). Collin (1998, p.246) also discusses these influences in the music of Shut Up and Dance.
19. Readers wishing to undertake their own investigations into the origins of samples used in electronic dance music may find the website Who Sampled: Exploring the DNA of Music (http://www.whosampled.com/) useful.
20. Examples of drum & bass DJ sets when combined with MC performances can be heard on the many 'tape packs' which were produced; for example, *Hysteria 31: New Dawn* (Various Artists, 2000) includes eight cassette tapes capturing a rave at Lakota, Bristol.
21. The concepts of 'dark' and 'light' here correspond with the characteristics of low-mid and mid-high spectral centroids of the synthesizer sounds, and the respective rough and smooth textural qualities of these. These impressions are also elicited through the rough, aggressive masculinity of the vocal samples on the former track and the smooth, melancholy, feminine sample of the latter.
22. 'Spaceship earth' describes the concept of the earth as a vehicle travelling through space with limited resources, as discussed by Buckminster Fuller (1968). 'Gaia' in this context similarly relates to the 'Gaia hypothesis' as discussed by James Lovelock (1979), which describes the earth as a self-regulating system that supports life. In Terence McKenna's monologue on The Shamen's 'Re:Evolution' (1993), McKenna describes the concept of a 'Gaian supermind': a radical development of these ideas that proposes the notion that humans can communicate with a planetary consciousness.
23. 'Gating' describes the electronic process of attenuating signals below a specified amplitude threshold. Gating effects can also be opened and closed by following a time envelope, allowing rhythmic stuttering effects to be produced. The latter technique of gating is frequently used in trance music, and has been referred to as 'trance gating' for this reason. In the context discussed, trance gating is the technique used.
24. For example, see the TIP World *Imagi:Nations* compilations (2005), which divide the styles for 'Night' and 'Day' into two separate volumes. The 'Night' volume utilizes harder, faster, and more abrasive sounds, while the 'Day' volume incorporates more 'light', melodic, and upbeat sounds.
25. Groups who create this type of psychedelic decor include the following: Trip Hackers, 3Delica, Artescape, Floating Bush Collective, and the Extra-Dimensional Space Agency.
26. For further discussions of 'technoshamanism' in relation to cyberculture see also Rushkoff (1994) and Turner (2008); and in relation to psy-trance culture St. John (2012).

CHAPTER 5

1. 'Fixed-media' musical compositions are sonic artworks created in the studio as sound recordings on media such as magnetic tape, compact disc, or digital audio files.
2. Musical examples of early electronic instruments are available on *OHM: The Early Gurus of Electronic Music* (Various Artists, 2000), which includes *Oraison* (1937), Oliver Messiaen's composition for the Ondes Martinot.
3. Optical sound is a medium that stores sound on transparent film. Early experiments in optical sound were carried out by various engineers, including the following: Rudolf Pfenninger in 1932; Norman McLaren in his experimental films (e.g. *Dots*, 1940);

and Evgeny Murzin, who created the ANS photoelectric optical sound synthesizer (Smirnov, 2013).

4. For further discussion of soundscape compositions and phonographies, see writings by members of the World Soundscape Project such as Truax (1984; 1996) and Schafer (1994).
5. The terms 'reality' and 'unreality' as they are used here correspond with the sources of 'external' and 'internal' sensory inputs as discussed by Hobson (2003).
6. See also Emmerson's (1986) discussion of *Dreamsong* (1978), which describes the synthesizer materials as providing an 'aural discourse'. Following his discussion, we may consider that this aural discourse is used to metaphorically suggest the otherness of dreams.
7. 'Granular time-stretching' is a sound design technique that extends the normal duration of sounds by dividing sound into 'grains': individual units of sound, typically in the order of less than 50 ms duration, which are then redistributed in time.
8. 'Convolution' is a signal processing technique in which two audio signals are integrated, so that the shape of one signal modifies the other. For a further technical discussion see Spjut (2000).
9. Although Kendall (2011a) has stated that his main intention with *Ikaro* (2009–2010) was to explore shamanic healing through electroacoustic composition, he notes that the choice of sonic materials reflects aspects of the Peruvian rainforest soundscape.
10. These materials translate a visual feature of hallucination into sound, using a specially designed piece of software called the *Atomizer Live Patch*; for further discussion see Weinel (2013).
11. These compositional strategies are also discussed in Weinel (2016), with regards to other works on Jon Weinel, *Entoptic Phenomena in Audio* (2014).
12. Fischman (2008) uses the term 'convergence' to describe the points in a composition where real acoustic materials and synthetic electroacoustic sounds meet; he uses the term 'divergence' to describe their separation.
13. As noted in Chapter 1, the presence of these represented emotions in music does not guarantee a 'positive relationship' (Gabrielsson, 2002). However, since Evans and Schubert (2008) suggest that such positive relationships are the most common, we may therefore presume that music 'affords' (in terms of DeNora, 2010, pp.21–45) corresponding responses.
14. As discussed in Weinel (2013), the design of these materials draws inspiration from the 'flashcore' music (a form of avant-garde speedcore techno) of artists such as La Peste (e.g. *Il Etait… 'Magnetique' / Une Possibilite*, 2006; see also Weinel, 2007; and Migliorati, 2016).
15. This discussion develops comparisons between electronic dance music and trance states provided by Hutson (1999), and my own arguments first presented in Weinel (2014).
16. While this argument focuses on the typical forms of the respective idioms, some fluidity does exist. For instance, 'hybrid' electroacoustic works (as discussed in Shave, 2008; Blackburn, 2010; and Ratcliffe, 2011) may incorporate percussive dance rhythms, and have been presented in alternative settings such as nightclubs.
17. Social interactions and bodily communication are also considered by the 'sociocultural' and 'corporeal' wavebands discussed by Henriques (2011).
18. For a further discussion of ways in which external sonic materials can be modified to reflect perceptual distortions, see Weinel, Cunningham, and Griffiths (2014).
19. Russell's (1980) 'circumplex model of affect' has been widely used in various studies of music and emotion, such as Bailes and Dean's (2009) work on variations in affect for computer generated sound (see also Dean and Bailes, 2010; 2011). This model has also been used in studies by Griffiths, Cunningham, and Weinel (2013; 2015), which seek to devise

a computational system that classifies musical tracks by affect, in order to devise playlists that are related to human emotion.

CHAPTER 6

1. For more information on neuroscience and auditory perception, see also Schnupp, Nelken, and King (2011).
2. In this regard Sitney's (1979) definition of the 'trance film' differs in its usage of the term 'trance' from Rouget's (1985) definition.
3. For example, Liebman (1998) proposes a verbally based reading of the scenes, which uncovers linguistic puns by examining the French words associated with visual juxtapositions at key points.
4. Notably, Curtis Harrington worked with both Kenneth Anger and Roger Corman, whose respective films *Inauguration of the Pleasure Dome* (1954) and *The Trip* (1967) are also discussed in this chapter. Harrington appears as an actor in *Inauguration of the Pleasure Dome.*
5. For a discussion of the different versions of *Inauguration of the Pleasure Dome* (Anger, 1954), such as the version with a soundtrack by Electric Light Orchestra, see Hutchison (2011, p.90).
6. Subjective third-person as discussed here involves the presentation of a protagonist from a third person view, while including sounds and images related to their subjective perception (such as the contents of dreams or hallucinations).
7. While *Fear and Loathing in Las Vegas* (Gilliam, 1998) develops the themes of Hunter S. Thompson's (1971) novel, Gilliam also comments 'in the end I think we've made an anti-drug movie, although not everyone agrees with me' (Gilliam and Christie, 1999, p.258).
8. Here and later on in *Enter the Void* (Noé, 2009) the camera is used to present the subjective viewpoint of the protagonist's soul, separate from his body. In this regard the film adopts a dualistic view of consciousness, where the mind and body are considered to be separate. For an overview of dualism, see Blackmore (2003, pp.9–14).
9. *Embrace of the Serpent* (Guerra, 2015) is based on the true-story of anthropologist Theodor Koch-Grünberg, ethnobotanist Richard Evans Schultes, and their respective encounters with Karamakate, an Amazonian shaman.
10. For example, John Whitney's work focuses primarily on ways to create forms of 'visual harmony' through abstract animations that are analogous to music (Whitney, 1980).
11. Jordan Belson also collaborated with sound artist Henry Jacobs on the *Vortex Concerts* (1957–1959), which explored these aesthetic approaches within the (somewhat appropriate) context of the Morrison Planetarium in San Francisco. In this elaborate production, thirty-eight speakers and multiple projectors were used to create an immersive multimedia performance (liner notes, Various Artists, *Highlights of Vortex: Electronic Experiments and Music*, 1959).
12. Sitney (1979, p.263) supports this view, commenting: '[s]imply stated, the early films, up until and including *Allures*, are objects of meditation'.
13. For documentation of these shows, see Ronald Nameth film *Andy Warhol's Exploding Plastic Inevitable with The Velvet Underground* (1996). Nameth uses a reduced frame-rate technique to reflect perceptual distortions; see also Youngblood (1970, pp.102–105).
14. Some scientific research has been carried out regarding the affective properties of video; for example, Bartram and Nakatani (2010) showed affective interpretations that were attributed to abstract motion graphics.
15. Ben Van Meter is also known for his avant-garde films, such as the spectacular *Acid Mantra* (1968), which utilizes multiple super-imposed shots to provide an energetic flow of

images that capture the spirit of sexual revolution and consciousness expansion in 1960s America (Albright, 1968).

16. These programs reflect a broader trend, in which the microcomputer provided low-cost tools for producing the material artefacts of rave culture. For instance, many artists used the Atari ST and Amiga 500 for music sequencing, and designing event fliers and record sleeves; this is discussed with regards to the US rave scene in *Better Living through Circuitry* (Reiss, 1999).
17. Rose X's video performance on *Alien Dreamtime* (McKenna et al., 1993) was created using the NewTek Video Toaster.
18. 'Projection mapping' or 'video mapping' is a technique in which digital projectors are used to project video on to the surfaces of irregularly shaped objects, transforming their appearance.
19. Shipibo designs have also been incorporated by the South African VJ group Afterlife, who presented a video of a projection-mapped Shipibo cloth at *Futuretech 2014*. For video documentation see Popular Mechanics SA (2014). For a further discussion of Shipibo designs, see also Chapter 2 pp.41–42.
20. As discussed in the opening of this chapter, a 'fulldome' is a type of immersive 360-degree projection environment in which a video is projected across a dome-shaped ceiling.
21. Disorientation in fulldome presentations may result from the phenomenon of 'vection', the illusion of self-motion that can be caused by the immersive features of the display (Brandt, Dichgans, and Koenig, 1973). For a further discussion of cognition within the virtual environments of fulldomes, see also Schnall, Hedge, and Weaver (2012).

CHAPTER 7

1. In this context, 'biofeedback' describes the use of devices that measure physiological or neurological activity, in order to provide continuous signals that can be used to control aspects of an electronic system. Common examples include electrocardiogram (ECG) for measuring heart-rate; electromyogram (EMG) for reading muscular activity; and electroencephalogram (EEG) which measures electrical activity across the surface of the brain. Besides their use in medicine, these devices are sometimes used as controllers for interactive music systems and video games; for a brief history see Ortiz (2012).
2. Bagatelle is an indoor table game, in which the player must shoot balls into holes that are protected by wooden pins.
3. Early 3D game engines such as id Software's 'id Tech' engine or 3D Realms' 'Build' construct a virtual world using a floor plan that consists of two-dimensional geometry, with an added height component. This creates an impression of 3D, however cameras are unable to properly display the virtual world when the line-of-sight is not parallel to the floor. These engines also use two-dimensional sprites for many elements such as items, enemies, and scenery.
4. For a discussion of texture mapping in video games, see Ahearn (2012). For a more general discussion of 3D rendering and lighting techniques in computer graphics, see Hughes et al. (2014).
5. The Atari ST actually used the YM2149F, a modified version of the AY-3-8910 programmable sound generator.
6. In the video games industry, 'triple-A' (AAA) games are those titles that have the largest budgets for development and promotion.
7. For example, Ray Liotta (known for his role in Martin Scorsese's *Goodfellas*, 1990) provided the voice acting for the main protagonist of the 1980s crime parody *Grand Theft Auto: Vice City* (Rockstar North, 2002).

8. 3D audio techniques allow the amplitude and stereo panning of sound effects to change based on their relative location to the player in a virtual environment.
9. The term 'presence' originated from Minsky's (1980) discussions of 'telepresence' systems for industrial applications that require remote operation, such as may be encountered in nuclear power plants or space stations, which present situations otherwise inaccessible to humans.
10. The definitions of 'presence' and 'immersion' used here follow those of Slater and Wilbur (1997). Witmer and Singer (1998) have also provided similar definitions, describing 'immersion' as the 'perception of being enveloped', which contributes towards a sense of presence; however Cajella (2011, pp.18–23) has noted some ambiguity in the use of these terms.
11. For demographic statistics regarding gamers in the USA, see the Entertainment Software Association's (2016) report. For further discussion see also Greenberg et al. (2010).
12. The suggestion that *Amanita muscaria* may have been used by Viking berserkers before going into battle was first proposed by Ödmann (1784, cited in Wasson, 1968). However, Wasson (1968, p.157) is sceptical of these claims, and argues that the effects of *Amanita muscaria* are generally more calming than energizing, and would therefore be unsuitable for use by the berserkers.
13. Neo-noir is a style of crime-drama that updates the 'film noir' of the 1940s and 1950s with modern elements.
14. *Max Payne* (Remedy Entertainment, 2001) is divided into three parts. The hallucination sequences occur at the end of 'Part 1: The American Dream' ('Chapter Nine: An Empire of Evil') and 'Part II: A Cold Day in Hell' ('Chapter Five: Angel of Death').
15. 'Key-framing' is an animation technique in which graphical parameters follow smooth transitions between values that are defined at specific points in time.
16. 'Easter eggs' are hidden elements found in software and video games, which can usually be unlocked by performing a special sequence of actions. They are often used to hide humorous content or in-jokes by the programmers; for a further discussion see Weinel, Griffiths, and Cunningham (2014).
17. This sequence is possibly intended as a parody of a scene in *The Big Lebowski* (Coen and Coen, 1998), in which the character of 'The Dude' has a hallucination that finds him flying above Los Angeles, before suddenly plummeting to the ground.
18. Sony also distributed promotional postcards at Glastonbury festival 1995, which had perforated strips that could be torn off to use as 'roaches' in spliffs (Bland, 2013).
19. The soundtrack CD *WipEout—The Music* (Various Artists, 1995) features several of the electronic dance music tracks from the game, and also includes tracks by other popular artists such as The Prodigy that were not featured in the actual game.
20. Burcombe acknowledges that the capitalized 'E' in the *WipEout* title has been interpreted as a reference to ecstasy, though denies that this was the intention (Yin-Poole, 2014). Notably however, the graphic design for *WipEout* was produced by The Designers Republic (TDR), who also created designs for electronic dance music labels such as Warp Records and others; thus the 'E' can reasonably be seen as a trope that was carried over from rave culture.
21. The controversial *WipEout* (Psygnosis, 1995) poster was released at a time when ecstasy was attracting a lot of negative attention from the press in the United Kingdom. In particular, this was the same year of Leah Betts's tragic ecstasy-related death, which led to a nation-wide campaign warning teenagers about the dangers of the drug (Collin, 1998, pp.229–306).
22. An 'on-rails shooter' is a type of action video game in which movement follows a predetermined path, while the player operates a projectile weapon.

23. It is also of interest to note that the game acknowledges the influence of Kandinsky's synaesthetic artworks in an end credit, which reads 'dedicated to the creative soul of Kandinsky'.
24. Drill 'n' bass is an experimental form of drum 'n' bass. For examples on CD, see the following soundtrack discs: Osamu Sato's *LSD and Remixes* (1998), which includes remixes by artists such as µ-Ziq and Ken Ishii; and Osamu Sato and Out Ass Mao's *Lucy in the Sky with Dynamites*, which was included with some versions of the game.
25. For a further discussion of the dream chart, see also the fan-site LSD: Dream Emulator Wiki (http://dreamemulator.wikia.com).
26. In Hinduism, a 'chakra point' is a node or energy point in the body.
27. *Psych Dome* was also subsequently adapted by Sacred Resonance for use in the performance *Noosphere—A Vision Quest* (see Curtis and Pitt, 2016).
28. In contrast with 'active' and 'reactive' types, a 'passive' brain-computer interface (BCI) 'derives its outputs from arbitrary brain activity without the purpose of voluntary control, for enriching a human-computer interaction with implicit information' (Zander et al., 2010, p.185).
29. Several press articles have drawn attention to the correspondence between the visuals of *SoundSelf* and those of psychedelic experiences provided by LSD or DMT; for example, see Kohler (2016) and Liberatore (2016).
30. The illustration also draws specifically on Dennett's (1993) related concept of the 'Cartesian Theatre', which he provided as a means to critique theatre models of consciousness (Figure 7.3 is an adaptation of an illustration of the Cartesian Theatre).

CHAPTER 8

1. For a further discussion of cyberculture, see also Dery (1996).
2. Video recordings of the #Hackstock 'talkaoke' discussions are available online; see The People Speak (2016).
3. Dubstep is a type of electronic dance music originating in the 'UK garage' scene of Croydon, London, in the mid-2000s, which incorporates dub-reggae influences and prioritizes bass elements. For an introduction see Walmsley (2009).
4. Empathy in VR has been explored in a recent study by the Affective Audio research team based at Glyndŵr University (publication forthcoming).
5. Notably, Picard's (1997) influential discussion of 'affective computing' proposes systems that respond to or exhibit human emotions. Yet as we have explored in *Inner Sound*, emotion is only one dimension of consciousness, and we can now begin to conceive of more sophisticated systems that take into account other variable aspects of consciousness.
6. For example, in *Brainstorm* (Trumbull, 1983), a machine for recording conscious experiences becomes dangerous after it is used to record someone having a heart-attack. Along similar lines, the cyberpunk film *Strange Days* (Bigelow, 1995) explores the seedy world of 'black jacks', illicit recordings that are made for the 'SQUID', a device that replays subjective conscious experiences for the wearer. More recently, *Paprika* (Kon, 2006) depicts the chaos that ensues following the theft of a 'DC Mini', a machine that records the dreams of patients for the purposes of psychotherapy.
7. The Affective Audio group based at Glyndŵr University has been carrying out research exploring some related areas (Weinel et al., 2014). For example, finding ways to evaluate ASC Simulations is one way in which we may seek to provide improved levels of accuracy (Cunningham, Weinel, and Picking, 2016), while the representation of smells and tastes also presents specific challenges that we may begin to address through suitable mappings (Cunningham and Weinel, 2016).

GLOSSARY

Accurate A pole of the 'mode of representation' axis of the 'representational component', which describes representations that correspond closely with subjective experience.

Acid house A variation of Chicago house music originating in the late 1980s, which utilizes the Roland TB-303 Bass Line synthesizer.

Acousmatic The term popularized by Pierre Schaeffer for describing experiences of sound, for which the acoustic source remains unseen. This term is widely used to describe compositions of electroacoustic music that are performed through loudspeakers.

Affective component One of two main components of the conceptual model that is presented in *Inner Sound*. The 'affective component' describes a range of possibilities for communicating mood and emotion, based on the 'arousal' and 'valence' dimensions of Russell's 'circumplex model of affect'.

Affective properties The term used to describe features of sound and audio-visual media that communicate mood and emotion.

Afrofuturism A cultural aesthetic that explores revised concepts of blackness, race, and society through science fiction in art, music, film, and literature.

Altered state of consciousness (ASC) Any state of awareness that diverges significantly from the baseline of normal waking consciousness. Examples include psychosis, psychedelic experience, dreaming, hypnogogic hallucination, sensory deprivation, meditation, trance, and hypnosis.

Ambient house A variation of house music originating in the late 1980s, which incorporates influences from dub, house music, and 'ambient' artists such as Brian Eno.

Animism The belief that forces and entities within nature have a soul.

Arena space The term used by Denis Smalley to describe 'the whole public space inhabited by performers and listeners'. This term is used in *Inner Sound* to define the *z* axis of the 'representational component', which ranges from situational to transported.

Arousal A dimension of emotion discussed in Russell's 'circumplex model of affect', which describes the level of alertness or energy activation. This term is used in *Inner Sound* to define the *y* axis of the 'affective component', which ranges from deactivation to activation.

ASC Simulations The term used in *Inner Sound* to describe interactive audio-visual systems that represent ASCs with regards to the sensory components of the experience.

Auditory hallucinations Experiences of sound that have no apparent acoustic origin in the external environment, and are presumed to be generated within the brain.

Auditory verbal hallucinations A type of auditory hallucination that is commonly experienced by schizophrenics, in which the subject hears speech.

Augmented reality/mixed reality (AR/MR) The terms used in computing to describe hardware and software solutions that overlay synthetic visual or auditory information upon a real, physical environment, providing a composite. 'Mixed reality' (MR) is a variation of AR that provides improved integration and interaction between the real and the synthetic.

Augmented unreality The term used in *Inner Sound* to describe a specific type of ASC Simulation, in which the user experiences synthetic hallucinations as composites within the real-world 'situation'.

Aural discourse The term used by Simon Emmerson in his 'language grid', to describe the communication of sonic materials via conventional musical approaches, through features such as pitch and rhythm.

Ayahuasca Or 'yagé', a hallucinogenic brew used in shamanic practices of the Amazon basin, which contains a natural source of DMT.

Biofeedback A type of electronic equipment traditionally used in medicine, which measures physiological or neurological activity. Biofeedback can be used to provide control inputs in interactive music systems and video games.

Breakbeat A percussive section of music during which the drums are heard in isolation, often found during the bridge sections of funk and soul recordings. These sections are often digitally sampled to provide the rhythms in hip-hop and electronic dance music tracks.

Breakbeat hardcore Or 'old skool', a type of electronic dance music originating in the UK rave scene during the late 1980s, which uses sped-up breakbeats.

Cartography of ecstatic and meditative states Fischer's theory of consciousness, which describes a range of possible states, which are related to properties of arousal or energy activation.

Chicago house An early form of electronic dance music originating in Chicago during the 1980s, which usually has a $\frac{4}{4}$ disco beat.

Circumplex model of affect Russell's dimensional model of emotion, which describes affect according to properties of valence and arousal.

Convergence The term used by Fischman to describe the points in an electroacoustic composition where real acoustic materials and synthetic electroacoustic sounds meet.

Cyberculture The culture of networked computers and associated technologies such as human-computer interfaces.

Detroit techno An early form of electronic dance music originating in Detroit during the 1980s, which has futuristic or hi-tech aesthetics.

Distortion A type of effects process in which the gain of an audio signal is overdriven, causing a form of clipping to occur, which produces desirable abrasive sonic characteristics.

Divergence The term used by Fischman to describe the points in an electroacoustic composition where real acoustic materials and synthetic electroacoustic sounds separate.

DMT *N,N*-dimethyltryptamine, a powerful psychedelic compound that can be manufactured synthetically, and which also occurs naturally in some plants.

Doppler effect An effect that occurs where motion of a sound source relative to the listener causes fluctuations in pitch.

Drum & bass Or 'jungle', a variation of breakbeat hardcore originating in the UK rave scene during the early 1990s, which uses highly sped-up breakbeats that are often chopped up and rearranged.

Echo/delay A type of effects process, which provides one or more repeating instances of the input audio signal, usually with decreasing amplitude.

Ecstasy A term that is normally used interchangeably with 'trance' to describe ASCs that involve heightened states of arousal. However, it is also used by Rouget to describe low-arousal ASCs similar to meditation. 'Ecstasy' is also the street-name of the psychoactive drug MDMA (3,4-Methylenedioxymethamphetamine).

Electroacoustic music A form of Western art music originating in the 1950s, in which music is created using sound recordings and/or electronic synthesis techniques, for performance on loudspeakers.

Entoptic phenomena The term used by Lewis-Williams and Dowson to describe visual experiences caused 'within the eye', such as phosphenes and form constants.

Episodic memory The term used by Schacter and Tulving to describe a type of long-term memory (LTM), which deals with storage and recall of autobiographical events.

Expanded cinema The term popularized by Gene Youngblood in the 1970s, to describe audio-visual works that were cited beyond the cinema, which often sought to transform the consciousness of the audience.

External A pole of the 'input' axis of the 'representational component', which describes sensory information that originates in the environment that is external to the individual.

Filter A type of audio effects process, which attenuates or boosts certain frequencies. Common types include 'low-pass filters', which reduce frequencies above a cut-off point; and 'high-pass filters', which reduce frequencies below the cut-off point.

Fixed-media A term that describes pre-recorded musical compositions or audio-visual works created in the studio, which are reproduced by playing back a sound recording or video.

Flanger A type of effects process that applies a short delay to an input audio signal, in the order of 10 ms, which is modulated to create a sweeping effect.

Form constants The term used by Heinrich Klüver to describe the lattice, cobweb, funnel, and spiral patterns of visual hallucination that his participants saw during mescaline hallucinations.

Fulldome A type of immersive 360-degrees projection environment in which a video is projected across a dome-shaped ceiling.

Huichol Or 'Wixáritari', indigenous peoples who live in the Sierra Madre Occidental range in Mexico.

Immersion Term describing the capabilities of technology for submersing an individual into a virtual environment.

Inner speech Dialogue that is experienced internally, such as while thinking, which is constructed without audible speech.

Input Based on Hobson's 'state space' theory of consciousness, 'input' describes the source of sensory information received by an individual. This term is used in *Inner Sound* to define the *x* axis of the 'representational component', which ranges from external to internal.

Internal A pole of the 'input' axis of the 'representational component', which describes sensory information that originates within the brain.

Kinaesthetic Refers to the tactile sensations that may occur in a video game through control of a game character or avatar.

Kiowa Native American peoples based today in Oklahoma, USA.

Ludic Refers to the 'game-like' aspects of video games, due to the challenges and goals that the player may be required to complete.

Mazatec Indigenous peoples of the Sierra Mazateca of Oaxaca, Mexico.

Meditation A form of ASC that may occur in either secular or religious contexts, during which activities focus attention and promote deeply passive states of awareness.

Mimetic discourse The term used by Emmerson in his 'language grid', to describe sonic materials that reference aspects of nature or human culture through extrinsic properties.

Mode of representation The term used in *Inner Sound* to describe the *y* axis of the 'representational component', which deals with stylistic approaches, and ranges from accurate to stylized.

Peyote *Lophophora williamsii*, a small spineless cactus that contains the psychedelic alkaloid mescaline.

Presence This term describes the feeling of 'being there' that may arise from immersion.

Projection mapping Or 'video mapping' is a technique in which digital projectors are used to project video on to the surfaces of irregularly shaped objects, transforming their appearance.

Psychedelic Meaning 'mind manifesting', this term is used to describe psychoactive drugs, the experiences they produce, and associated counter-cultures and artefacts.

Psychosis A broad category of ASC that describes separation from reality, which may be caused by psychological disorders such as schizophrenia, various medical conditions such as brain tumours, or substance abuse.

Psy-trance Formerly known as 'Goa trance', this term describes a global electronic dance music culture that originated in the hippy parties of Goa, India, during the late 1980s.

Reality As it is used in *Inner Sound*, 'reality' describes sensory experiences that correspond with those that arrive via an external physical environment.

Representational component One of two main components of the conceptual model that is presented in *Inner Sound*. The 'representational component' describes a range of possibilities for communicating representations, based on the dimensions of 'input', 'mode of representation', and 'arena space'.

Representational properties The term used to describe features of sound and audio-visual media that represent spatial locations, places, events, or concepts.

Reverberation Or 'reverb', a type of effects process in which the audio signal is reflected many times, simulating the diffusion of an acoustic signal within a physical space.

San people Also known as 'bushmen', indigenous hunter-gatherer peoples of South Africa, across a range of territories.

Semantic memory The term used by Schacter and Tulving to describe a type of long-term memory (LTM), which is a general store of information and factual knowledge.

Shamanism A Western construct that is often used to collectively describe a diverse range of global traditions, which are often animist, and which utilize visionary states or trances to interact with a spirit world.

Shipibo An indigenous people who live along the Ucayali River in Peru.

Situational A pole of the 'arena space' axis of the 'representational component', which describes approaches where synthetic materials are overlaid as a composite on to the natural sound and light of the arena space.

Sleep paralysis A particular form of hypnagogic hallucination that may occur on the threshold of sleep, during which the individual may perceive sinister apparitions while feeling suffocated or unable to move.

Space jazz A type of jazz music associated especially with Sun Ra, which explores themes related to outer space and Afrofuturist mythologies.

Space rock A type of rock music originating in the 1970s, which explores themes related to outer space, and often utilizes synthesizers and effects devices.

Spectromorphology Denis Smalley's theory of electroacoustic sound, which describes the spectral (frequency) properties of sound, and their shaping in time.

Stream of consciousness Or 'stream of thought', is the metaphor used by William James to describe consciousness as a continuous flow of sensory experiences.

Stylized A pole of the 'mode of representation' axis of the 'representational component', which describes representations that utilize metaphorical, impressionistic, or symbolic approaches.

Surf rock A type of predominantly instrumental rock 'n' roll music, originating in the early 1960s, which utilizes echo and reverb effects, and is thematically related to teenage surfing culture.

Surrealism A twentieth-century art movement that seeks to unlock the irrationality of dreams and the unconscious, following the psychoanalysis theories of Sigmund Freud.

Synaesthesia A phenomenon in which different sensory modalities may become blurred; for example, sounds may have a colour, or smells may have a taste. Psychedelic drugs often promote experiences of synaesthesia, such as 'sound-to-image' visual hallucinations.

Synchresis The term used by Michel Chion to describe integrated experiences of sound and image.

Technoshamanism A term associated with 1990s rave culture and cyberculture, where technologies such as electronic dance music, VR, and psychedelic drugs are considered as shamanic tools.

Theatre of consciousness The metaphor used by Baars, in his Global Workspace (GW) theory, which suggests that consciousness can be thought of as a theatre stage, on which different cognitive processes enter into the spotlight at any given time, while others function in the background like stagehands.

Trance A form of ASC that may occur in either secular or religious contexts, during which energetic behaviours overload the senses and produce heightened states of arousal. In some cases experiences of trance may be characterized as 'spirit possession'.

Trance film Sitney's term for films that explore the lives of somnambulists, ritual initiates, or the possessed.

Transported A pole of the 'arena space' axis of the 'representational component', which describes approaches where the natural sound and light of the arena space are suppressed, and replaced by synthetic materials.

Tukano An indigenous people who live along the Vaupés River, mainly in Colombia.

Unreality As it is used in *Inner Sound*, 'unreality' describes sensory experiences that correspond with internal, imaginary, or hallucinatory environments.

Valence A dimension of emotion discussed in Russell's 'circumplex model of affect', which describes the level of pleasant or unpleasantness. This term is used in *Inner Sound* to define the x axis of the 'affective component', which ranges from unpleasant to pleasant.

Virtual acousmatic space Wishart's term for the illusory space created synthetically through the use of acousmatic sound.

Virtual environment A synthetic environment created using digital audio and 3D computer graphics, which can often be explored using interactive controllers.

Virtual reality (VR) The term used in computing to describe a hardware and software configuration, where the user looks through goggles and wears headphones, in order to become immersed in virtual environments.

Virtual unreality The term used in *Inner Sound* to describe a specific type of ASC Simulation, in which the user is 'transported' into a synthetic hallucination.

Visual music A type of experimental film in which synaesthetic animations are provided in correspondence with music and sound. This term is also used to describe paintings such as the work of Kandinsky, which derive their form and structure from music.

VJ Or 'video-jockey', a person who mixes videos and projections as an accompaniment to musical performances by bands, DJs, or electronic dance music artists.

Vodou A syncretic religion of Haiti that has its roots in traditions such as West African Vodun.

Wah-wah A type of effects process that applies a sweeping filter to the input audio signal, producing a characteristic sound similar to the human voice.

REFERENCES

BIBLIOGRAPHY

Adams, J.K. (1994) 'Psychosis: 'Experimental' and Real,' in Leary, T., Metzner, R., and Weil, G.M. (eds) *The Psychedelic Reader*. New York: Citadel Press, pp.61–82.

Ahearn, L. (2012) *3D Game Textures: Create Professional Game Art using Photoshop*, 3rd edn. Waltham: Focal Press.

Albright, T. (1968) '"Make Love, Not War, or Brown Rice": Filmmaker Ben Van Meter Takes Moviegoers on a Magical Anti-Establishment Mystery Tour,' *Rolling Stone*, 11 May 1968. Online: http://www.rollingstone.com/movies/features/make-love-not-war-or-brown-rice-19680511 (Accessed: 25 October 2016).

Atkinson, R.C. and Shiffrin, R.M. (1971) 'The Control of Short-Term Memory,' *Scientific American*, 225(2), pp.82–90.

Baars, B.J. (1988) *A Cognitive Theory of Consciousness*. Cambridge: Cambridge University Press.

Baars, B.J. (1997) *In the Theatre of Consciousness: The Workspace of the Mind*. New York: Oxford University Press.

Baddeley, A.D. (2000) 'The Episodic Buffer: A New Component of Working Memory?,' *Trends in Cognitive Sciences* 4(11), pp.417–423.

Baddeley, A.D. and Hitch, G.J. (1974) 'Working Memory,' in Bower, G.H. (ed.), *The Psychology of Learning and Motivation: Advances in Research and Theory: Vol. 8*. New York: Academic Press, pp.47–89.

Bailes, F. and Dean, R.T. (2009) 'Listeners Discern Affective Variation in Computer-Generated Musical Sounds,' *Perception*, 38(9), pp.1386–1404.

Barnard, A. (2007) *Anthropology and the Bushman*. Oxford: Berg.

Barnier, A.J. and Nash, M.R. (2012) 'Introduction: A Roadmap for Explanation, a Working Definition,' in Barnier, A.J. and Nash, M.R. (eds) *The Oxford Handbook of Hypnosis: Theory, Research, and Practice*. Oxford: Oxford University Press, pp.1–18.

Bartram, L. and Nakatani, A. (2010) 'What Makes Motion Meaningful? Affective Properties of Abstract Motion,' *Fourth Pacific-Rim Symposium on Image and Video Technology* (PSIVT), Singapore, 14–17 November 2010. doi: 10.1109/PSIVT.2010.85

BBC News (2005) 'Magic Mushroom Ban becomes the Law,' *BBC News*, 18 July 2005. Online: http://news.bbc.co.uk/1/hi/uk/4691899.stm (Accessed: 15 May 2015).

Becker, J. (2001) 'Anthropological Perspectives on Music and Emotion' in Juslin, P.N. and Sloboda, J.A. (eds) *Music and Emotion: Theory and Research*. Oxford: Oxford University Press, pp.135–160.

Becker, J. (2004) *Deep Listeners: Music, Emotion and Trancing*. Bloomington: University of Indiana Press.

Becker, J. (2012) 'Exploring the Habitus of Listening: Anthropological Perspectives,' in Juslin, P.N. and Sloboda, J.A. (eds) *Handbook of Music and Emotion: Theory, Research, Applications*. Oxford: Oxford University Press, pp.127–158.

Bell, B. (1969) 'You Don't Have to be High,' *New York Times*, 28 December 1969.

Berrin, K. (ed.) (1978) *Art of the Huichol Indians*. New York: Harry N. Abrams.

Blackburn, M. (2010) 'Electroacoustic Music Incorporating Latin American Influence,' *eContact!* 12(4). Online: http://econtact.ca/12_4/blackburn_influences.html (Accessed: 4 May 2016).

Blackmore, S. (2001) 'There is No Stream of Consciousness,' *Journal of Consciousness Studies*, 9(5–6), pp.17–28.

Blackmore, S. (2003) *Consciousness: An Introduction*. London: Hodder Education.

Bland, A. (2013) 'Ahead of the Game: Sony's PlayStation Convinced us that Video Games are More than just Child's Play,' *The Independent*, 27 November 2013. Online: http://www.independent.co.uk/life-style/gadgets-and-tech/features/ahead-of-the-game-sonys-playstation-convinced-us-that-video-games-are-more-than-just-childs-play-8968089.html (Accessed: 15 November 2016).

Bliss, E.L. and Clark, L.D. (1962) 'Visual Hallucinations' in West, L.J. (ed.) *Hallucinations*. New York: Grune & Stratton, pp.92–107.

Bogenschutz, M.P. and Johnson, M.W. (2016) 'Classic Hallucinogens in the Treatment of Addictions,' *Progress in Neuro-Psychopharmacology & Biological Psychiatry*, 64, pp.250–258.

Bogucki, R. (2016) Private correspondence, 21 November 2016.

Borhegyi, S.F. (1961) 'Miniature Mushroom Stones from Guatemala,' *American Antiquity*, 26(4), pp.498–504.

Bovey, S. (2006) '"Don't Tread on Me": The Ethos of '60s Garage Punk,' *Popular Music and Society*, 29(4), pp.451–459.

Bower, G.H. (1981) 'Mood and Memory,' *American Psychologist*, 36(2), pp.129–148.

Bowles, P. (1962) *A Hundred Camels in the Courtyard*, 2nd edn. Reprint, San Francisco: City Lights Books, 1986.

Bradley, L. (2001) *Bass Culture: When Reggae Was King*. London: Penguin Books.

Brandt, T., Dichgans, J., and Koenig, E. (1973) 'Differential Effects of Central Versus Peripheral Vision on Egocentric and Exocentric Motion Perception,' *Experimental Brain Research*, 16(5), pp.476–491.

Braun, H.J. (2002) *Music and Technology in the Twentieth Century*. Baltimore: John Hopkins University Press.

Bressloff, P.C., Cowan, J.D., Golubitsky, M., Thomas, P.J., and Wiener, M.C. (2001) 'Geometric Visual Hallucinations, Euclidean Symmetry and the Functional Architecture of Striate Cortex,' *Philosophical Transactions of the Royal Society B: Biological Sciences*, 356(1407), pp.299–330.

Breznikar, K. (2011) 'Electric Prunes Interview with James Lowe,' *It's Psychedelic Baby Magazine* [website]. Online: http://psychedelicbaby.blogspot.co.uk/2011/06/electric-prunes-interview-with-james_09.html (Accessed: 22 November 2015).

Broadbent, D. (1958) *Perception and Communication*. New York: Pergamon Press.

Brougher, K. and Mattis, O. (2005) *Visual Music: Synaesthesia in Art and Music Since 1900*. London: Thames & Hudson.

Buhler, J. and Neumeyer, D. (2013) 'Music and the Ontology of the Sound Film: The Classical Hollywood System,' in Neumeyer, D. (ed.) *The Oxford Handbook of Film Music Studies*. New York: Oxford University Press, pp.17–43.

Buñuel, L. (1947) 'Notes on the Making of Un Chien Andalou,' in MacDonald, S. (ed.) *Art in Cinema: Documents Toward a History of the Film Society*. Philadelphia: Temple University Press, 2006, pp.101–102.

Burroughs, W.S. (1953) *Junky*. Reprint, London: Penguin Books, 1977.
Burroughs, W.S. (1959) *The Naked Lunch*. Reprint, London: Fourth Estate, 2010.
Burroughs, W.S. and Ginsberg, A. (1963, 1975) *The Yage Letters*. Reprint, London: Penguin Books, 2006.
Cajella, G. (2011) *In-Game: From Immersion to Incorporation*. Cambridge, MA: MIT Press.
Callan, D.E., Jones, J.A., Munhall, K., Callan, A.M., Kroos, C., and Vatikiotis-Bateson, E. (2003) 'Neural Processes Underlying Perceptual Enhancement by Visual Speech Gestures,' *NeuroReport*, 14(17), p.2213–2218.
Calvert, G.A., Bullmore, E.T., Brammer, M.J., Campbell, R., Mcguire, P.K., Iversen, S.D., and David, A.S. (1997) 'Activation of Auditory Cortex During Silent Lipreading,' *Science* 276(5312), pp.593–596.
Cardeña, E. (2011) 'Altering Consciousness: Setting Up the Stage,' in Cardeña, E. and Winkelman, M. (eds) *Altering Consciousness: Multidisciplinary Perspectives, Volume 1: History, Culture and the Humanities*. Santa Barbara: Praeger.
Carroll, L. (1865–1871) *Alice's Adventures in Wonderland & Through the Looking-Glass*. Reprint, Ware: Wordsworth Editions, 1993.
Castaneda, C. (1968) *The Teaching of Don Juan: A Yaqui Way of Knowledge*. Reprint, London: Penguin Books, 2004.
Ceruzzi, P.E. (2012) *Computing: A Concise History*. Cambridge, MA: MIT Press.
Chalmers, D. (1996) *The Conscious Mind: In Search of a Fundamental Theory*. Oxford: Oxford University Press.
Chion, M. (1994) *Audio-Vision: Sound on Screen*. New York: Columbia University Press.
Coleridge, S.T. (1797) 'Kubla Khan,' in Holmes, R. (ed.) *Samuel Taylor Coleridge: Selected Poetry*. London: Penguin Books, 1996, pp.229–231.
Coleridge, S.T. (1798) 'The Rime of the Ancient Mariner,' in Holmes, R. (ed.) *Samuel Taylor Coleridge: Selected Poetry*. London: Penguin Books, 1996, pp.81–100.
Collin, M. (1998) *Altered State: The Story of Ecstasy Culture and Acid House*. London: Serpent's Tail.
Collins, K. (2008) *Game Sound: An Introduction to the History, Theory, and Practice of Video Game Music and Sound Design*. Cambridge, MA: MIT Press.
Craig, T.K.J., Rus-Calafell, M., Ward, T., Fornells-Ambrojo, M., McCrone, P., Emsley, R., and Garety, P. (2015) 'The Effects of an Audio Visual Assisted Therapy Aid for Refractory Auditory Hallucinations (AVATAR Therapy): Study Protocol for a Randomised Controlled Trial,' *Trials* 16, p.349. doi: 10.1186/s13063-015-0888-6
Crowley, K. (2011) *Surf Beat: Rock 'n' Roll's Forgotten Revolution*. New York: Backbeat Books.
Cunningham, S. and Weinel, J. (2016) 'The Sound of the Smell (and Taste) of My Shoes Too: Mapping the Senses Using Emotion as a Medium,' *AM '16 Proceedings of Audio Mostly 2016*, Norrköping, Sweden, 4–6 October 2016. doi: 10.1145/2986416.2986456
Cunningham, S., Weinel, J., and Picking, R. (2016) 'In-Game Intoxication: Demonstrating the Evaluation of the Audio Experience of Games with a Focus on Altered States of Consciousness,' in Garcia-Ruiz, M. (ed.) *Games User Research: A Case Study Approach*. Boca Raton, FL: CRC Press, pp.97–118.
Curtis, D. and Pitt, B. (2016) 'Noosphere—A Vision Quest at Adelaide Planetarium by Sacred Resonance,' *Sacred Resonance* [webpage]. Online: http://www.sacredresonance.com.au/ (Accessed: 27 May 2016).
Cytowic, R. E. (1989) *Synesthesia: A Union of the Senses*. New York: Springer-Verlag.
Davis, E. (2010) 'Dub, Scratch and the Black Star: Lee Perry,' in *Nomad Codes: Adventures in Modern Esoterica*. Portland: Yetti Books, pp.236–253.
Dean, R.T. and Bailes, F. (2010) 'Time Series Analysis as a Method to Examine Acoustical Influences on Real-time Perception of Music,' *Empirical Musicology Review*, 5(4), pp.152–175.

Dean, R.T. and Bailes, F. (2011) 'Modelling Perception of Structure and Affect in Music: Spectral Centroid and Wishart's Red Bird,' *Empirical Musicology Review*, 6(2), pp.131–137.
Delville, M. (1994) 'The Moorcock/Hawkwind Connection: Science Fiction and Rock 'n' Roll Culture,' *Foundation* 62, pp.64–69.
Dennett, D. (1993) *Consciousness Explained*. London: Penguin Books.
DeNora, T. (2010) *Music in Everyday Life*. Cambridge: Cambridge University Press.
De Quincy, T. (1821) *Confessions of an English Opium Eater*. Reprint, London: Penguin Books, 2003.
Deren, M. (1953) *Divine Horsemen: The Living Gods of Haiti*. Reprint, New York: McPherson & Company, 2004.
Deren, M. (1965) 'Notes, Essays, Letter,' *Film Culture*, 39 (Winter), pp.1–56.
Deren, M. (2005) *Essential Deren*. New York: McPherson & Company.
Dery, M. (1994) 'Black to the Future: Interviews with Samuel R. Delany, Greg Tate, and Tricia Rose,' in Dery, M. (ed) *Flame Wars: The Discourse of Cyberculture*. Durham, NC: Duke University Press, pp.179–222.
Dery, M. (1996) *Escape Velocity: Cyberculture at the End of the Century*. London: Hodder and Stoughton.
Devereux, P. (2001) *Stone Age Soundtracks: The Acoustic Archaeology of Ancient Sites*. London: Vega.
Devereux, P. (2008) *The Long Trip: A Prehistory of Psychedelia*. Brisbane: Daily Grail.
Dierks, T., Linden, D.E.J., Jandl, M., Formisano, E., Goebel, R., Lanfermann, H., and Singer, W. (1999) 'Activation of Heschl's Gyrus During Auditory Hallucinations,' *Neuron*, 22(3), pp.615–621.
Dobkin de Rios, M. and Katz, F. (1975) 'Some Relationships between Music and Hallucinogenic Ritual: The 'Jungle Gym' in Consciousness,' *Ethos*, 3(1), pp.64–76.
Dorje, G. (Translator), Coleman, G. and Jinpa, T. (eds) (2005) *The Tibetan Book of the Dead*. London: Penguin Classics.
Dowson, T.A. (2007) 'Debating Shamanism in Southern African Rock Art: Time to Move On . . . ,' *South African Archaeological Bulletin*, 62(185), pp.49–61.
Doyle, P. (2005) *Echo & Reverb: Fabricating Space in Popular Music Recording 1900–1960*. Middletown: Wesleyan University Press.
Eakin, L., Lauriault, E., and Boonstra, H. (1986) *People of the Ucayali: The Shipibo and Conibo of Peru*. Dallas: International Museum of Cultures.
Eger, S. and Collings, P.R. (1978) 'Huichol Women's Art,' in Berrin, K. (ed.) *Art of the Huichol Indians*. New York: Harry N. Abrams, pp.35–53.
Eliade, M. (1964) *Shamanism: Archaic Techniques of Ecstasy*. Reprint, Princeton, NJ: Princeton University Press, 2004.
Eliade, M. (1978) 'The Eleusinian Mysteries,' in *A History of Religious Ideas: Vol.1 From the Stone Age to the Eleusinian Mysteries*. Chicago: University of Chicago Press, pp.290–301.
Emmerson, S. (1986) 'The Relation of Language to Materials,' in Emmerson, S. (ed.) *The Language of Electroacoustic Music*. Basingstoke: Macmillan Press, pp.17–39.
Eneix, L.C. (2016) *Listening for Ancient Gods*. Myakka City, FL: OTS Foundation.
Entertainment Software Association (2016) *Essential Facts: About the Computer and Video Game Industry*. Washington, DC: Entertainment Software Association. Online: http://essentialfacts.theesa.com/Essential-Facts-2016.pdf (Accessed: 27 May 2016).
Estrada, A. (1981) *María Sabina: Her Life and Chants*. Santa Barbara: Ross-Erikson.
Evans, P. and Schubert, E. (2008) 'Relationships Between Expressed and Felt Emotions in Music,' *Musicae Scientiae*, 8(1), pp.75–99.
Fachner, J.C. (2011) 'Time Is the Key: Music and Altered States of Consciousness,' in Cardeña, E. and Winkelman, M. (eds) *Altering Consciousness: Multidisciplinary Perspectives: Volume 1: History, Culture and Humanities*. Santa Barbara: Praeger, pp.355–376.

Fischer, R. (1971) 'A Cartography of the Ecstatic and Meditative States,' *Science*, 174(4012), pp.897–904.
Fischman, R. (2008) 'Mimetic Space–Unravelled,' *Organised Sound*, 13(2), pp.111–122.
Flattery, D.S. and Schwartz, M. (1989) *Haoma and Harmaline: The Botanical Identity of the Indo-Iranian Sacred Hallucinogen 'Soma' and its Legacy in Religion, Language and Middle Eastern Folklore.* Berkley: University of California Press.
Frith, S. (1987) 'Towards an Aesthetic of Popular Music,' in Leppert, R. and McClary, S. (eds) *Music and Society: The Politics of Composition, Performance and Reception.* Cambridge: Cambridge University Press, pp.133–150.
Freud, S. (1899) *The Interpretation of Dreams.* Reprint, Ware: Wordsworth Editions, 1997.
Fuller, B. (1968) *Operating Manual for Spaceship Earth.* Reprint, Zurich: Lars Müller, 2008.
Furst, P.T. (1976) *Hallucinogens and Culture.* San Francisco: Chandler & Sharp.
Furst, P.T. (2007) *Visions of a Huichol Shaman.* Philadelphia: University of Pennsylvania Museum of Archaeology and Anthropology.
Gabrielsson, A. (2002) 'Emotion Perceived and Emotion Felt: Same or Different?,' *Musicae Scientiae*, 5(1 suppl.), pp.123–147.
Gabrielsson, A. and Lindstrom, E. (2012) 'The Role of Structure in the Musical Expression of Emotions,' in Juslin, P.N. and Sloboda, J.A. (eds) *Handbook of Music and Emotion: Theory, Research, Applications.* Oxford: Oxford University Press, pp.367–400.
Gebhart-Sayer, A. (1984) *The Cosmos Encoiled: Indian Art of the Peruvian Amazon.* New York: Center for Inter-American Relations.
Gebhart-Sayer, A. (1985) 'The Geometric Designs of the Shipibo-Conibo in Ritual Context,' *Journal of Latin American Lore*, 11(2), pp.143–175.
Gell, A. (1995) 'The Language of the Forest: Landscape and Phonological Iconism in Umeda' in Hirsch, E. and O'Hanlon, M. (eds) *The Anthropology of Landscape.* Oxford: Oxford University Press, pp.232–254.
Gibson, J.J. (1950) *The Perception of the Visual World.* Cambridge, MA: Riverside Press.
Gibson, J.J. (1966) *The Senses Considered as Perceptual Systems.* Boston: Houghton Mifflin.
Gibson, W. (1984) *Neuromancer.* Reprint, London: Harper Voyager, 1995.
Gilliam, T. and Christie, I. (1999) *Gilliam on Gilliam.* London: Faber and Faber.
Gizycki, H., Girardin, J.L., Snyder, M., Zizi, F., Green, H., Giuliano, V., Spielman, A., and Taub, H. (1998) 'The Effects of Photic Driving on Mood States,' *Journal of Psychosomatic Research*, 44(5), pp. 599–604.
Godlee, F. (2016) 'The War on Drugs has Failed: Doctors Should Lead Calls for Drug Policy Reform,' *BMJ* 2016;355:i6067. doi: 10.1136/bmj.i6067
Goldberg, J. and Latimer, D. (2014) *Flowers in the Blood.* New York: Skyhorse.
Greenberg, B.S., Sherry, J., Lachlan, K., Lucas, K., and Holmstrom, A. (2010) 'Orientations to Video Games among Gender and Age Groups,' *Simulation and Gaming*, 41(2), pp.238–259.
Gregory, R.L. (1980) 'Perceptions as Hypotheses,' *Philosophical Transactions of the Royal Society B: Biological Sciences*, 290(1038), pp.181–197.
Griffiths, D., Cunningham, S., and Weinel, J. (2013) 'A Discussion of Musical Features for Automatic Music Playlist Generation Using Affective Technologies,' *AM '13 Proceedings of the 8th Audio Mostly: A Conference on Interaction with Sound*, Piteå, Sweden, 18–20 Sept 2013. doi: 10.1145/2544114.2544128
Griffiths, D., Cunningham, S., and Weinel, J. (2015) 'A Self-Report Study that Gauges Perceived and Induced Emotion with Music,' *IEEE Proceedings of the Sixth International Conference on Internet Technologies and Applications 2015*, Wrexham, UK, 8–11 September 2015. doi: 10.1109/ITechA.2015.7317402
Grimshaw, M. and Garner, T. (2015) *Sonic Virtuality: Sound as Emergent Perception.* New York: Oxford University Press.

Grunenberg, C. (2005) *Summer of Love: Art of the Psychedelic Era*. London: Tate Publishing.
Harner, M.J. (1973) *Hallucinogens and Shamanism*. London: Oxford University Press.
Harner, M. (1990) *The Way of the Shaman*. New York: Harper & Row.
Harvey, G. (2003) 'General Introduction' in Harvey, G. (ed.) *Shamanism: A Reader*. London: Routledge, pp.1–23.
Hayward, P. (2004) 'Sci-Fidelity,' in Hayward, P. (ed.) *Off the Planet: Music, Sound and Science Fiction Cinema*. Eastleigh: John Libbey, pp.1–29.
Hendlin, S.J. (1979) 'Initial Zen Intensive (Sesshin): A Subjective Account,' *Journal of Pastoral Counseling*, 14, pp.27–43.
Henriques, J. (2011) *Sonic Bodies: Reggae Sound Systems, Performance Techniques and Ways of Knowing*. New York: Continuum.
Hicks, M. (2000) 'The Fuzz,' in *Sixties Rock: Garage, Psychedelic, and Other Satisfactions*. Urbana: University of Illinois Press, pp.12–22.
Hobson, J.A. (2003) *The Dream Drugstore*. Cambridge, MA: MIT Press.
Hobson, J.A. (2009) 'REM Sleep and Dreaming: Towards a Theory of Protoconsciousness,' *Nature Reviews Neuroscience*, 10(11), pp.803–813.
Homer, M. (2009) 'Beyond the Studio: The Impact of Home Recording Technologies on Music Creation and Consumption,' *Nebula*, 6(3), pp.85–99.
Hufford, D.J. (1989) *The Terror That Comes in the Night: An Experience-Centered Study of Supernatural Assault Traditions*. Philadelphia: University of Pennsylvania Press.
Hughes, J.F., Van Dam, A., McGuire, M., Sklar, D.F., Foley, J.D., Feiner, S.K., and Akeley, K. (2014) *Computer Graphics: Principles and Practice*, 3rd edn. Upper Saddle River, NJ: Addison-Wesley.
Hutchison, A.L. (2011) *Kenneth Anger*. London: Black Dog Publishing.
Hutson, S.R. (1999) 'Technoshamanism: Spiritual Healing in the Rave Subculture,' *Popular Music and Society*, 23(1), pp.53–77.
Huxley, A. (1954–1956) *The Doors of Perception and Heaven and Hell*. Reprint, London: Flamingo, 1994.
Ihde, E. (2015) 'Do Not Panic: Hawkwind, the Cold War and the "Imagination of Disaster",' *Cogent Arts & Humanities*, 2(1). doi: 10.1080/23311983.2015.1024564
Jackson, S. and Moody-Freeman, J.E. (eds) (2011) *The Black Imagination: Science Fiction, Futurism and the Speculative*. New York: Peter Lang.
James, W. (1890) *The Principles of Psychology, Vol.1*. Reprint, New York: Cosimo, 2009.
Johnson, K. (2011) *Are You Experienced? How Psychedelic Consciousness Transformed Modern Art*. Munich: Prestel.
Jones, S.M., Trauer, T., Mackinnon, A., Sims, E., Thomas, N., and Copolov, D.L. (2012) 'A New Phenomenological Survey of Auditory Hallucinations: Evidence for Subtypes and Implications for Theory and Practice,' *Schizophrenia Bulletin*, 40(1), pp.231–235.
Joseph, B.W. (2002) '"My Mind Split Open": Andy Warhol's Exploding Plastic Inevitable,' *Grey Room*, 8, pp.80–107.
Julien, R.M. (2001) *A Primer of Drug Action*, 9th edn. New York: Worth.
Jung, C.G. (1978) *Man and His Symbols*. London: Pan Books.
Juslin, P.N. (2008) 'Emotional Reactions to Music' in Hallam, S., Cross, I., and Thaut, M. (eds) *The Oxford Handbook of Music Psychology*, 2nd edn. Oxford: Oxford University Press, pp.197–214.
Kane, B. (2014a) 'Les Paul and the "Les Paulverizer",' in *Sound Unseen: Acousmatic Sound in Theory and Practice*. New York: Oxford University Press, pp.165–179.
Kane, B. (2014b) 'Myth and the Origin of the Pythagorean Veil,' in *Sound Unseen: Acousmatic Sound in Theory and Practice*. New York: Oxford University Press, pp.45–72.
Kane, B. (2014c) *Sound Unseen: Acousmatic Sound in Theory and Practice*. New York: Oxford University Press.

Kaplan, R.W. (1975) 'The Sacred Mushroom in Scandinavia,' *Man*, 10(1), pp.72–79.
Katz, D. (2006) *People Funny Boy: The Genius of Lee 'Scratch' Perry*. London: Omnibus Press.
Katz. M. (2010) *Capturing Sound: How Technology Has Changed Music*. Los Angeles: University of California Press.
Kendall, G.S. (2007) 'The Artistic Play of Spatial Organization: Spatial Attributes, Scene Analysis and Auditory Spatial Schemata,' *Proceedings of the International Computer Music Conference 2007*, Copenhagen, Denmark, 27–31 August 2007. Online: http://hdl.handle.net/2027/spo.bbp2372.2007.014 (Accessed: 7 December 2016).
Kendall, G.S. (2010) 'Spatial Perception and Cognition in Multichannel Audio for Electroacoustic Music,' *Organised Sound* 15(3), pp.228–238.
Kendall, G.S. (2011a) 'Bridging a Shamanic Worldview and Electroacoustic Art,' *Proceedings of the Electroacoustic Music Studies Conference*, Sforzando!, New York. 14–18 June 2011. Online: http://www.garykendall.net/papers/ShamanicBridging.pdf (Accessed: 7 December 2016).
Kendall, G.S. (2011b) 'Ikaro by Gary Kendall' [webpage]. Online: http://www.garykendall.net/compositions/Ikaro.html (Accessed: 25 June 2015).
Kihlstrom, J.F. (2012) 'The Domain of Hypnosis, Revisited,' in Barnier, A.J. and Nash, M.R. (eds) *The Oxford Handbook of Hypnosis: Theory, Research, and Practice*. Oxford: Oxford University Press, pp.21–52.
Kivy, P. (1990) *Music Alone: Philosophical Reflections on the Purely Musical Experience*. Ithaca, NY: Cornell University Press.
Kjellgren, A., Lyden, F., and Norlander, T. (2008) 'Sensory Isolation in Flotation Tanks: Altered States of Consciousness and Effects on Well-Being,' *The Qualitative Report*, 13(4), pp.636–656.
Klüver, H. (1971) *Mescal and Mechanisms of Hallucinations*. Chicago: University of Chicago Press.
Knowles, C. (2010) *The Secret History of Rock 'n' Roll*. Berkeley: Viva Editions.
Knox, J. (2017) 'Remote Sense: A Live AV fulldome performance commissioned by Cryptic' [webpage]. Online: http://jonnyknox.com/pile_portfolio/remote-sense (Accessed: 17 May 2017).
Koch-Grünberg, T. (1909) *Zwei Jahre unter den Indianern: Reisen in Nordwest Brasilien 1903–1905* [Two Years Among the Indians: Travels in Northwest Brazil 1903–1905]. Berlin: Ernst Wasmuth A.G.
Kohler, C. (2016) '*SoundSelf:* A VR Acid Trip Without The Drugs and Flashbacks,' *Wired*, 3 May 2016. Online: https://www.wired.com/2016/05/soundself-vr-ego-death/ (Accessed: 23 November 2016).
Krippner, S. (2012) 'The Psychedelic Experience, Contemporary Music, and the Grateful Dead: A 1969 Study Revisited' in Meriwether, N.G. (ed.) *Reading the Grateful Dead: A Critical Survey*. Lanham: Scarecrow Press, pp.257–268.
Krumhasl, C.L. (1997) 'An Exploratory Study of Musical Emotions and Psychophysiology,' *Canadian Journal of Experimental Psychology*, 51(4), pp.336–352.
Kumar, S., Sedley, W., Barnes, G.R., Teki, S., Friston, K.J., and Griffiths, T.D. (2014) 'A Brain Basis for Musical Hallucinations,' *Cortex*, 52, pp.86–97.
Kushner, D. (2012) *Jacked: The Outlaw Story of Grand Theft Auto*. Hoboken, NJ: John Wiley & Sons.
La Barre, W. (1970) Film review of *To Find Our Life: The Peyote Hunt of the Huichols of Mexico* by Furst, P.T., *American Anthropologist*, 72(5), p.1201.
La Barre, W. (1972) *The Ghost Dance: The Origins of Religion*. London: George Allen & Unwin.
La Barre, W. (2011) *The Peyote Cult*, 5th edn. Maidstone: Crescent Moon.
Laing, R.D. (1967) *The Politics of Experience and The Bird of Paradise*. Reprint, London: Penguin Books, 1990.

Lajoux, J.D. (1963) *The Rock Paintings of Tassili*. Cleveland: World Publishing.
Laufer, B. (1913) 'Origin of the Word Shaman,' *American Anthropologist*, 19(3), pp.361–371.
Leary, T. (1968) 'The Seven Tongues of God,' in *The Politics of Ecstasy*. Reprint, Oakland: Ronin, 1998, pp.13–58.
Leary, T. (1994) *Chaos & Cyber Culture*. Berkeley: Ronin.
Leech, J. (2010) *Seasons They Change: The Story of Acid and Psychedelic Folk*. London: Jawbone Press.
Lewis-Williams, J.D., Dowson, T.A., and Deacon, J. (1993) 'Rock Art and Changing Perceptions of Southern Africa's Past: Ezeljagdspoort Reviewed,' *Antiquity*, 67(255), pp. 273–291.
Lewis-Williams, J.D. (1996) *Discovering Southern African Rock Art*. Claremont: David Philip.
Lewis-Williams, J.D. (2004) *The Mind in the Cave*. London: Thames & Hudson.
Lewis-Williams, J.D. (2007) 'Shamanism: A Contested Concept in Archaeology.' *Before Farming*, 4, pp.223–261.
Lewis-Williams, J.D. and Dowson, T.A. (1988) 'The Signs of All Times: Entoptic Phenomena in Upper Paleolithic Art,' *Current Anthropology*, 29(2), pp.201–245.
Liberatore, S. (2016) 'That's Trippy! Watch the VR App that Claims to be Able to Reproduce the Effects of a Hallucinogenic Drug,' *Daily Mail*, 4 May 2016. Online: http://www.dailymail.co.uk/sciencetech/article-3572184/That-s-trippy-Watch-VR-app-claims-able-reproduce-effects-hallucinogenic-drug.html (Accessed: 27 May 2016).
Liebman, S. (1998) '*Un Chien Andalou:* The Talking Cure,' in Kuenzli, R. (ed.) *Dada and Surrealist Film*. Cambridge: MIT Press, pp.143–158.
Lilly, J.C. (1972) *Center of the Cyclone: Looking into Inner Space*. Reprint, Oakland: Ronin.
Lindahl, J.R., Kaplan, C.T., Winget, E.M., and Britton, W.B. (2013) 'A Phenomenology of Meditation-Induced Light Experiences: Traditional Buddhist and Neurobiological Perspectives,' *Frontiers in Psychology*, 4. doi: 10.3389/fpsyg.2013.00973
Lovelock, J. (1979) *Gaia: A New Look at Life on Earth*. Oxford: Oxford University Press.
Lowy, B. (1971) 'New Records of Mushroom Stones from Guatemala,' *Mycologia*, 63(5), pp.983–993.
Lubman, D. (1998) 'An Archaeological Study of Chirped Echo from the Mayan Pyramid of Kukulkan at Chichen Itza,' *Acoustic Society of America*, Norfolk, VA, 12–16 October, 1998. Summary online: http://www.ocasa.org/MayanPyramid.htm (Accessed: 19 June 2015).
Ludwig, A.M. (1969) 'Altered States of Consciousness' in Tart, C.T. (ed.) *Altered States of Consciousness: A Book of Readings*. New York: John Wiley & Sons, pp.9–22.
Luke, D. (2010) 'Rock Art or Rorschach: Is There More to Entoptics than Meets the Eye?,' *Time and Mind: The Journal of Archaeology, Consciousness and Culture*, 3(1), pp.9–28.
MacLeod, C., Matthews, A., and Tata, P. (1986) 'Attentional Bias in Emotional Disorders,' *Journal of Abnormal Psychology*, 95(1), pp.15–20.
Manning P. (2004) *Electronic & Computer Music*, 2nd edn. Oxford: Oxford University Press.
Marr, D. (1982) *Vision: A Computational Investigation into the Human Representation and Processing of Visual Information*. San Francisco: W.H. Freeman.
Maupin, E.W. (1969) 'On Meditation' in Tart, C.T. (ed.) *Altered States of Consciousness: A Book of Readings*. New York: John Wiley & Sons, pp.177–186.
Mayer, G. (2008) 'The Figure of the Shaman as a Modern Myth: Some Reflections on the Attractiveness of Shamanism in Modern Societies,' *Pomegranate*, 10(1). doi: 10.1558/pome.v10i1.70
McGurk, H. and MacDonald, J. (1976) 'Hearing Lips and Seeing Voices,' *Nature*, 263, pp.746–748.
McKenna, T. (1992) *Food of the Gods*. London: Rider.
McLeary, J.A., Sypherd, P.S., and Walkington, D.L. (1960) 'Antibiotic Activity of An Extract of Peyote (Lophophora Williamsii (Lemaire) Coulter),' *Economic Botany*, 14(3), pp.247–249.

McLuhan, M. (1964) *Understanding Media*. Reprint, London: Routledge, 2005.
McLuhan, M. and Fiore, Q. (1968) *War and Peace in the Global Village*. Reprint, San Francisco: Hardwired, 1997.
Merlin, M.D. (1984) *On the Trail of the Ancient Opium Poppy*. London: Associated University Presses.
Metzner, R., Alpert, R., and Leary, T. (1968) *The Psychedelic Experience: A Manual Based on the Tibetan Book of the Dead*. Reprint, London: Penguin Classics, 2008.
Meyer, L.B. (1956) *Emotion and Meaning in Music*. Chicago: Chicago University Press.
Migliorati, A. (2016) 'Portrait #7: La Peste–"Para La Santísima Muerte Flashcore Live Set" [Previously Unreleased],' *Pay No Mind to Us, We're Just a Minor Threat*. Online: http://www.paynomindtous.it/2016/11/portrait7-la-peste.html (Accessed: 20 November 2016).
Miller, K. (1978) 'Huichol Art and Acculturation' in Berrin, K. (ed.) *Art of the Huichol Indians*. New York: Harry N. Abrams.
Milner, G. (2009) *Perfecting Sound Forever*. London: Granta Books.
Minsky, M. (1980) 'Telepresence,' *OMNI Magazine*, June 1980, pp.45–51.
Minter, J. (2005) 'VLM,' *Llamasoft: Home of the Virtual Light Machine and the Minotaur Project Games* [webpage]. Online: http://minotaurproject.co.uk/vlm.php (Accessed: 1 November 2015).
Mithoefer, M.C., Wagner, M.T., Mithoefer, A.T., Jerome, L., and Doblin, R. (2010) 'The Safety and Efficacy of 3,4-Methylenedioxymethamphetamine-Assisted Psychotherapy in Subjects with Chronic, Treatment-Resistant Posttraumatic Stress Disorder: The First Randomized Controlled Pilot Study,' *Journal of Psychopharmacology*, 25(4), pp.439–452.
Monk-Turner, E. (2003) 'The Benefits of Meditation: Experimental Findings,' *The Social Science Journal*, 40, pp.465–470.
Montgomery, G.H., Duhamel, K.N., and Redd, W.H. (2000) 'A Meta-Analysis of Hypnotically Induced Analgesia: How Effective is Hypnosis?,' *International Journal of Clinical and Experimental Hypnosis*, 48(2) pp.138–153.
Moritz, W. (1977) 'William Moritz on James Whitney's *Yantra* and *Lapis*,' *Center for Visual Music*. Online: http://www.centerforvisualmusic.org/WMyantra.htm (Accessed: 2 November 2015).
Moritz, W. (1985) 'Who's Who in Filmmaking: James Whitney,' *iotaCenter*. Online: http://www.iotacenter.org/visualmusic/articles/moritz/whoswhitney (Accessed: 2 November 2015).
Moritz, W. (1997) 'The Dream of Colour Music and the Machines that Made it Possible,' *Animation World Magazine* 2(1). Online: http://www.awn.com/mag/issue2.1/articles/moritz2.1.html (Accessed: 7 December 2016).
Moser, B and Tayler, D. (1965) *The Cocaine Eaters*. London: Longmans.
Munn, H. (1972) 'The Mushrooms of Language' in Harner, M. (ed.) *Hallucinogens and Shamanism*. Oxford: Oxford University Press.
Neher, A. (1961) 'Auditory Driving Observed with Scalp Electrodes in Normal Subjects,' *Electroencephalography and Clinical Neurophysiology*, 13(3), pp.449–451.
Neher, A. (1962) 'A Physiological Explanation of Unusual Behavior in Ceremonies Involving Drums,' *Human Biology*, 34(2), pp.151–162.
Nishikawa, H. (1998) *Lovely Sweet Dream*. Tokyo: Media Factory.
Nishimoto, S., Vu, A.T., Naselaris, T., Benjamini, Y., Yu, B., and Gallant, J. (2011) 'Reconstructing Visual Experiences from Brain Activity Evoked by Natural Movies,' *Current Biology*, 21(19), pp.1641–1646.
Noble, D.J. (1995) 'Sounds Like ...,' *UniVibes: International Jimi Hendrix Magazine*, 20, November 1995, pp.20–25.
Nuttall, J. (1968) *Bomb Culture*. London: MacGibbon & Kee.

Oakley, D.A. (2012) 'Hypnosis, Trance and Suggestion: Evidence from Neuroimaging,' in Barnier, A.J. and Nash, M.R. (eds) *The Oxford Handbook of Hypnosis: Theory, Research, and Practice*. Oxford: Oxford University Press, pp.365–392.

Ödmann, S. (1784) 'Försök at utur Naturens Historia förklara de nordiska gamla Kämpars Berserka-gang' [An Attempt to Explain the Berserk-Raging of Ancient Nordic Warriors Through Natural History]. *Kongliga Vetenskaps Academiens nya Handlingar,* 5, pp.240–247.

Ondaatje, M. (2002) *The Conversations: Walter Murch and the Art of Editing Film*. London: Bloomsbury Publishing.

Oren, M. (2010) 'Getting out of Your Mind to Use Your Head,' *Art Journal*, 69 (4), pp.76–95.

Ortiz, M. (2012) 'A Brief History of Biosignal-Driven Art,' *eContact* 14(2). Online: http://econtact.ca/14_2/ortiz_biofeedback.html (Accessed: 23 November 2016).

Oster, G. (1970) 'Phosphenes,' *Scientific American*, 222(2), pp.79–87.

Ott, J. (1976) *Hallucinogenic Plants of North America*. Berkeley: Wingbow Press.

Palmer, R. (1992) 'Church of the Sonic Guitar,' DeCurtis, A. (ed.), *Present Tense: Rock & Roll and Culture*. Durham: Duke University Press, pp.13–37.

Patton, M. (1990) 'On Entoptic Images in Context: Art, Monuments, and Society in Neolithic Brittany,' *Current Anthropology*, 31(5), pp.554–558.

Peleka, R.J. (1990) 'The Phenomenology of Meditation' in West, M.A. (ed.) *The Psychology of Meditation*. Oxford: Oxford University Press, pp.59–80.

Penman, J. and Becker, J. (2009) 'Religious Ecstatics, 'Deep Listeners,' and Musical Emotion,' *Empirical Musicology Review*, 4(2), pp.49–70.

Picard, R.W. (1997) *Affective Computing*. Cambridge, MA: MIT Press.

Poole, S. (2004) *Trigger Happy: Videogames and Entertainment Revolution*. New York: Arcade Publishing.

Ratcliffe, R. (2011) 'New Forms of Hybrid Musical Discourse: An Exploration of Stylistic and Procedural Cross-Fertilisation Between Contemporary Art Music and Electronic Dance Music,' *Proceedings of the International Computer Music Conference 2011*, University of Huddersfield, UK, 31 July–5 August 2011. Online: http://hdl.handle.net/2027/spo.bbp2372.2011.047 (Accessed: 7 December 2016).

Ratsch, A., Steadman, K.J., and Bogossian, F. (2010) The Pituri Story: A Review of the Historical Literature Surrounding Traditional Australian Aboriginal Use of Nicotine in Central Australia, *Journal of Ethnobiology and Ethnomedicine*, 6(26). doi: 10.1186/1746-4269-6-26.

Reichel-Dolmatoff, G. (1978) *Beyond the Milky Way: Hallucinatory Imagery of the Tukano Indians*. Los Angeles: UCLA Latin American Centre Publications.

Reichel-Dolmatoff, G. (1987) *Shamanism and Art of the Eastern Tukanoan Indians: Colombian Northwest Amazon*. Leiden: E.J. Brill.

Reynolds, S. (2008) *Energy Flash: A Journey Through Rave Music and Dance Culture*. London: Picador.

Reznikoff, I. and Dauvois, M. (1988) 'La Dimension Sonore des Grottes Ornées' [The Sonic Dimensions of Caves], *Bulletin de la Société Préhistorique Française*, 85(8), pp.238–246.

Richardson, M. (2006) *Surrealism and Cinema*. Oxford: Berg.

Rickard N.S. (2004) 'Intense Emotional Responses to Music: A Test of the Physiological Arousal Hypothesis,' *Psychology of Music*, 32, pp.371–388.

Roberts, A. (2012) *Albion Dreaming: A Popular History of LSD in Britain*. Singapore: Marshall Cavendish Editions.

Robertson, R. (2015) 'Maya Deren: Meshes of the Audiovisual: Music, Image and Sound in Maya Deren's *Meshes of the Afternoon* (1943, 1959),' in *Cinema and the Audiovisual Imagination: Music, Image, Sound*. London: I.B. Tauris, pp.73–79.

Robinson, J. (2007) 'Tripping the Lights,' *The Guardian*, 14 April 2007. Online: http://www.theguardian.com/artanddesign/2007/apr/14/art.culture/print (Accessed: 25 October 2015).

Robinson, J.P. and Hirsch, P. (1972) 'Teenage Response to Rock and Roll Protest Songs,' in Denisoff, R.S. and Peterson, R.A. (eds) *The Sounds of Social Change: Studies in Popular Culture*. Chicago: Rand McNally, p.222–232.

Rogan, J. (2001) *The Byrds: Timeless Flight Revisited: The Sequel*. London: Rogan House.

Rosenzweig, M.R., Leiman, A.L., and Breedlove, S.M. (1999) *Biological Psychology: An Introduction to Behavioural, Cognitive and Clinical Neuroscience*, 2nd edn. Sunderland: Sinauer Associates Inc.

Rouget, G. (1985) *Music and Trance: A Theory of the Relations Between Music and Possession*. Chicago: University of Chicago Press.

Rubin, D.S. (ed.) (2010) *Psychedelic: Optical and Visionary Art since the 1960s*. Cambridge, MA: MIT Press.

Rucker, R., R.U. Sirius and Queen Mu (eds) (1992) *Mondo 2000: A User's Guide to the New Edge*. London: Thames and Hudson.

Rumsey, F. and McCormick, T. (2009) *Sound and Recording*, 6th edn. Oxford: Focal Press.

Rushkoff, D. (1994) *Cyberia: Life in the Trenches of Hyperspace*, 2nd edn. Manchester: Clinamen Press, 2002.

Russell, J. (1980) 'A Circumplex Model of Affect,' *Journal of Personality and Social Psychology*, 39(6), pp.1161–1178.

Sahagún, B. (1499–1590a) *Florentine Codex: General History of the Things of New Spain. Book 10: The People (Number 14, Part XI)*. Translated by Dibble, C.E. and Anderson, A.J.O. Santa Fe: The School of American Research and the University of Utah, 1974.

Sahagún, B. (1499–1590b) *Florentine Codex: General History of the Things of New Spain. Book 11: Earthly Things (Number 14, Part XII)*. Translated by Dibble, C.E. and Anderson, A.J.O. Santa Fe: The School of American Research and the University of Utah, 1974.

Schacter, D.L. and Tulving, E. (1994) 'What are the Memory Systems of 1994?,' in Schacter, D.L. and Tulving, E. (eds) *Memory Systems*. Cambridge, MA: MIT Press, pp.1–38.

Schaeffer, P. (1966) 'Acousmatics,' translated from *Traité des Objets Musicaux* (Paris: Éditions du Seuil, 1966) by Smith, D.W., 2007, in Cox, C. and Warner, D. (eds) *Audio Culture: Readings in Modern Music*. New York: Continuum, 2007, pp.76–87.

Schaefer, S.B. (1996) 'The Crossing of the Souls: Peyote, Perception, and Meaning among the Huichol Indians' in Schaeffer, S.B. and Furst, P.T. (eds) *People of the Peyote: Huichol Indian History, Religion and Survival*. Albuquerque: University of New Mexico Press.

Schaefer, S.B. and Furst, P.T. (1996) 'Introduction' in Schaeffer, S.B. and Furst, P.T. (eds) *People of the Peyote: Huichol Indian History, Religion and Survival*. Albuquerque: University of New Mexico Press.

Schafer, R.M. (1994) *The Soundscape: Our Sonic Environment and the Tuning of the World*. Rochester, VT: Destiny Books.

Schedel, M. (2007) 'Jean-Claude Risset: Elementa,' *Computer Music Journal*, 31(1), pp.105–106.

Schnall, S., Hedge, C., and Weaver, R. (2012) 'The Immersive Virtual Environment of the Digital Fulldome: Considerations of Relevant Psychological Processes,' *International Journal of Human-Computer Studies*, 70(8), pp.561–575.

Schnupp, J., Nelken, I., and King, A. (2011) *Auditory Neuroscience: Making Sense of Sound*. Cambridge, MA: MIT Press.

Schoenberger, N.E. (2000) 'Research on Hypnosis as an Adjunct to Cognitive-Behavioral Psychotherapy,' *International Journal of Clinical and Experimental Hypnosis*, 48(2), pp.154–169.

Schultes, R.E. (1972) 'An Overview of Hallucinogens in the Western Hemisphere' in Furst, P.T. (ed.) *Flesh of the Gods: The Ritual Use of Hallucinogens*. Reprint, Long Grove: Waveland Press, 1990, pp.3–54.

Schultes, R.E., Hofmann, A., and Rätsch, C. (1996) *Plants of the Gods: Their Sacred, Healing and Hallucinogenic Powers*, 2nd edn. Rochester, VT: Healing Arts Press.

Sci-Fi-London (2016) '#Hackstock – Immersive Art Without Boundaries' [webpage]. Online: http://sci-fi-london.com/festival/2016/programme/event/hackstock-immersive-arts-without-boundaries (Accessed: 27 May 2016).

Shave, T. (2008) 'Communicative Contract Analysis: An Approach to Popular Music Analysis,' *Organised Sound*, 13(1), pp.41–50.

Shepherd, J. and Giles-Davis, J. (1991) 'Music, Text and Subjectivity,' in Shepherd, J., *Music as Social Text*. Cambridge: Polity Press, pp.174–185.

Sherratt, A. (1991) 'Sacred and Profane Substances: The Ritual Use of Narcotics in Later Neolithic Europe,' in Garwood, P., Jennings, D., Skeates, R., and Toms, J. (eds) *Sacred and Profane: Proceedings of a Conference on Archaeology, Ritual and Religion*. Oxford: Oxford University Committee for Archaeology, pp.50–64.

Sherratt, A. (1995) 'Alcohol and its Alternatives: Symbol and Substances in Pre-Industrial Cultures,' in Goodman, J., Lovejoy, P.E., and Sherratt, A. (eds), *Consuming Habits: Drugs in History and Anthropology*. London: Routledge.

Sicko, D. (2010) *Techno Rebels: The Renegades of Electronic Funk*, 2nd edn. Detroit: Painted Turtle.

Siegel, R.K. (1977) 'Hallucinations,' *Scientific American*, 237(4), pp.132–140.

Signore, J. D. (2007) 'Joshua White: The Joshua Light Show,' *Gothamist*, 2 April 2007. Online: http://gothamist.com/2007/04/02/interview_joshu.php (Accessed: 25 October 2015).

Singh, R. (2010) 'Harry Smith, an Ethnographic Modernist in America,' in Perchuk, A. and Singh, R. (eds) *Harry Smith: The Avant-Garde in the American Vernacular*. Los Angeles: Getty Publications, pp.15–62.

Sitney, P.A. (1965) 'Harry Smith Interview,' in Sitney, P.A. (ed.) *Film Culture Reader*. Reprint, New York: Cooper Square Press, 2000, pp.260–276.

Sitney, P.A. (1979) *Visionary Film: The American Avant-Garde 1943–1978*, 2nd edn. Oxford: Oxford University Press.

Skotnes, P. (2007) *Claim to the Country: The Archive of Lucy Lloyd and Wilhelm Bleek*. Johannesburg: Jacana; Athens: Ohio University Press.

Slater, M. and Wilbur, S. (1997) 'A Framework for Immersive Virtual Environments (FIVE): Speculations on the Role of Presence in Virtual Environments,' *Presence: Teleoperators and Virtual Environments*, 6(6), pp.603–616.

Sloboda, J.A. and Juslin, P.N. (2012) 'At the Interface Between the Inner and Outer World: Psychological Perspectives,' in Juslin, P.N. and Sloboda, J.A. (eds) *Handbook of Music and Emotion: Theory, Research, Applications*. Oxford: Oxford University Press, pp.73–98.

Smalley, D. (1986) 'Spectro-morphology and Structuring Processes,' in Emmerson, S. (ed.) *The Language of Electroacoustic Music*. Basingstoke: Macmillan Press, pp.61–93.

Smalley, D. (2007) 'Space-Form and the Acousmatic Image,' *Organised Sound*, 12(1), pp.38–58.

Smirnov, A. (2013) *Sound in Z: Experiments in Sound and Electronic Music in Early 20th Century Russia*. Köln: Walther Koenig.

Solecki, R. (1975) 'Shadinar IV, a Neanderthal Flower Burial in Northern Iraq,' *Science*, 190(4217), pp.880–881.

Soloman, A. (2013) 'The Death of Trance: Recent Perspectives on San Ethnographies and Rock Arts,' *Antiquity*, 87(338), pp.1208–1213.

Sonnenschein, D. (2001) *Sound Design: The Expressive Power of Music, Voice and Sound Effects in Cinema*. Studio City, CA: Michael Wiese Productions.

Sontag, S. (1965) 'The Imagination of Disaster,' *Commentary,* 40(4), pp.42–48.
Spjut, E. (2000) 'Convolution in Csound: Traditional and Novel Applications,' in Boulanger, R. (ed.), *The Csound Book.* Cambridge, MA: MIT Press.
Sterchi, H.C, Ridgeway, E.A., and Dyack, D.P. (2005) *Sanity System for Video Game.* US Patent 6,935,954, filed 3 September 2002, and issued 30 August 2005.
St. John, G. (2009) *Technomad: Global Raving Countercultures.* London: Equinox.
St. John, G. (2011) 'DJ Goa Gil: Kalifornian Exile, Dark Yogi and Dreaded Anomaly,' *Dancecult: Journal of Electronic and Dance Music Culture,* 3(1), pp.97–128. Online: http://dj.dancecult.net/index.php/dancecult/article/view/318 (Accessed: 15 May 2015).
St. John, G. (2012) *Global Tribe: Technology, Spirituality & Psytrance.* Sheffield: Equinox.
Strassman, R. (2001) *DMT: The Spirit Molecule.* Rochester, VT: Park Street Press.
Swan, D.C. (1999) *Peyote Religious Art: Symbols of Faith and Belief.* Jackson: University Press of Mississippi.
Sweet, M. (2014) *Writing Interactive Music for Video Games: A Composer's Guide.* Upper Saddle River, NJ: Addison-Wesley.
Szwed, J.F. (2000) *Space Is The Place: The Life and Times of Sun Ra.* Edinburgh: Canongate Books.
Tart, C.T. (1969) *Altered States of Consciousness: A Book of Readings.* New York: John Wiley & Sons.
Tayler, D. (1972) *The Music of Some Indian Tribes of Columbia* [background notes and commentary on the music collections of the Anglo-Columbian recording expedition 1960–1961]. London: British Institute of Recorded Sound.
Teagle, J. and Sprung, J. (1995) *Fender Amps: The First Fifty Years.* Milwaukee: Hal Leonard.
Terry, M., Steelman, K.L., Guilderson, T., Dering, P., and Rowe, M.W. (2006) 'Lower Pecos and Coahuila Peyote: New Radiocarbon Dates,' *Journal of Archaeological Science,* 33(7), pp.1017–1021.
Thomas, K. (1971) *Religion and the Decline of Magic.* Reprint, London: Penguin Books, 1991.
Thompson, A. (1997) *Stompbox: A History of Guitar, Fuzzes, Flangers, Phasers, Echoes and Wahs.* San Francisco: Miller Freeman Books.
Thompson, E. (2002) *The Soundscape of Modernity; Architectural Acoustics and the Culture of Listening in America 1900–1933.* Reprint, Cambridge, MA: MIT Press, 2004.
Thompson, H.S. (1971) *Fear and Loathing in Las Vegas: A Savage Journey to the Heart of the American Dream.* Reprint, London: William Collins, 2005.
Toffler, A. (1970) *Future Shock.* Reprint, London: Pan Books, 1972.
Toffler, A. (1980) *The Third Wave.* Reprint, Toronto: Bantam Books, 1981.
Tolkien, J.R.R. (1954–1955) *The Lord of the Rings: The Fellowship of the Ring, The Two Towers, The Return of the King.* Reprint, London: Harper Collins, 2005.
Treisman, A.M. (1960) 'Contextual Cues in Selective Listening,' *Quarterly Journal of Experimental Psychology,* 12(4), pp.242–248. doi: 10.1080/17470216008416732
Trowell, I. (2001) 'Auto-Synthesis,' *Organised Sound* 6(3), pp.215–233.
Truax, B. (1984) *Acoustic Communication.* Norwood, NJ: Ablex.
Truax, B. (1996) 'Soundscape, Acoustic Communication & Environmental Sound Composition,' *Contemporary Music Review,* 15(1), pp.49–65.
Truax, B. (2007) 'Chalice Well' [webpage]. Online: http://www.sfu.ca/~truax/chalice.html (Accessed: 25 June 2015).
Truax, B. (2008) 'The Shaman Ascending' [webpage]. Online: http://www.sfu.ca/~truax/shaman.html (Accessed: 25 June 2015).
Trybyszewski, J. (2004) 'Where the Pyramid Meets the High: Founding Elevator Tommy Hall and his Horizontal Thinking,' *The Austin Chronicle,* 13 August 2004. Online: http://www.austinchronicle.com/music/2004-08-13/224147/ (Accessed: 14 May 2015).
Turner, F. (2008) *From Counterculture to Cyberculture.* Chicago: University of Chicago Press.

Turner, V. (1982) *From Ritual to Theatre: The Seriousness of Human Play*. New York: PAJ Publications.
Tuzin, D. (1980) *The Voice of the Tambaran: Truth and Illusion in Ilahita Arapesh Religion*. Berkley: University of California Press.
Tuzin, D. (1984) 'Miraculous Voices: The Auditory Experience of Numinous Objects,' *Current Anthropology*, 25(5), pp.579–596.
Van Meter, B. (2016) Private correspondence, 2 August 2016.
Veal, M.E. (2007) *Dub: Soundscapes and Shattered Songs in Jamaican Reggae*. Middletown: Wesleyan University Press.
Vitebsky, P. (1995) *The Shaman: Voyages of the Soul; Trance, Ecstasy and Healing from Siberia to the Amazon*. London: Duncan Baird, 2008.
Vitos, B. (2014) 'Along the Lines of the Roland TB-303: Three Perversions of Acid Techno,' *Dancecult: Journal of Electronic Dance Music Culture*, 6(1). doi: 10.12801/1947-5403.2014.06.01.14
Walmsley, D. (2009) 'Dubstep,' in Young, R. (ed.) *The Wire Primers: A Guide to Modern Music*. London: Verso.
Wasson, R.G. (1957) 'Seeking the Magic Mushroom,' *Life*, 13 May 1957, pp.100–147.
Wasson, R.G. (1968) *Soma: Divine Mushroom of Immortality*. New York: Harcourt, Brace & World.
Wasson, R.G. (1972) 'The Divine Mushroom of Immortality' in Furst, P.T. (ed.) *Flesh of the Gods: The Ritual Use of Hallucinogens*. Reprint, Long Grove: Waveland Press, 1990.
Wasson, R.G., Cowan, G., Cowan, F., and Rhodes, W. (1974) *María Sabina and her Mazatec Mushroom Velada* [including musical score and four cassette recordings]. New York: Harcourt Brace Jovanovich.
Wasson, R.G., Hoffman, A., and Ruck, C.A.P. (1978) *The Road to Eleusis: Unveiling the Secret of the Mysteries*. New York: Harcourt Brace Jovanovich.
Wasson, V.P. and Wasson, R.G. (1957) *Mushrooms, Russia and History* (2 vols.). New York: Pantheon Books.
Wayne, W.U. (2012) 'Explaining Schizophrenia: Auditory Verbal Hallucination and Self-Monitoring,' *Mind & Language*, 27(1), pp.86–107.
Wees, W.C. (1992) 'Making Films for the Inner Eye: Jordan Belson, James Whitney, Paul Sharits,' in *Light Moving in Time: Studies in the Visual Aesthetics of Avant-Garde Film*. Berkeley: University of California Press, pp.123–152. Online: http://ark.cdlib.org/ark:/13030/ft438nb2fr/ (Accessed: 25 October 2015).
Weheliye, A.G. (2005) *Phonographies; Grooves in Sonic Afro-Modernity*. Durham: Duke University Press.
Weinel, J. (2007) 'Flashcore: Earth Atomizer, Let's Go,' *Spannered*, 20 May 2007. Online: http://www.spannered.org/music/1181/ (Accessed: 7 December 2016).
Weinel, J. (2011) 'Quake Delirium: Remixing Psychedelic Video Games,' *Sonic Ideas/Ideas Sónicas*, 3(2), pp.22–29.
Weinel, J. (2013) 'Visual Patterns of Hallucination as a Basis for Sonic Arts Composition,' *AM '13 Proceedings of the 8th Audio Mostly: A Conference on Interaction with Sound*, Piteå, Sweden, 18–20 September 2013. doi: 10.1145/2544114.2544125 (Accessed: 29 June 2015).
Weinel, J. (2014) 'Shamanic Diffusions: A Technoshamanic Philosophy of Electroacoustic Music,' *Sonic Ideas/Ideas Sónicas* 6(12), pp.42–46.
Weinel, J. (2016) 'Entoptic Phenomena in Audio: Categories of Psychedelic Electroacoustic Composition,' *Contemporary Music Review*, 35(2), pp.202–223.
Weinel, J., Cunningham, S., and Griffiths, D. (2014) 'Sound Through the Rabbit Hole: Sound Design Based on Reports of Auditory Hallucination,' *AM '14 Proceedings of the 9th Audio*

Mostly: A Conference on Interaction with Sound, Aalborg, Denmark, 1–3 October 2014. doi: 10.1145/2636879.2636883 (Accessed: 1 May 2015).

Weinel, J., Griffiths, D., and Cunningham, S. (2014) 'Easter Eggs: Hidden Tracks and Messages in Musical Mediums,' *Proceedings of the International Computer Music Conference 2014,* 14–20 September 2014, Athens, Greece. Online: http://hdl.handle.net/2027/spo.bbp2372.2014.024 (Accessed: 4 January 2017).

Weinel, J., Cunningham, S., Griffiths, D., Roberts, S., and Picking, R. (2014) 'Affective Audio,' *Leonardo Music Journal,* 24, pp.17–20.

Weiner, N. (1961) *Cybernetics: Or Control and Communication in the Animal and the Machine,* 2nd edn. Reprint, Mansfield Centre, CT: Martino, 2013.

Whaley, J., Sloboda, J., and Gabrielsson, A. (2008) 'Peak Experiences in Music' in Hallam, S., Cross, I., and Thaut, M. (eds) *The Oxford Handbook of Music Psychology,* 2nd edn. Oxford: Oxford University Press, pp.745–758.

Whitney, J.H. (1980) *Digital Harmony: On the Complementarity of Music and Visual Art.* Peterborough: Byte Books/McGraw-Hill.

Wilcken, L. (1992) *The Drums of Vodou.* Tempe: White Cliffs Media Company.

Williams, B. (2001) 'Black Secret Technology: Detroit Techno and the Information Age,' in Nelson, A., Tu, T.L.N., and Hines, A.H. (eds) *Technicolor: Race, Technology and Everyday Life.* New York: New York University Press, pp.154–176.

Wishart, T. (1985) *On Sonic Art.* Reprint, Amsterdam: Harwood Academic Publishers, 1996.

Witmer, B.G. and Singer, M.J. (1998) 'Measuring Presence in Virtual Environments: A Presence Questionnaire,' *Presence: Teleoperators and Virtual Environments,* 7(3), pp.225–240.

Wolfe, T. (1968) *The Electric Kool-Aid Acid Test.* Reprint, London: Black Swan, 1989.

Yin-Poole, W. (2014) 'WipEout: The Rise and Fall of Sony Studio Liverpool,' *Eurogamer,* 30 November 2014. Online: http://www.eurogamer.net/articles/2013-03-22-wipeout-the-rise-and-fall-of-sony-studio-liverpool (Accessed: 27 May 2016).

Youngblood, G. (1970) *Expanded Cinema.* New York: E.P. Dutton.

Zander, T.O., Kothe, C., Jatzey, S., and Gaertner, M. (2010) 'Enhancing Human-Computer Interaction with Input from Active and Passive Brain-Computer Interfaces,' in Tan, D.S. and Nijholt, A. (eds) *Brain-Computer Interfaces: Applying our Minds to Human-Computer Interaction.* London: Springer, pp.181–199.

Zinman, G. (2008) 'The Joshua Light Show: Concrete Practices and Ephemeral Effects,' *American Art,* 22(2), pp.17–21.

DISCOGRAPHY

13th Floor Elevators (1966) *Psychedelic Sounds of the 13th Floor Elevators.* LP, International Artists.

Acen (1992) *Trip II The Moon (Part 1).* 12″, Production House.

Adamski (1989) *Liveandirect.* LP, MCA Records.

The Amboy Dukes (1968) *Journey to the Center of the Mind.* 7″, Mainstream Records.

Augustin, Frisner (1994) *The Drums of Vodou.* CD, White Cliffs Media.

Augustus Pablo (1976) *King Tubby Meets Rockers Uptown.* CD, Shanachie.

Augustus Pablo (1981) *East of the River Nile.* LP, Shanachie.

Badings, Henk (1958) *Electronic Ballet Music 'Cain and Abel.'* 7″, Philips.

The Beach Boys (1963) *Little Deuce Coupe.* LP, Capitol Records.

The Beach Boys (1963) *Surfer Girl.* LP, Capitol Records.

The Beatles (1964) *Meet The Beatles!* LP, Capitol.

The Beatles (1966) *Revolver.* LP, Capitol Records.

The Beatles (1967) *Magical Mystery Tour.* LP, Capitol Records.

Bill Haley and His Comets (1954) *Rock Around the Clock.* 10″ Shellac, Decca.

Bizarre Inc. (1991) 'Playing with Knives (Quadrant Mix),' on *Playing with Knives*. 12", Vinyl Solution.
Blackbeard (1980) *I Wah Dub*. LP, More Cut Records.
Black Sabbath (1970) *Paranoid*. LP, Vertigo.
Bomb the Bass (1988) 'Megablast (Hip Hop On Precinct 13),' on *Into the Dragon*. LP, Rhythm King Records.
Brown, James (1970) *The Funky Drummer*. 7", King Records.
The Byrds (1965) *Turn, Turn, Turn*. 7", CBS.
The Byrds (1966) *Eight Miles High*. 7", CBS.
C.A. Quintet (1969) *Trip Thru Hell*. LP, Candy Floss.
Children's Stories (1992) 'The Chocolate Factory,' on *Volume 1*. 12", Phuture Trax Promotions.
Chuck Berry (1964) *No Particular Place to Go*. 7", Chess.
Collins, Lyn (1972) *Think (About It)*. LP, People.
Coltrane, John (1974) *Interstellar Space*. LP, Impulse!
Dance Conspiracy (1992) *Dub War*. 12", XL Recordings.
Derango (2005) *Tumult*. CD, Inpsyde Media.
Deren, Maya (Sound recordist) (1953) *Voices of Haiti*. 10" Vinyl, Elektra.
Deren, Maya (Sound recordist) (1980) *Divine Horsemen: The Voodoo Gods of Haiti*. LP, Lyrichord.
The Deuce Coupes (1963) *Hotrodders' Choice*. LP, Del-Fi Records.
De Vit, Tony (2000) *The Dawn*. 12", Tidy Trax.
Dick Dale and His Del-Tones (1962) *Surfers' Choice*. LP, Deltone Records.
Dick Dale and His Del-Tones (1963) *Checkered Flag*. LP, Capitol Records.
Dick Dale and His Del-Tones (1964) *Mr. Eliminator*. LP, Capitol Records.
The Doors (1987) 'A Little Game,' on *Live at the Hollywood Bowl* [recorded 1968]. LP, Elektra.
Drexciya (1995) *The Journey Home*. 12", Warp Records.
Drexciya (1997) *The Quest*. 2xCD, Submerge.
Drexciya (1999) *Neptune's Lair*. CD, Tresor.
Ed Rush & Optical (1998) *Wormhole*. 2xCD, Virus Recordings.
Egyptian Empire (1992) *The Horn Track*. 12", Ffrreedom.
The Electric Prunes (1966) *I Had Too Much To Dream (Last Night)*. 7", Reprise Records.
The Electric Prunes (1968) *Mass in F Minor*. LP, Reprise Records.
Eric B. & Rakim (1987) *You Know I Got Soul*. 12", Cooltempo.
Euromasters (1992) *Alles Naar De Kl—te*. 12", Rising High Records.
Fapardokly (1966) *Fapardokly*. LP, UIP.
Fingers Inc. (1988) *Can You Feel It*. 12", Jack Trax
Fischman, Rajmil (2000) *No Me Quedo* [electroacoustic composition]. Available on: *... a 'wonderful' world*, CD, EMF, 2007.
The Future Sound of London (1993) *Cascade*. 12", Virgin.
The Future Sound of London (1994) *Lifeforms*. 2xCD, Virgin.
Hallucinogen (1995) *Twisted*. CD, Dragonfly Records.
Hawkwind (1971) *X in Search of Space*. LP, United Artists Records.
Hawkwind (1973) *Space Ritual*. 2xLP, UAD.
Hawkwind (1981) *Sonic Attack*. LP, RCA.
Humanoid (1988) *Stakker Humanoid*. 12", Westside Records.
Hyper-On Experience (1993) 'Time Stretch,' on *Deaf in the Family (A Sad Title for an Otherwise Splendid EP)*. 12", Moving Shadow.
Ike Turner's Kings of Rhythm (as Jackie Brenston and his Delta Cats) (1951) *Rocket 88*. 10" Shellac, Chess.
The Impacts (1963) *Wipe Out!* LP, Del-Fi Records.

Infrared V's Gil Felix (2003) *Capoeira*. 12", Infrared.
Jamie Principle (1987) *Baby Wants to Ride*. 12", Trax Records.
Jefferson Airplane (1967) *White Rabbit*. 7", RCA Victor.
Jefferson, Marshall (1986) 'Move Your Body,' on *The House Music Anthem*. 12", Trax Records.
The Jimi Hendrix Experience (1968) *Electric Ladyland*. 2xLP, Polydor.
Joe Hill Louis (1950) *Boogie in the Park*. 7", Phillips.
Joe Smooth (1988) *Promised Land*. 12", DJ International Records.
John Barry (1967) 'Capsule in Space,' on *You Only Live Twice (Original Motion Picture Soundtrack)*. CD, EMI-Manhattan Records, 1988.
Josh Wink (1995) *Higher State of Consciousness*. 12", Manifesto.
Kaleidoscope (1967) *Flight from Ashiya*. 7", Fontana.
Kendall, Gary (2002) *Unu* [electroacoustic composition]. Digital audio available online: http://www.garykendall.net/compositions/Unu.html (Accessed: 17 May 2016).
Kendall, Gary (2002) *Wayda* [electroacoustic composition]. Digital audio available online: http://www.garykendall.net/compositions/Wayda.html (Accessed: 4 May 2015).
Kendall, Gary (2006) *Qosqo* [electroacoustic composition]. Digital audio available online: http://www.garykendall.net/compositions/Qosqo.html (Accessed: 4 May 2015).
Kendall, Gary (2009–2010) *Ikaro* [electroacoustic composition]. Digital audio available online: http://www.garykendall.net/compositions/Ikaro.html (Accessed: 4 May 2015).
The Kinks (1964) *You Really Got Me*. 7", Pye Records.
The KLF (1990) *Chill Out*. CD, KLF Communications.
Kode9 and The Spaceape (2006) *Memories of the Future*. CD, Hyperdub.
Kraken (2001) *Dominion*. 12", Zero Gravity Recordings.
Landau, Carolyn (Interviewer) (2010) 'Donald Tayler and Brian Moser interviewed by Carolyn Landau.' Streaming digital audio, British Library Sound Archive. Online: http://sounds.bl.uk/World-and-traditional-music/Interviews-with-ethnomusicologists/025M-C1397X0009XX-0001V0 (Accessed: 18 June 2015).
La Peste (2006) *Il Etait... 'Magnetique'/Une Possibilite*. 12", Hangars Liquides.
Lee 'Scratch' Perry (as Lee [King] Perry) (1968) *People Funny Boy*. 7", Doctor Bird.
Lee 'Scratch' Perry (1972) *French Connection*. 7", Justice League.
Lee 'Scratch' Perry (1975) *Kung Fu Meets the Dragon*. LP, Justice League.
Les Paul and Mary Ford (1951) *How High the Moon*. 7", Capitol Records.
Lewis, Jerry Lee (1957) *Whole Lot of Shakin' Going On*. 10", Shellac, Sun Record Company.
Link Wray & His Wray Men (1958) *Rumble*. 7", Cadence.
Liquid (1992) *Sweet Harmony*. 12", XL Recordings.
Little Richard (1956) *Long Tall Sally*. 7", Speciality.
Little Richard (1971) *Little Richard's Greatest Hits*. LP, CBS Records.
The Lively Ones (1963) *Surf Drums*. LP, Del-Fi Records.
Love (1967) *Forever Changes*. LP, Elektra.
Luna-C (1994) *Piano Progression*. 12", Kniteforce.
DJ Marky (2001) *The Brazilian Job*. CD, Movement.
The Martian (1999) *LBH—6251876 (A Red Planet Compilation)*. CD, Red Planet.
Massive Attack (1994) *Protection*. CD, Wild Bunch Records.
May, Derrick, Craig, Carl, Atkins, Juan and Pennington, James (Suburban Knight) (1992) *Relics: A Transmat Compilation*. LP, Buzz.
McNabb, Michael (1978) *Dreamsong* [electroacoustic composition]. Available on: *Dreamsong/Love in the Asylum/Mars* Suite, CD, WERGO, 1993.
Model 500 (1985) *No UFOs*. 12", Metroplex.
Moore, Adrian (1996) *Dreamarena* [electroacoustic composition]. Available on: *Traces*, CD, empreintes DIGITALes, 2000.

Moser, Brian and Tayler, Donald (Sound recordists) (1960–1961) 'Brian Moser & Donald Tayler Colombia Collection.' Streaming digital audio, British Library Sound Archive. Online: http://sounds.bl.uk/world-and-traditional-music/moser-tayler-colombia (Accessed: 18 June 2015).

Moser, Brian and Tayler, Donald (Sound recordists) (1972) *The Music of Some Indian Tribes of Colombia*. 3xLP, British Institute of Recorded Sound.

Moser, Brian and Tayler, Donald (Sound recordists) (1987) *Music of the Tukano and Cuna Peoples of Colombia*. LP, Rogue Records.

The Mothers of Invention (1966) *Freak Out!* 2xLP, Verve.

Neurocore (2009) *Starship Travellers*. 12", Underground Perversions Records.

The Orb (1991) *Adventures Beyond the Ultraworld*. 2xCD, Big Life.

Orca (1993) '4AM (Original Mix),' on *4AM (The Remixes and The Original)*. 12", Pure White.

Parmerud, Åke (2005) *Dreaming in Darkness* [electroacoustic composition]. Available on: *Nécropolis*, CD, empreintes DIGITALes, 2016.

Perhacs, Linda (1970) *Parallelograms*. LP, Kapp Records.

Phuture (1987) *Acid Tracks*. 12", Trax.

Pink Floyd (1973) *Dark Side of the Moon*. LP, Harvest.

Pleiadians (1997) *I.F.O. (Identified Flying Object)*. CD, Dragonfly Records.

Presley, Elvis (1962) *Girls! Girls! Girls!* LP, RCA Victor.

Prince Jammy (1982) *Prince Jammy Destroys The Invaders ...* LP, Greensleeves Records.

The Prodigy (1991) *Charly*. 12", XL Recordings.

The Ragga Twins (1990) 'Hooligan 69,' on *Ragga Trip / Hooligan 69*. 12", Shut Up And Dance Records.

Rebel MC featuring Tenor Fly (1991) *The Wickedest Sound*. 12", Desire Records.

Risset, Jean-Claude (1998) *Elementa* [electroacoustic composition]. Available on: *Elementa*, CD, INA-GRM, 2001. Performed at: 'ICMC/SMC 2014 Joint Conference,' National Observatory, Athens, 18 September 2014.

Sabina, María (1957) *Mushroom Ceremony of the Mazatec Indians of Mexico*. LP, Folkways.

Sato, Osamu (1998) *LSD and Remixes*. 2xCD, Music Mine.

Scientist (1981) *Scientist Meets the Space Invaders*. LP, Greensleeves Records.

Scientist (1981) *Scientist Rids the World of the Curse of The Evil Vampires*. LP, Greensleeves Records.

Scientist (1982) *Scientist Encounters Pacman*. LP, Greensleeves Records.

Scientist (1982) *Scientist Wins the World Cup*. LP, Greensleeves Records.

Scientist and Prince Jammy (1980) *Scientist vs. Prince Jammy: Big Showdown*. LP, Greensleeves Records.

Scientist and Prince Jammy (1982) *Scientist and Prince Jammy Strike Back!* LP, Trojan Records.

Shakta (1997) *Silicon Trip*. CD, Dragonfly Records.

The Shamen with Terence McKenna (1993) *Re:Evolution*. 12", One Little Indian. Lyrics available online: http://deoxy.org/t_re-evo.htm (Accessed: 15 May 2015).

Smalley, Denis (1997) *Empty Vessels* [electroacoustic composition]. Available on: *Sources/Scènes*, CD, empreintes DIGITALes, 2000.

Smart E's (1992) *Sesame's Treet*. 12", Suburban Base Records.

Smith, Harry (Curator) (1952) *Anthology of American Folk Music*. Reissue, 6xCD, Smithsonian Folkways, 1997.

Smith, Harry (Sound recordist) (1973) *The Kiowa Peyote Meeting*. CD, Reissue, Smithsonian Folkways, 2009.

Spiral Tribe (1993) *Spiral Tribe Sound System*. CD, Big Life.

DJ Spooky That Subliminal Kid (1996) *Songs of a Dead Dreamer*. CD, Asphodel.

Stockhausen, Karlheinz (1953) *Studie 1* [electroacoustic composition]. Available on: *Elektronische Musik 1952–1960*, CD, Stockhausen-Verlag.

Stockhausen, Karlheinz (1954) *Studie 2* [electroacoustic composition]. Available on: *Elektronische Musik 1952–1960*, CD, Stockhausen-Verlag.
Sun Ra (1978) *Lanquidity*. LP, Philly Jazz Inc.
The Surfaris (1963) *Wipe Out*. 7", Dot Records.
Tongue N' Cheek (1988) *Nobody (Can Love Me)*. 12", Criminal Records.
The Tornadoes (1962) *Bustin' Surfboards*. 7", Aertaun.
Truax, Barry (2004–2005) *The Shaman Ascending* [electroacoustic composition]. Available on: *Spirit Journies*, CD, Cambridge Street Records, 2007.
Truax, Barry (2009) *Chalice Well* [electroacoustic composition]. Available on: *The Elements and Beyond*, CD, Cambridge Street Records, 2014.
Truax, Barry (2016) *The Garden of Sonic Delights* [electroacoustic composition]. Premiered at: 'BEAST FEaST: Real/Unreal,' University of Birmingham, 29 April 2016.
Ultimate Spinach (1968) *Ultimate Spinach*. LP, MGM Records.
Underworld (1993) 'Rez,' on *Rez / Cow Girl*. 12", Junior Boy's Own.
Underworld (1995) *Born Slippy*. 12", Junior Boy's Own.
The Upsetters (1970) *Clint Eastwood*. 7", Randy's.
The Upsetters (1978) *Return of the Super Ape*. LP, VP Records.
Urban Hype (1992) *A Trip to Trumpton*. 12", Faze 2.
Various Artists (1950) *Music of Haiti: Vol. 2, Drums of Haiti*. CD, Reissue, Smithsonian Folkways, 2004.
Various Artists (1951) *Music of Haiti: Vol. 1, Folk Music of Haiti*. CD, Reissue, Smithsonian Folkways, 2004.
Various Artists (1952) *Music of Haiti: Vol. 3, Songs and Dances of Haiti*. CD, Reissue, Smithsonian Folkways, 2004.
Various Artists (1959) *Highlights of Vortex: Electronic Experiments and Music*. CD, Reissue, Smithsonian Folkways, 2004. Liner notes online: http://www.folkways.si.edu/highlights-of-vortex-electronic-experiments-and-music/contemporary/album/smithsonian (Accessed: 1 November 2016).
Various Artists (1972) *Play School*. LP, BBC Records.
Various Artists (1994) *Order Odonata Vol.1*. CD, Dragonfly Records.
Various Artists (1995) *WipEout—The Music*. CD, Columbia.
Various Artists (1996) *Platinum Breakz*. 2xCD, Metalheadz.
Various Artists (1997) *Platinum Breakz II*. 2xCD, Metalheadz.
Various Artists (2000) *Hysteria 31: New Dawn*. 8xCassette Tape, Hysteria.
Various Artists (2000) *OHM: The Early Gurus of Electronic Music*. 3xCD, Ellipsis Arts.
Various Artists (2005) *Imagi:Nations Part 1: Night*. 2xLP, TIP.World.
Various Artists (2005) *Imagi:Nations Part 2: Day*. 2xLP, TIP.World.
Weinel, Jon (2009) *Entoptic Phenomena* [electroacoustic composition]. Available on: *Entoptic Phenomena in Audio*, 12", Hardcore Jewellery, 2014.
Weinel, Jon (2011) *Nausea* [electroacoustic composition]. Performed at: 'Fifth International Conference on Internet Technologies & Applications 2013: Art Expo,' Glyndŵr University, Wrexham, 11 September 2013.
Weinel, Jon (2014) *Entoptic Phenomena in Audio*. 12", Hardcore Jewellery, 2014.
The Winstons (1969) *Color Him Father/Amen Brother* (1969). 7", Metromedia Records.
Wishart, Trevor (1978) *Red Bird: A Political Prisoner's Dream*. Reissue, LP, Sub Rosa, 2015.

FILMOGRAPHY

Adler, L. (1978) *Up In Smoke*. Paramount Pictures.
Android Jones and 360art (2015–2016) *Samskara* [fulldome film].
Anger, K. (1947) *Fireworks*. Available on: *The Films of Kenneth Anger: Volume One*, DVD, Fantoma, 2007.

Anger, K. (1954) *Inauguration of the Pleasure Dome*. Available on: *The Films of Kenneth Anger: Volume One*, DVD, Fantoma, 2007.
Anger, K. (1963) *Scorpio Rising*. Available on: *The Films of Kenneth Anger: Volume Two*, DVD, Fantoma, 2007.
Belson, J. (1961) *Allures*. Available on: *Jordan Belson: 5 Essential Films*, DVD, Center for Visual Music, 2007.
Belson, J. (1962) *LSD* [unfinished film]. Screened at: 'Found: New Restorations and Discoveries from Center for Visual Music,' Tate Modern, London, 26 September 2013.
Bigelow, K. (1995) *Strange Days*. Twentieth Century Fox.
Boyle, G. and Robertson, F. (2000) *Boyle Family*. BBC Scotland.
Bredow, G. (2006) *High Tech Soul: The Creation of Techno Music*. DVD, Plexifilm.
Buñuel, L. (1929) *Un Chien Andalou*.
Buñuel, L. (1930) *L'Age d'Or*.
Cameron, J. (1989) *The Abyss*. Twentieth Century Fox.
Caulfield, A. and Caulfield, N. (2014) *From Bedrooms to Billions*. Gracious Films.
Clouse, R. (1973) *Enter the Dragon*. Warner Bros.
Cocteau, J. (1930) *Le Sang d'un Poète*.
Coen, J. and Coen, E. (1998) *The Big Lebowski*. Gramercy Pictures.
Corman, R. (1967) *The Trip*. American International Pictures (AIP).
Cronenberg, D. (1999) *eXistenZ*. Alliance Atlantis Communications.
De Hirsch, S. (1965) *Peyote Queen*. Available on: *Treasures IV: American Avant-Garde Film, 1947–1986*, DVD, National Film Preservation Foundation, 2008.
Deren, M. (1985) *Divine Horsemen: The Living Gods of Haiti. Available on: Divine Horsemen*, DVD, Re:Voir, 2008.
Deren, M., and Hammid, A. (1943) *Meshes of the Afternoon*. Available on: *Maya Deren Experimental Films*, DVD, Boying, 2006.
Esteva, J. (2014) *Komian*. Siwa Productions. Screened at: 'Royal Anthropological Institute (RAI) International Festival of Ethnographic Film,' Watershed, Bristol, 16–19 June 2015.
Friedkin, W. (1971) *French Connection*. Twentieth Century Fox.
The Future Sound of London (1994) *Lifeforms* [music video]. VHS, Virgin.
Gilliam, T. (1998) *Fear and Loathing in Las Vegas*. Universal Pictures.
Guerra, C. (2015) *Embrace of the Serpent*. Oscilloscope.
Harrington, C. (1946) *Fragment of Seeking*.
Harrington, C. (1948) *Picnic*.
Harrison, N. (2004) 'Can I Get an Amen' [video documenting an installation]. Online: http://nkhstudio.com/pages/popup_amen.html (Accessed: 6 December 2016).
Hopper, D. (1969) *Easy Rider*. Columbia Pictures.
Howlett, L. (Music), and Hyperbolic Systems (Video artist) (1993) *Prodigy: One Love* [music video].
Hunter, R.D. (2015) 'Alabama and Georgia,' *Reginald D. Hunter's Songs of the South*, episode 2. BBC, 28 February 2015.
Jodorowsky, A. (1970) *El Topo*. Douglas Films.
Jodorowsky, A. (1973) *Holy Mountain*. ABKCO Films.
The Joshua Light Show (1969) *Liquid Loops*. Available on: *The Joshua Light Show Liquid Loops*, DVD, Center for Visual Music.
The KLF (1991) *The White Room* [unfinished film]. KLF Communications.
Knox, J. (Visuals) and Britto, D. (Music) (2016) *Remote Sense* [live audio-visual fulldome performance]. Performed at: Fulldome UK 2016, National Space Centre, Leicester, 4–5 November 2016.
Kon, S. (2006) *Paprika*. Sony Pictures.

Kounen, J. (2004) *Blueberry* (aka. *Renegade*). Cinema Mondo.
Kubrick, S. (1968) *2001: A Space Odyssey*. Metro-Goldwyn-Mayer (MGM).
Lisberger, S. (1982) *Tron*. Walt Disney.
Lucas, G. (1971) *THX 1138*. Warner Bros.
Lynch, D. (1986) *Blue Velvet*. De Laurentiis Entertainment Group (DEG).
McEuen, A. (2013) *Pink Floyd 360: Dark Side Of The Moon* [fulldome film]. Starlight Productions. Screened at: 'Dome Club,' Birmingham, UK, 24 January 2013.
McKenna, T. (Vocals), Spacetime Continuum (Music), Kent, S. (Music), and Rose X (Video artist) (1993) *Alien Dreamtime*. Reissue, DVD, Magic Carpet Media, 2003.
McLaren, N. (1940) *Dots*. Available on: *Norman McLaren–L'Integrale* [The Master's Edition], 7xDVD, National Film Board of Canada.
Nameth, R. (1996) *Andy Warhol's Exploding Plastic Inevitable with The Velvet Underground.*
Noé, G. (2009) *Enter the Void*. Boid.
Nolan, C. (2005) *Batman Begins*. Warner Bros.
The People Speak (2016) 'Talkaoke: Sci-Fi-London 16 Day 1, Part 1' [video]. Online: https://www.youtube.com/watch?v=ZBorlth4ErE (Accessed: 27 May 2016).
Popular Mechanics SA (2014) 'Afterlife Dazzles Delegates at Futuretech 2014.' Online: http://www.youtube.com/watch?v=iztlq_4BUMg (Accessed: 1 November 2016).
Reiss, J. (1999) *Better Living Through Circuitry*. Cleopatra Pictures.
Roddenberry, G. (Creator) (1966–1969) *Star Trek* (The Original Series) [TV series]. National Broadcasting Company (NBC).
Rush, R. (1968) *Psych-Out*. American International Pictures (AIP)
Russell, K. (1980) *Altered States*. Warner Bros.
Scorsese, M. (1990) *Goodfellas*. Warner Bros.
Scott, R. (1982) *Blade Runner*. Warner Bros.
Smith, H (1939–1957) *Early Abstractions*. Available on: *Early Abstractions & Mirror Animations*, DVD, Harry Smith Archives.
Sol, O. (Concept and Visuals) and Ralp (Music) (2015) *Quadrivium* [live audio-visual fulldome performance]. Performed at: Fulldome UK 2016, National Space Centre, Leicester, 4–5 November 2016.
Studio !K7 (Producer) (1993–1998) *X-Mix* [VJ mix series]. Studio !K7.
Švankmajer, J. (1987) *Alice*. First Run Features.
Švankmajer, J. (1994) *Faust*. Lucernafilm—Beta.
TAS Visual Art (2015) 'Shipibo Fire (Animation).' Online: http://vimeo.com/141945291 (Accessed: 10 January 2016).
Trumbull, D. (1983) *Brainstorm*. Metro-Goldwyn-Mayer (MGM).
Van Meter, B. (1968) *Acid Mantra*. Available on: *Rebirth of a Nation: Ex-Spirit-Mental Cinema of the Sixities*, DVD, 2016.
Wagner, A., and Minter, J. (1988) *Merak*. Reissue: DVD, Media Quest, 2005.
Whitney, J. (1957) *Yantra*. Screened at: 'Head Trips: Abstraction and Infinity—Visual Music Films,' Barbican, London, 4 October 2015.
Whitney, J. (1966) *Lapis*.
Wiene, R. (1920) *Das Cabinet des Dr. Caligari*. Decla-Bioscop AG.
Wilcox, F.M. (1956) *Forbidden Planet*. Metro-Goldwyn-Mayer (MGM).
Yalkut, J. (1968) *Turn, Turn, Turn*. Screened at: 'Head Trips: Abstraction and Infinity—Visual Music Films,' Barbican, London, 4 October 2015.

VIDEO GAMES AND SOFTWARE

3D Realms (1996) *Duke Nukem 3D*. MS-DOS, GT Interactive Software.
Arnott, R. (2011) *Deep Sea* [beta]. Microsoft Windows.

Arnott, R. and Balster, E. (2016) *SoundSelf* [beta]. Microsoft Windows, Oculus Rift.
Asmik Ace Entertainment (1998) *LSD: Dream Emulator*. Sony PlayStation, Asmik Ace Entertainment.
Atari (1980) *Battlezone*. Arcade, Atari.
Bitmap Brothers (1989) *Xenon 2 Megablast*. Atari ST, Image Works.
Cubicle Ninjas (2016) *Guided Meditation VR*. Microsoft Windows, Oculus Rift.
Curious Pictures (2011) *Deepak Chopra's Leela*. Nintendo Wii, THQ.
Digital Pictures (1992) *Night Trap*. Sega CD, Sega.
DMA Design (2001) *Grand Theft Auto III*. Sony PlayStation 2, Rockstar Games.
EA Canada (2001) *SSX Tricky*. Nintendo GameCube, Electronic Arts.
Enhance Games and Monstars (2016) *Rez Infinite*. Sony PlayStation 4, Enhance Games.
Fathomable (2016) *Gnosis* [beta]. Microsoft Windows, Oculus Rift.
Happy Finish (2016) *Autism TMI Virtual Reality Experience* [virtual reality app]. iOS, The National Autistic Society.
Harris, O.L.L. and Smit, N. (2016) *Deep VR* [beta]. Microsoft Windows, Oculus Rift.
id Software (1993) *Doom*. MS-DOS, GT Interactive.
id Software (1996) *Quake*. MS-DOS, GT Interactive.
Midway Games (1992) *Mortal Kombat*. Arcade, Midway Games.
Minter, J. (1984) *Psychedelia*. C64, Llamasoft.
Minter, J. (1986) *Colourspace*. Atari ST, Llamasoft.
Minter, J. (1987) *Trip-A-Tron*. Atari ST, Llamasoft.
Minter, J. (1990–2003) *Virtual Light Machine (VLM)*. Atari Jaguar/Nuon, Llamasoft.
Minter, J. (1992) *Hardcore* [beta]. Atari ST, Llamasoft.
Namco (1979) *Galaxian*. Namco.
Oliver Twins (1989) *Fantasy World Dizzy*. Atari ST, Codemasters.
Psygnosis (1995) *WipEout*. Sony PlayStation, Psygnosis.
Q Entertainment (2011) *Child of Eden*. Sony PlayStation 3, Ubisoft.
Realtime Games (1988) *Carrier Command*. Atari ST, Rainbird.
Remedy Entertainment (1996) *Death Rally*. MS-DOS, GT Interactive.
Remedy Entertainment (2001) *Max Payne*. Sony PlayStation 2, Rockstar Games.
Rockstar North (2002) *Grand Theft Auto: Vice City*. Sony PlayStation 2, Rockstar Games.
Rockstar North (2013) *Grand Theft Auto V*. Sony PlayStation 3, Rockstar Games.
Rocksteady Studios (2009) *Batman: Arkham Asylum*. Sony PlayStation 3, Eidos Interactive.
Silicon Knights (2002) *Eternal Darkness: Sanity's Requiem*. Nintendo GameCube, Nintendo.
Sonic Team (1991) *Sonic the Hedgehog*. Sega Mega Drive, Sega.
Spicy Horse (2011) *Alice: Madness Returns*. Sony PlayStation 3, Electronic Arts.
Taito (1978) *Space Invaders*. Taito.
Team Andromeda (1995) *Panzer Dragoon*. Sega Saturn, Sega.
Team Andromeda (1996) *Panzer Dragoon II Zwei*. Sega Saturn, Sega.
Ubisoft Monstreal (2012) *Far Cry 3*. Song PlayStation 3, Ubisoft.
Unello Design (2015) *Zen Zone*. Samsung Gear VR, Unello Design.
United Game Artists (2001) *Rez*. Sega Dreamcast, Sega.
United Game Artists (2008) *Rez HD*. Microsoft Xbox 360, Q Entertainment.
Weinel, J. (2013) *Psych Dome* [beta]. Apple OSX.
Westwood Studios (1995) *Command and Conquer*. MS-DOS, Electronic Arts.

INDEX